D1591668

Build,
Memory

Build, Memory
James Stewart Polshek

The Monacelli Press

Library of Congress Cataloging-in-Publication Data
Polshek, James Stewart.
Build, memory / James Stewart Polshek.
pages   cm
ISBN 978-1-58093-362-9 (hardback)
1. Polshek, James Stewart—Themes, motives. 2. Architecture—United States—
History—20th century. 3. Architecture—United States—History—21st century. I. Title.
NA737.P55A4 2014
720.97309'04—dc23   2013043231

www.monacellipress.com

10 9 8 7 6 5 4 3 2 1

First edition

Designed by Pentagram
Paula Scher
Jeff Close, Andrea Whitfill

Printed in China

To Ellyn

Contents

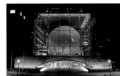

Preface

I confess I do not believe in time. I like to
fold my magic carpet, after use, in such
a way as to superimpose one part of the
pattern upon another. Let visitors trip.

—Vladimir Nabokov
  Speak, Memory

I have devoted my life—almost my entire life, sixty of my more than eighty years—to architectural practice, education, and public service. Certain qualities—ambition, impatience, imagination, persistence, optimism, and energy—have served me well in architecture, but they have not allowed me the time to look back. Finally my addiction to work has diminished. I am ready to remember and to reflect.

I first encountered Nabokov's magic carpet in the early 1960s, and as I began to create this book his words took on a new significance. The unorthodox approach to memoir writing appeals to me, certainly, but there is also, in my mind at least, a kinship of perspective. Nabokov writes from a politically liberal point of view yet never relinquishes attention to the scientific and the aesthetic.

Two other intellectuals have occupied the margins during my work on this book. The eminent British historian and social commentator Tony Judt, in one of his last works, described the "distinctive late nineteenth-century mix of cultural self-confidence informed by a duty to engage in public improvement." This strikes me as an apt characterization also of the mid-twentieth century, when I came of age as a designer and passionate believer in the discipline of architecture.

Abraham Flexner, the father of modern medical education, reinforced my deep-held conviction that architecture is a healing art. Like the medical profession, architecture aspires to restore, renew, make whole, reconcile, and harmonize. In a 1915 speech Flexner listed six defining characteristics of a profession—any worthwhile profession, not just medicine. The sixth is especially reflective of my beliefs: a profession must be "altruistic in motivation." How simple, yet how thoroughly complex. The work, in fact, of a life in architecture.

Time and healing, buildings and memories. Please don't trip.

Introduction

It was said by William Wordsworth that "the Child is father of the Man." I think that is true in my case, for there is much that I learned as a boy, assimilated as a young man, and practiced as a young architect that has been with me for eight decades. I was born in Akron, Ohio, on February 11, 1930. The Great Depression was upon us. Hitler came to power in 1933, the Spanish Civil War ended in 1939 with the victory of a Fascist dictator, and the Dust Bowl was a climatic catastrophe affecting millions. The only good news was the election of Franklin Delano Roosevelt in 1932. At home my mother devoted herself to the appearance of the house, conveying an unambiguous message about the importance of order and expression—the aesthetic dimension of my life. My father's sense of humor and contrarian progressive opinions spoke to a messier reality—the political dimension of my life. The aesthetic and the political have forever since been interwoven in my life and in my work.

In the 1940s World War II came to Akron. On Sunday, December 7, I was awaiting *The Mark of Zorro* in our local movie house. The manager walked onto the stage to announce the bombing of Pearl Harbor. In just a short time we had a victory garden, gasoline-rationing stickers on the windshield of our car, large balls of saved tin foil, and a new knowledge of the silhouettes of enemy aircraft. Gold stars started to appear in neighborhood windows.

The end of this decade saw two serendipitous experiences that would have enduring consequences for me. The first was the construction of a new house in my neighborhood. The architect, Victor Hornbein, was a former apprentice of Frank Lloyd Wright's, and the house was a maverick amid a virtual zoo of bourgeois European styles. The flat roof and windowless street facade shocked our neighbors. For me, it was an epiphany, a suggestion that architecture, in addition to providing shelter, could act as social critique.

The second encounter took place at Western Reserve University in Cleveland. I was planning a career in medicine, but I was struggling with the pre-med curriculum, except for anatomy (the architecture of the body, after all). Not so with an undergraduate art history course called simply "Modern Building." I instinctively understood the design rationale of the projects we studied (Berthold Lubetkin's penguin pool at the London Zoo was one). That was the end of my medical career. I spent a year studying architecture at Western Reserve, but it was soon clear to me that it was time to move on.

In 1950 I traveled to New Haven for an interview at Yale. On the way I visited New York for the first time. I was curious about the buildings going up at the United Nations. Security was not a concern then, and I walked onto a wood-crate elevator with several construction workers. Seconds later a group of well-dressed men entered, one with round black eyeglasses. I have always thought of this chance meeting with Le Corbusier as a good omen: six weeks later I was accepted at the Yale School of Architecture.

The first-year program focused on the fundamentals of form making, drawing on traditional Japanese construction and borrowing bits of theory from Wright, Max Bill, and Mies van der Rohe. Eugene Nalle directed the design studios for my first two years. He was a cryptic intellectual, former pilot, and hardscrabble Texas contractor who had received his architecture degree, from Yale, only a few years earlier. I thrived under his monastic discipline. At the end of the first year I married my undergraduate muse, Ellyn. During the last two years I studied with Louis Kahn in his just completed Yale University Art Gallery—a building my firm was to restore many years later. Visiting studio critics were as weirdly diverse as Philip Johnson and Frederick Kiesler.

After graduation, in June 1955, I worked in I. M. Pei's office in New York City for six months, then my wife and I spent a year in Copenhagen thanks to Senator J. William Fulbright. During the year abroad we traveled extensively in Scandinavia and also found time to sneak off to Paris. We ended our "grand tour" in Rome, where I audited a course by the great engineer Pier Luigi Nervi. When we returned to New York, I worked for Ulrich Franzen. In 1957, our first child, Peter, was born; I also designed my first house, in collaboration with a Yale classmate. The clients for the house introduced me to the chairman of a major textile manufacturer in Japan, and I was later commissioned to design two buildings for the company—the formal start of an independent practice.

The turbulent 1960s began with the inauguration of Brasília, the Oscar Niemeyer– and Roberto Burle Marx–designed new capital of Brazil, and ended with a man on the moon. In between the country lost JFK, MLK, and RFK, not to mention the war in Vietnam. Discovering the Beatles was hardly compensatory. The birth of our daughter, Jenny, surely was, on a personal level. The mid-1960s found us living, for the most part, in Tokyo and Kyoto.

The year 1970 introduced the "dark decade." The economy was in free fall; national and international events dealt one blow after another: Nixon's resignation, the Iranian revolution, the oil embargo. Work in the office diminished dramatically. In 1973, at the urging of Max Bond, I met with the search committee charged with recommending a new dean for the School of Architecture at Columbia. Not long afterward, William McGill, president of the university, appointed me to this position. My arrangement allowed me to continue my practice. I generally stopped at the office in the morning and in the evening. In between I defended myself from an ensconced faculty opposed to change as well as a still restive student body. Simultaneously I was recruiting new members to the faculty, most notably Kenneth Frampton and Klaus Herdeg. I also developed a new undergraduate course, "The Shape of Two Cities: New York–Paris Program," and launched a new interdisciplinary study center, the Temple Hoyne Buell Center for the Study of American Architecture.

I absorbed two long-lasting messages from my asymmetrical schedule. First, not only could I simultaneously immerse myself in academia and my office, but I could gain much from the merging of the two. Second, and more significant, I learned that it was necessary to share design responsibilities with younger colleagues. These collaborations established a pattern that has characterized the work of the office ever since.

Economic and political globalization defined the 1980s. Ronald Reagan was president, and America's one percent began to come out of the closet and spend. Public institutions—libraries, theaters, and museums—once again had the confidence to address capital needs. These years also saw the Iran-Iraq War, the Soviet war in Afghanistan, and the First Intifada.

It was partly in response to this state of affairs that Sidney Gilbert and I founded Architects and Planners for Social Responsibility. We were inspired by the International Physicians for the Prevention of Nuclear War. As the firm continued to grow it was managed by Joseph Fleischer, my first partner. Along with partner Paul Byard, we were establishing an international reputation for serving, almost exclusively, educational, cultural, scientific, and governmental institutions. Tim Hartung and James Garrison joined us as partners in 1987. Together, we attempted to create powerful and unique identities for our diverse clients, emphasizing the public interests they served.

The decade of the 1990s was to see eight years of peace and prosperity beginning with the inauguration of William Jefferson Clinton in 1993 (well before we were awarded the commission for his presidential center). The Hubble telescope established itself in outer space; the World Wide Web in inner space. At the end of the decade, along with Alain Salomon, a young French architect who had been a student at Columbia, we won a competition for a building housing architects, planners, and environmentalists in the Haute-Savoie. Other than the United States Embassy in Oman, it was the first overseas building since the two in Japan. In 1998 Duncan Hazard, Richard Olcott, Susan Rodriguez, and Todd Schliemann became partners.

The first night of the 2000s saw the opening of the Rose Center for Earth and Space at the American Museum of Natural History. The optimism, and the dramatic new vision of the universe, seemed to set the course for the decade—until September 11, 2001. From the windows of our office in Greenwich Village we viewed, with horror, the terrorist attack on the World Trade Center in Lower Manhattan. No other event has so affected the city of New York or the country.

I left the partnership in 2005 to become its design counsel. It was fifty years since I had graduated from architecture school, and the time had come to step to the side, though not off the road entirely. The office had grown to 175, still fueled by the energy and expansiveness of the 1990s, and the complexity of decision making and the pressure to bring in new work were enormous. To celebrate the new arrangement, I accepted a two-month residency at the American Academy in Rome.

My early years at Yale and my experiences in Japan and Scandinavia prepared me for a life of creating buildings based more on structured design principles than on idiosyncratic form making. But they also encouraged me to find ways to bridge architectural formalism and social responsibility. This theme of reconciliation recurs in the tapestry of text and image I have assembled in this book. The sixteen illustrated narratives focus on beginnings—*the intellectual challenge of the project*—and endings—*the ways the project nurtures the social interests of its community*. Perhaps in architecture, too, the child—these buildings—is the father of the man—a practice of architecture that goes beyond the empirical to serve the common good.

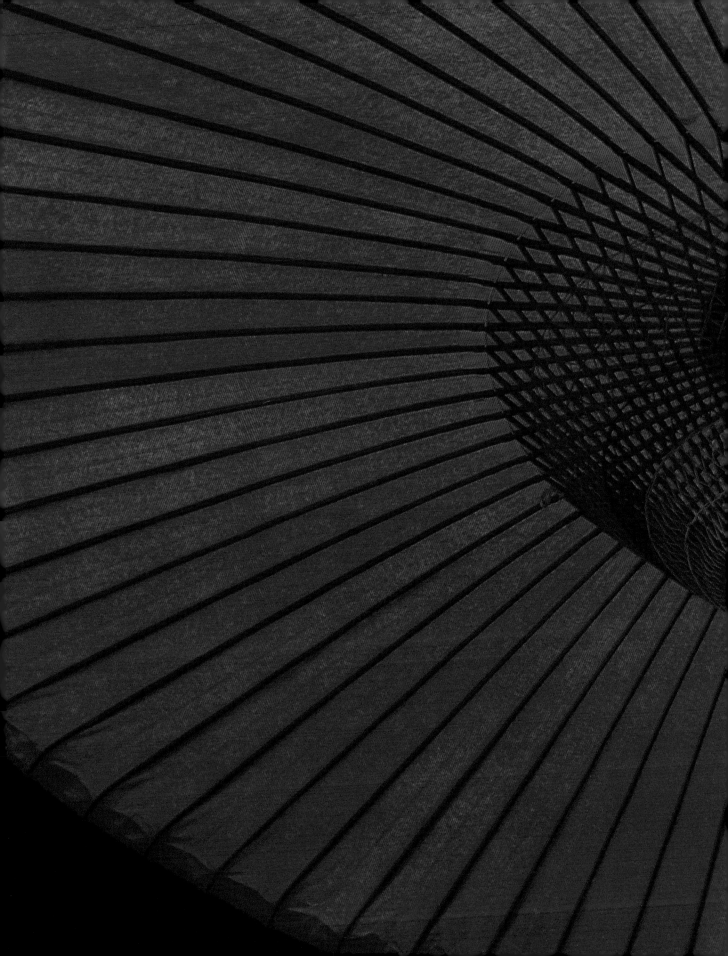

Teijin Institute for Biomedical Research
Teijin Applied Textile Science Center
Hino, Tokyo; Ibaraki, Osaka, Japan
1962–1965

1   2   3

**There is nothing in Japan. But it is the emptiness of the crucible that absorbs everything from the outside and transforms it into something different. That force of transformation is Japan.
—Yukio Mishima**

An American architect living in Japan quickly becomes aware of two acutely different worldviews: an ancient culture in "modern dress." Simplicity, lightness, and lack of pretension are found everywhere. Visual and performing arts disciplines created between the fifth and sixteenth centuries—calligraphy,[4] crafts, poetry, kabuki,[5] noh plays,[6] ikebana, ceramics, Bunraku,[7] textile design—are still available in galleries and theaters. At the same time, fashion,[2] manga,[3] anime, film, modern dance[1] and music, industrial design, computer graphics, and performance art have expanded the Japanese artistic palette in unique ways. And most important, architecture and landscape design bridge ancient and modern time frames.

Traditionally Japan has not distinguished between fine arts and crafts. The Japanese word that best translates "art" is *katachi,* which literally means "form and design." This implies that art is integral to everyday life. While the West seeks to dominate nature, believing in an aesthetic that values symmetry and perfection, Japan accepts that life is unpredictable, that nature is flawed, and that beauty resides in what is natural, imperfect, and ephemeral.

Many see Japanese culture and Zen Buddhism as indivisible components of the same social/religious unit. At the end of the nineteenth century, Lafcadio Hearn

4

wrote, in an essay entitled "The Genius of Japanese Civilization," of the contrast between the Western passion for "endurance" and the Japanese preference for "impermanence." Hearn's examples included straw sandals and tatami mats, paper shoji screens, bamboo chopsticks, and fragile wooden residential structures—all restorable, recyclable, and renewable. The idea of impermanence did not come from religion alone. Before there were systems of belief, there was geography, and Japan's geography is an intrinsic component of the "ring of fire"—the band of active volcanoes around the edges of the Pacific Ocean. Typhoons and earthquakes have plagued life in the country for thousands of years.

5

6

7

1

2

3

4

Frank Lloyd Wright visited Japan in 1905; the prints he famously collected[4] would inspire many of his subsequent designs, including his Jiyu Gakuen girls school.[1] Thirty years later architect Bruno Taut, escaping from his native Germany, revealed the Katsura Imperial Villa to the world.[3] His writings impressed Walter Gropius and Le Corbusier, among others. Of present-day architects, Tadao Ando carries on the spirit of Zen minimalism.[2] His quiet and elegant structures hardly appear impermanent, but to many their unadorned concrete surfaces and voluptuous forms seem to be premature ruins emerging from the earth or water.

1

2

In the late 1950s my knowledge of Japan was almost nonexistent. I had tasted sukiyaki at Miyako[3] (then New York's only Japanese restaurant), visited George Nakashima's workshop in New Hope, Pennsylvania, [4] peeked at Junzo Yoshimura's model house at MoMA, [2] perused an issue of *House Beautiful* dedicated to *shibui,* and attended a studio at Yale that introduced Eastern philosophy and indigenous Japanese construction methods. [5]

Nevertheless, late on a spring day in 1961, I received a phone call from my first client, Dr. Gerald Oster. Gerry and his wife, Gisela, [1] both polymer chemists, had recently moved into a townhouse I had designed in Greenwich Village. My first thought was that he was calling to complain of clanking pipes. Instead, he asked, in his usual prankish manner, "How would you like to go to Japan?" I was flabbergasted. He explained that he wanted me to meet Shinzo Ohya, the chairman of Teijin Ltd., a major textile manufacturer in Japan; Mr. Ohya intended to build a chemical research laboratory for Teijin.

3

4

5

1

2

3

5

4

Gerry and Gisela led the conversation to research facilities. Mr. Ohya declared that he wanted his laboratory to be the most advanced in Japan, not only in its function but in its physical design. He wished to create an example for Japanese corporations that were still recovering from the war. Suddenly he turned to me and, without preamble, asked if I would be interested in designing the proposed laboratory.

At that time, with the exception of the Oster townhouse[4] and country house,[5] my experience consisted of six months as a junior member of a design team in I. M. Pei's office. I had also worked on a few houses and an office interior for Ulrich Franzen, but I was hardly qualified to design a technologically advanced, multimillion-dollar facility. Nevertheless I answered in the only way an aspiring young architect would.

For three months I heard nothing, and I have no recollection of signing a contract (which I later learned is not unusual in Japan). Then one morning three Japanese men arrived in my office. They asked if I could be in Tokyo in two weeks. I managed to keep my composure, though I hoped they didn't see that I had literally broken out in a cold sweat. We parted with my first bow. A month later (two weeks proved impossible), I embarked for the Far East. In those days, trans-Pacific aircraft had to refuel in Anchorage. I barely spoke to the young man sitting beside me until we deplaned in Alaska. When I introduced myself, I discovered that my seatmate was Michael Rockefeller.[3] After the plane took off for Tokyo, I offered him a few little green and black pills, which he gratefully accepted. (A longtime sufferer of aerophobia, I had come prepared with a variety of meds.) He told me he was on his way to New Guinea for anthropological research. Michael Rockefeller never returned.

A few nights later, Ellyn and I arrived at the Osters' promptly, curious and excited. Mr. Ohya was short, solidly built, olive-skinned, and bald.[1] He reminded me of my father, which was perhaps a good omen. Mrs. Ohya was petite, eccentrically dressed and coiffed.[2] Behind them stood Mr. Yamamoto, retainer and translator, who bowed courteously and often.

1

2

The plane landed at Haneda International Airport on October 1, 1961. I could only assume that the reception I received was usually reserved for foreign dignitaries:[2] a small contingent of Teijin employees, all male, and a young woman carrying a bouquet of chrysanthemums. Among the greeters was Mr. Yamamoto,[1] who would become my guide over the three years of the Tokyo project. From then on I was called *Sensei* (Professor).

I was happily surprised by my temporary home in Frank Lloyd Wright's Imperial Hotel.[3] Wright had died two years earlier, and his masterpiece was already close to the final years of its life. The combination of jet lag and anticipation drove me directly to the Wright-designed bar for my first Suntory whiskey.

3

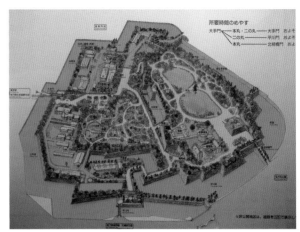

4

The next day, just before noon, I was picked up by a uniformed driver and taken to Teijin's corporate headquarters, across the street from the Imperial Palace grounds. There Mr. Ohya and I, through Mr. Yamamoto, engaged in a few minutes of small talk. Then we entered a conference room next door. Seated around a large table was a group of Teijin administrators and, more important, scientists who had a direct interest in the new research laboratory, including the lab director, Dr. Yoshida. The group arranged for me to meet representatives from Kajima Corporation, the construction company, the next day and visit the site the day after that. In between I managed to explore the nooks and crannies of the Imperial Hotel,[3] stroll the Ginza, and visit the grounds of the Imperial Palace.[4]

At Kajima I saw a small group of architects and engineers. My professional home for the next year would be a small and drab but well-lit room within the architecture section. Nearby were a model shop and a library with Western and Japanese publications. I selected my staff from the few who spoke English; most of the team wore a uniform of gray smocks. I had a lot to learn about Japanese practice—particularly the metric system and the "language" of numbers in general. That evening a few members of the team escorted me to one of the thousands of infamous Tokyo bars. I retired to the hotel after many beers and sakes, and the non-stop laughter of my companions and the charming "bar girls."

The following morning three cars pulled up to the hotel. Out of one stepped the omnipresent "Mr. Moto" (as I called Mr. Yamamoto under my breath). We drove through dense morning traffic for an hour or so until we reached Hino City, then a suburb of Tokyo. Just outside of this small town the cars turned into a dirt road. Through the dust churned up by the lead car, I saw a flat, treeless, industrial landscape. This, apparently, was the site of the new laboratory. About three hundred yards on, we pulled up to the edge of a field. The sun was bright, and as the morning fog cleared I recognized, to the south, the outline of Mount Fuji, Japan's "magic mountain."[2]

Forty yards ahead a tall, flimsy-looking, wood-and-bamboo structure about fifty feet high appeared through the haze.[1] We were led toward it by two young boys, each swishing a fifteen-foot bamboo pole through the tall grass. I must have looked puzzled because Mr. Yamamoto whispered to me, "Vipers!" At that moment the rickety tower seemed highly appealing.

I scrambled up, and soon the others joined me. The weight of our bodies—altogether there were fourteen of us—caused the structure to sway. Hands over mouths, my companions began to chuckle nervously. Was the platform pitching from our weight or from a mild earthquake? It could have been either, since earthquakes occurred with some frequency.

To the south was the picture-perfect view of Mount Fuji. To the north was an underused industrial zone. I expressed enthusiasm even though I had no idea what I was supposed to be looking for.

1

2

3

4

5

I spent the remainder of my fortnight visit meeting researchers, reviewing Kajima's early feasibility studies, and visiting some of Tokyo's most prominent early modernist buildings, including Kenzo Tange's Sogetsu Art Center,[3] Kisho Kurokawa's Nagakin Capsule Tower,[1] and Kunio Maekawa's National Museum of Modern Art.[4] I also examined the site from an environmental perspective and reorganized and quantified the program I had been given. Kajima supplied enough information, graphic and otherwise, to allow me to focus on the design of the new building. And I visited schools and possible residences for my family, since Ellyn and I had realized that we would have to move to Japan if I were to take on this project.

Once back in New York, I began to investigate the nature of laboratories and "process" architecture. I discovered that these building types essentially design themselves. Most buildings do not have the luxury of arbitrariness or of being contingent on a designer's discretion or an owner's perceived needs. Theoretical and practical constraints and opportunities determine organization and form. This is often the case with industrial buildings, libraries, theaters, hospitals, and especially research facilities. This explains, at least in part, how a neophyte designer, barely five years out of school, could create a large, complex structure in a foreign land. It is worth noting that this particular young architect could not have faced these challenges with a design of any integrity without Japanese inventiveness and the culture's age-old respect for the aesthetic.

Given the shaky ground underfoot, my colleagues at Kajima and I had already determined that the building would be concrete, and I devoted some time to familiarizing myself with exposed concrete structures. I knew the work of Auguste Perret[2] and Le Corbusier, particularly the latter's Unité d'Habitation, the iconic apartment building in Marseille.[6] I had learned something of the technology of poured-in-place concrete at the Pei office, which had designed the housing at Kips Bay in New York City.

I could only go so far with the design in the United States. It was time to return to Japan, and on May 15, 1962, we flew to Tokyo as a family. We were enthusiastically welcomed—especially our two children.[5] We settled into a traditional guesthouse (ryokan) and soon moved into a small house in Azabu, Tokyo's diplomatic precinct.

My family was hardly acclimated. Language, manners, tastes, odors, climate, and tremors: everything was new. Peter, almost five, refused to remove his shoes when we entered a restaurant. Conversely, Jenny bowed to everyone!

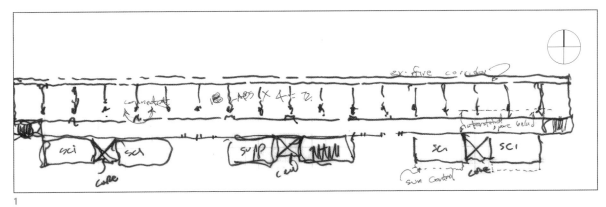

1

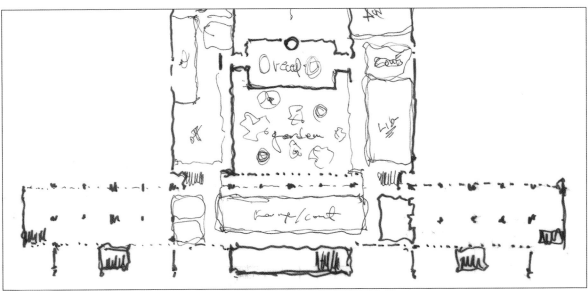

2 ↑

3 ↓

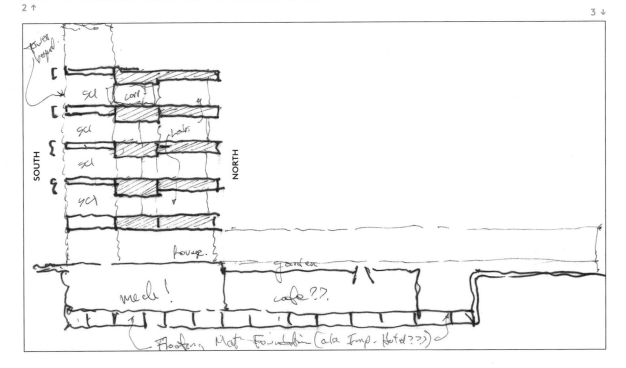

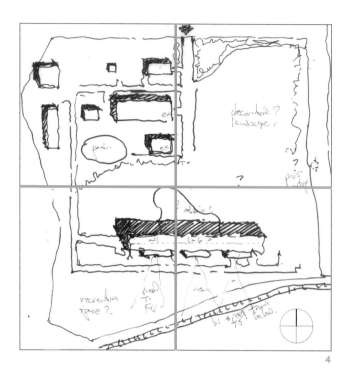

4

Two fundamental design considerations had emerged, both involving cardinal points of the compass. The site's most important view corridor was to the south, with Mount Fuji in the distance. There the site ended abruptly in a drop of more than fifteen meters. To the west was a densely developed industrial manufacturing operation. The only possible entry was from the north or east. The site was divided into four quadrants.[4] The northwest portion was occupied by support buildings and a water retention pond. The southeast and southwest areas offered access, privacy, and security—the obvious site for the laboratory. The northeast quadrant would be reserved for future expansion.

The second factor was the type of research that would form the core of the program. Teijin's primary business was the manufacture of rayon fibers; over the years it had become Japan's largest producer of polymer products. My patrons, the Osters, had stressed that southern light would be unacceptable for the research labs. All laboratory units would have to face magnetic north to avoid direct or indirect ultraviolet light.

The basic program consisted of seventy-two laboratories, each seven by eleven meters. The client wanted to be able to connect them horizontally to form product research units. Town zoning requirements specified that the overall structure not exceed twenty-four meters in height, so it quickly became obvious that the building would be a long, thin, east-west-oriented slab with the labs distributed on four floors. Although the scientific research teams had expressed a preference for adjacent offices and labs, the length and height of the building precluded that arrangement. We developed a scheme in which the research offices and vertical service cores were in south-facing towers separated from the laboratory units by an access corridor. After the building was completed, a documentary film represented the massing as a series of sugarcube-like boxes. [2,3]

The program also called for administrative offices, lounge, library, auditorium, and separate reception pavilion. Because of the sharp drop at the south of the site, it seemed as though these functions could be placed only to the north of the laboratory units. Instead, we raised the laboratory floors seven meters above the ground plane and slipped the common functions underneath.

In the early 1960s there were few precedents for basic research facilities. The Salk Institute by Louis Kahn (1962)[4] and the Endo Laboratories by Paul Rudolph (1964)[5] had not yet been completed. However, Kahn had been my studio critic at Yale, where I was exposed to his concept of served and servant spaces. Historic buildings also proved to be influential, especially a temple in Nara that directly inspired the plasticity of the sunless north facade of the lab. [1]

2

3

4 ↑

5 ↓

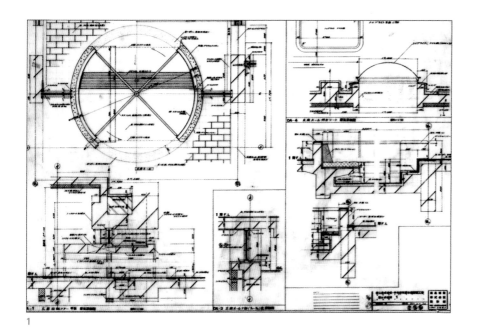

1

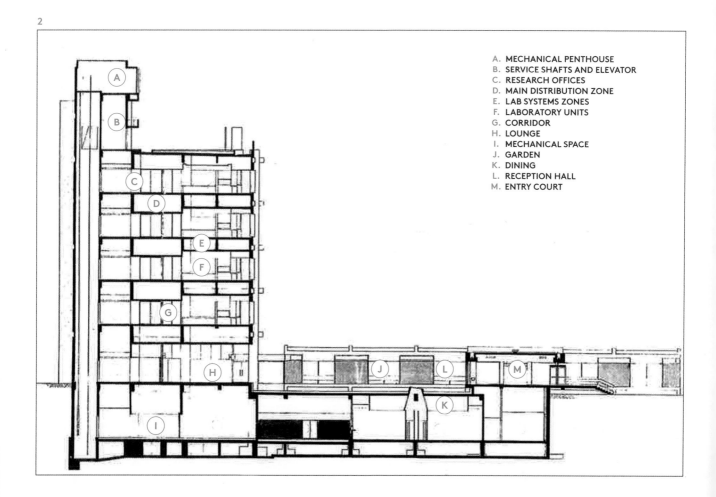

2

A. MECHANICAL PENTHOUSE
B. SERVICE SHAFTS AND ELEVATOR
C. RESEARCH OFFICES
D. MAIN DISTRIBUTION ZONE
E. LAB SYSTEMS ZONES
F. LABORATORY UNITS
G. CORRIDOR
H. LOUNGE
I. MECHANICAL SPACE
J. GARDEN
K. DINING
L. RECEPTION HALL
M. ENTRY COURT

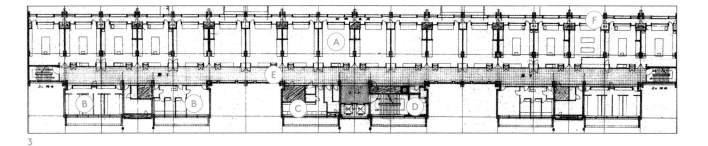

3

A. TYPICAL LAB UNIT
B. RESEARCH OFFICES
C. BALANCE ROOM
D. ELEVATOR CORE
E. MAIN CORRIDOR
F. EMERGENCY ESCAPE

Before long we had a preliminary scheme. The five-story building—four levels of labs, each with an interstitial service area, and the ground level of public functions—was located in the southern sector of the site along an east-west axis. Three vertical towers were on the south side, as I had anticipated, and the main entry and gatehouse were at the east of the site.

As the months went by the team developed structural drawings, planned mechanical system distribution routes, and decided on the material palette. Yoshi Koshiyama, Kajima's chief structural and mechanical engineer, attended all coordination meetings and design reviews. Representatives of the scientific research staff were present as well. The collaborative spirit behind Japanese design affected me for a lifetime.

The formal expression of the north and south facades was determined by our early analysis into the relationship between the internal research and the external orientation. The towers on the south contained offices for scientists and technical personnel, a vibration-free balance room, secure storage, elevators, fire stairs, and vertical mechanical and electrical shafts. Laboratory modules were distributed along the north face of the building. This allocation resulted in a small-scale, repetitive, highly articulated north elevation and a large-scale, deeply shadowed south elevation.

Ink-on-vellum working drawings appeared daily.[1] Wood detail models of three bays of the north elevation helped us to refine the proportions of the precast

4

elements of the railing system.[4] Behind each railing was a one-meter-wide exterior balcony. In addition to shading the floor below, the balcony would provide roll-out safety slides for the lab units. Behind alternating single and double columns were blue exhaust ducts and white liquid-waste shafts.

We presented the design to Mr. Ohya, members of his board, scientists, and Kajima executives, who responded enthusiastically. A few days later, an unanticipated crisis began to unfold. Kajima's director told me that Mr. Ohya's wife wished to see the plans. Kajima would transport me and the director, along with the presentation drawings and models, to the Ohya residence outside of Tokyo.

Mrs. Ohya was *mezurashii*—strange or unorthodox, but actually idiosyncratic and unpredictable. She looked intently at the documents but showed little interest in the models or any other materials. Finally, Mrs. Ohya asked the director to point out north on the site plan and model. Once he did so Mrs. Ohya's perpetual smile disappeared. She and the director abruptly left the room. Twenty minutes passed before he returned alone.

In the car I asked him to explain the problem. Direct answers to unpleasant questions are rare in Japan, but by the end of the ride back to Tokyo the director offered that Mrs. Ohya was *ureshikunai* (unhappy). According to Mrs. Ohya, a profound believer in Shinto rituals and geomancy, or feng shui (*inyodo* in Japan), the tallest portion of the laboratory was in the wrong quadrant of the site.[5] She was convinced that the building was destined to bring bad luck—specifically the death of her husband. To satisfy her shaman and calm her fears, she asked Kajima to turn the building around and move it to the northwest quadrant of the site. I was stunned.

I returned to the city, where I met Ellyn at the American Club. Moments later, fortified by a very tall glass of whiskey, I was relating the events of the day. I had never been informed that the mystical science of geomancy[6] was part of the program! However, the one thing I was certain of was that I could not agree to reorient and relocate the building.

A few days later I met with Mr. Ohya, and the following week I made another presentation to the board of directors. I was excused from the room while the directors discussed the fate of the building. Thirty minutes later I was ushered into the chairman's office. He was

there alone. His expression was serious, as were his unforgettable words: "Please proceed as planned!" The crisis was over. It seemed no more than a month before the giant foundation excavation appeared on the site.[2]

The construction moved forward with military efficiency. Just after dawn two or three mornings a week, a car and driver would pick me and one of my assistants up to visit the site. The mornings began with an assembly of all the workers. Each trade, neatly attired and with yellow safety helmets, stood at attention.[4] The superintendent addressed them on the topics of safety, neatness, and pride in work. At the end, with a shout of "Banzai," they would jog to their assigned tasks. For me, these martial moments, though impressive, brought back some unnerving images of World War II.[3]

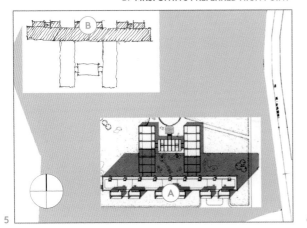

A. HIGH POINT OF BUILDING
B. MRS. OHYA'S PREFERRED HIGH POINT

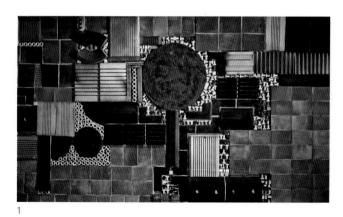

1

As the concrete superstructure began to rise, I turned my attention to the design of the interior, including furnishings, an art program, and graphics. Although fittings for the labs and technical spaces would be imported from Germany, we designed the casework that would enclose the hoods and lab tables. The Kajima team was inexperienced with interior design, but their extensive library of English and American design magazines became my "interiors department." I would leaf through journals, looking for photos of well-designed light fixtures, cabinetry, furnishings, textiles, accessories, and ceramic and vinyl flooring. Within weeks Kajima would produce shop drawings and material samples.

A noted ceramics artist was commissioned as part of the art program. I thought his work was too mannered for the lab, but on a visit to the studio I became intrigued by the clay fragments used to support work in firing kilns and suggested they might lend a spontaneity and originality to the walls. Fortunately the artist saw my proposal as an homage.[1]

I was also involved in the design for the courtyard.[3,4] It seems insolent that, in a country where landscape design is almost a religion, I would take this on. But with assistance from the Kajima landscape architecture department, I selected every stone and azalea bush. Skylights for the cafeteria below[2] appeared as stonelike protrusions through the white-gravel surface.

2 ↑

3 ↓

4

1

2

3

4

In March 1963, the project was nearly complete. I led Mr. Ohya and a group of Teijin scientists and board members on a tour of the building. Dr. Yoshida and his staff were delighted. They crawled through the underfloor voids, visited the labs and offices where they would work, and asked questions nonstop.

The following day a senior executive of Teijin asked me to design a prototype textile manufacturing and research building in the Kansai region, midway between Kyoto and Osaka. Obayashi Gumi, with a head office in Osaka, was to be the builder of this half-million-square-foot structure. Once the laboratory design was well along, I asked Teijin to find us a home in Kyoto. My wife, who had been working with the anti–nuclear weapons movement,[3] looked forward to visiting Zen gardens and temples, the Kyoto Museum of Traditional Crafts (Fureaikan), and the shops off of historic Kawaramachi Street. Our home was a classic Japanese dwelling[2]—except for the Western bedroom on the second floor—in the village of Yamashina, just over the mountain from the famous Hotel Miyako. A sand garden, dozens of pink and orange azalea bushes, and a carp pond that our son couldn't stay out of constituted the grounds around the dwelling.

Four months later proved to be an ideal time for the family to return to the United States. Peter was ready for first grade and Jenny for preschool, and we needed to bring our empty New York apartment back to life. We sailed from Kobe to Hong Kong on the *Viet-nam*,[1] a Messageries Maritimes ship. From Hong Kong we flew to Thailand, India, Egypt, Greece, England, and finally, home to New York.

I returned to Japan that December on my own. I shuttled between Obayashi Gumi's headquarters in Osaka and the construction site in suburban Tokyo on the bullet train, madly marking up drawings on the way. One day in Tokyo I was called to see Kajima's design director. Upon entering, I noticed that the site model for our project had been modified. A new structure had appeared. The director explained that Mr. Ohya had agreed to construct a banal curtain-walled tower in the northwestern corner of the site. The tower, no less than one meter above the highest point of the laboratory, would placate Mrs. Ohya.[4]

1

The dedication of the Tokyo research facility was scheduled for August 1964. A gigantic red-and-white-striped tent on the west lawn of the new building was the locus for the formal ceremony.[3] In attendance were Shinto priests with their multiple blessings and members of the Kajima family as well as various science luminaries from Europe and the United States. It was a glorious moment—an ending to an involvement that few architects will ever have.

I had not seen the building for five months. Construction photos had been sent to New York, but those were very far from the reality we were soon to experience. As we entered through the new gatehouse, the structure materialized; the building was a dark silhouette against the noontime sun.

The heavily sculpted form of the north facade responded to the north orientation and corresponding absence of direct sunlight.[2,4] Rising from the top of the building, behind the plane of the facade, were the alternating blue and white exhaust and waste shafts. The four laboratory levels were supported by piers at each end, allowing an open view under the lab block. The only interruptions were the mechanical and egress cores.

As we rounded the side of the building, Mount Fuji arose from the landscape like a mirage. The south facade was rendered in terra-cotta tile and punctuated with vertical windows that allowed natural light into the long laboratory access corridors.[1] The giant research towers with their concrete sunshades rose like sentinels.

2

3

4

2

3

4

Once we had circled the building, we walked up the steps of the glass pavilion. (Forty-five years later, my son and his family visited this exact spot.) [4] Inside were waiting several dozen lab technicians, administrators, and senior scientists. As the revolving door spun us into the room, they broke into applause.

Seating pits, wood-clad vitrines inspired by Charlotte Perriand, and a concrete reception desk were the only furnishings. [2] The Japanese gardeners had taken my drawings and turned them into a classical Japanese landscape. The ceramic murals identified the connections to the east and west administrative wings. [3] We passed through the auditorium, which could expand into a large conference room. [1] Down the hall was the research library, an executive office, and a staff lounge overlooking the enclosed garden.

1   2   3

By now our group had grown quite large. As many as could fit took the elevator to the lab floors. The laboratory entry doors were flanked by individual utility panels; Scandinavian-influenced circular lights provided illumination and left the ceiling free for access. The labs, not yet in use, looked as impeccable as showroom models.[4] The German hardware fittings coordinated with the terra-cotta floor tile[5] and the white plastic laminate casework we had designed. The floor of the main corridor was covered in bright blue vinyl tile. The white-coated Teijin scientists and the uniformed Kajima team looked like extras in a science-fiction film.

We next inspected the research offices in the three towers,[3] all of which overlooked what has come to be called the "Fuji view." Then we took the elevators to the roof, a recreational space with three large raised areas of grass—my first "green" roof.[1] Each grass parcel related to one of the three research towers. Fresh air intakes were at the top of the southern towers, and one meter in from the north parapet were the exhaust and waste shafts.

Next on our tour was the below-grade floor. In addition to the café, this level contained some of the earliest computerized building management systems in the world. The "brain" of the building consisted of control consoles facing graphic screens.[6] The screen displays looked exactly as if we had dissected the building and exposed the complex inner anatomy of ducts, tubes, wires, and conduits. This control area would soon bring the research center to life. After this wondrous day, Ellyn returned home and I traveled to Kyoto for six intense weeks to finalize the design of the new textile center. While I was in the United States, a proud chairman Ohya showed off his new laboratory to Prince Akihito, now emperor of Japan.[2]

4

5

6

1

2

3

4

5

The program for the textile institute was very different from that for the lab building. The principal objective for this building was product development, not basic research. My early sketches had been turned into schematic drawings under the direction of a precocious young architect at Obayashi, Masatoshi Fujinawa—"Fuji" to me. [5]

The new site was an unexceptional tract of flat land within sight of the Meishin Highway that connects Tokyo and Osaka. Two characteristics distinguished the property: a fifth-century tomb (a national monument) [1] and a single ancient pine tree. [2] Both of these influenced the siting of the building.

1

2

3

4

5

6

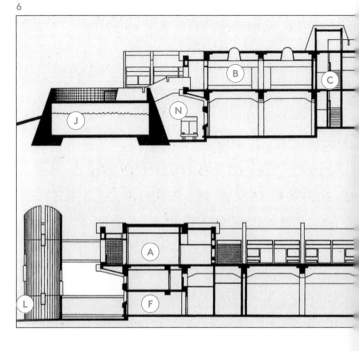

The upper level of the two-floor structure was laid out symmetrically, with different functions separated by seven garden courtyards (seven is a lucky number in Japan) open to the sky.[2] These functions included material research, design, and testing as well as executive offices, an auditorium, a cafeteria, and an entrance.[3,4] The mechanical plant, cooling towers, and generators were in the center of the upper floor. The open lower floor was a vast experimental production plant. Four stair towers provided entry for plant workers.[1,5]

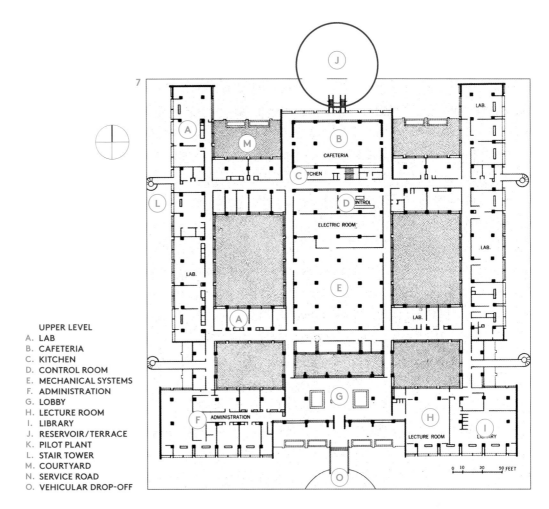

UPPER LEVEL
A. LAB
B. CAFETERIA
C. KITCHEN
D. CONTROL ROOM
E. MECHANICAL SYSTEMS
F. ADMINISTRATION
G. LOBBY
H. LECTURE ROOM
I. LIBRARY
J. RESERVOIR/TERRACE
K. PILOT PLANT
L. STAIR TOWER
M. COURTYARD
N. SERVICE ROAD
O. VEHICULAR DROP-OFF

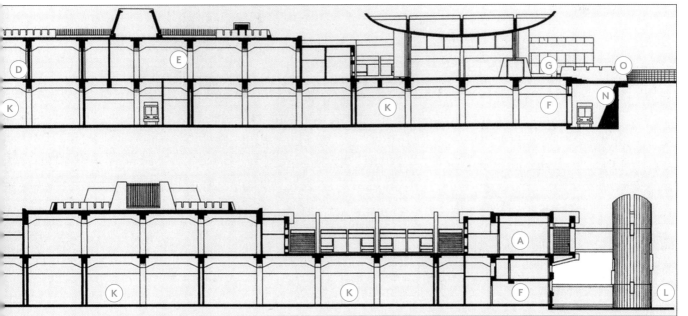

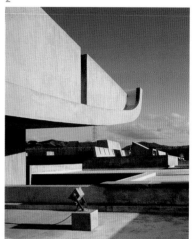

There were six points of entry to the structure. The first was a formal approach at the top of a vehicular ramp marked by a sweeping concrete roof structure;[1,2] this led to the public lobby and executive suite on the upper level. A second entry on the opposite side of this level was a platform off the cafeteria. This circular terrace, which looked south over employee housing and recreational areas, was actually the roof of a huge, stone-clad emergency water-storage tank.[3] Platform and tank were carefully situated to accommodate the ancient pine tree. The other four entries, those in the circular concrete stair towers, led to a mezzanine with lockers, washrooms, and lounges. A service road at the perimeter of the building allowed access for large equipment.[4] I saw the road as a metaphorical moat separating the structure from the surrounding landscape.

It was time for me to leave. Fuji's superb team could complete the detailed design drawings, and he would oversee the work. I spent a final glorious weekend visiting Katsura, Tofukuji, and other favorite temples and gardens. On the last evening, sitting in the hotel bar, I began to wonder about a career in New York. What could I—spoiled and jobless—possibly do to equal or top this Japanese experience?

In 1967 I returned to Japan to discuss the possibility of designing a third building for Teijin. The project never materialized, but before I left I paid one more visit to the Imperial Hotel. It was noon. The lobby was empty except for the sounds of laughter and occasional applause coming from a distant dining room.[3] As I wandered through the halls, I noticed men pushing small wooden carts with metal wheels. On each cart were piles of numbered shoe boxes. I opened one and saw brass and chrome hardware and room numbers[1,2] that had been removed from the hotel rooms. Weeks later Wright's masterpiece was demolished, an early victim of real estate development in a burgeoning economy.[4]

New York State Bar Center
Albany, New York
1968–1971

Wallace K. Harrison once commented that the design of Empire State Plaza [1,2] in Albany, New York, created at the behest of Governor Nelson Rockefeller in 1959, was inspired by Chandigarh, Brasília, and Versailles. [3,4,5]

This was a transparent attempt by its architect to inflate the stature of the scheme. It is rather a bombastic complex of overscaled buildings; more's the pity, it is adjacent to H. H. Richardson's magnificent 1899 State Capitol. We tried to keep this insensitive juxtaposition always in mind as we undertook a project in Albany that would require mediation between old and new.

2

1

3

4

5

1

2

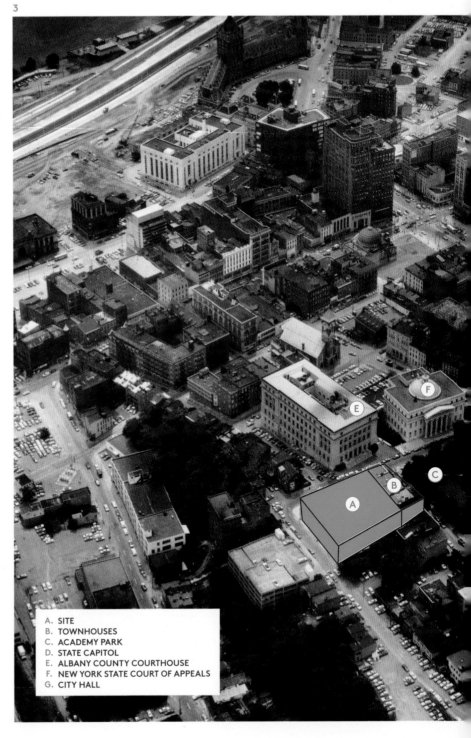

3

A. SITE
B. TOWNHOUSES
C. ACADEMY PARK
D. STATE CAPITOL
E. ALBANY COUNTY COURTHOUSE
F. NEW YORK STATE COURT OF APPEALS
G. CITY HALL

4   5

In 1965 the New York State Bar Association, based in Albany, decided to build a new headquarters. The group then had 22,000 members (now it is closer to 80,000) and is the oldest voluntary bar association in the United States. The board appointed a committee headed by the president, Cloyd Laporte, which included past presidents S. Hazard Gillespie Jr.[5] and Whitney North Seymour Jr.,[4] to assemble a site in a prominent downtown location. Almost two years later, the association purchased four adjacent lots on Elk Street, the end of a mostly intact row of townhouses dating from the 1820s and 1830s. To the south, the four lots faced landmarked Academy Park, which is one corner of the state capital precinct. Also across from the park are the Greek Revival Albany County Court House, the faux temple form of the New York State Court of Appeals, and H. H. Richardson's Romanesque city hall of 1880.

In early 1968, Whitney Seymour, known as Mike, and Hazard Gillespie came to my office to discuss the new headquarters. How they got there was an interesting story. In 1965 Philip Johnson had suggested me to Mr. and Mrs. Edgar Bronfman for the design of a recreational pavilion at their estate in Purchase, New York.[1] Ann Bronfman in turn recommended me to the building committee of Rosemary Hall at the Choate School for a new campus.[2] Philip must have thought both of those projects had something to offer to the attorneys when Mike Seymour asked him for advice on architect selection.

Mike Seymour would give the rationale for our selection a few years later, after the Albany headquarters was completed, in the American Bar Association *Journal*:

The design committee made its boldest move in the decision to try to find a relatively unknown younger architect who would see the new bar headquarters as his chance to establish his own reputation and would give it the extra attention and personal interest that was necessary to make a low-budget building a standout.

The late 1960s spelled the end of this kind of personalized selection of architects. From then on, with increasing ferocity, the procedure was bureaucratized.

1

2

At the time of that first meeting, my office was in the forty-eighth-floor "attic" of an Art Deco tower at East Fortieth Street and Madison Avenue.[1] To reach this unorthodox aerie, visitors had to take two elevators and one flight of stairs to a thirty-foot-high room containing an open steel water reservoir. At the base of this industrial artifact sat my secretary, Ms. May (a.k.a. Ellyn May Polshek).[2] There were only two other employees; one of them, Joseph Fleischer,[3] would become the managing partner of Polshek Partnership more than two decades later.

On the wall were large photographs of the research buildings I had recently completed for Teijin in Japan. These were hardly relevant to the project that had been described to me. Consequently, when we sat down, I showed the exceptionally tall, elegantly dressed barristers plans and photographs of three nineteenth-century townhouses I had completed in Manhattan's Upper West Side Urban Renewal Area. I had been a consultant for the Mental Hygiene Facilities Improvement Fund in Albany for a children's mental health center in West Seneca, New York, and so we also spoke of the checkered political history of Albany. And I mentioned that Ellyn and I had just purchased an old farmhouse in the Hudson River Valley less than an hour south of the capital. The convenient location would allow me to spend additional time on the project.

3

1

The lawyers noted that their site was in a historic district composed of small-scale nineteenth-century buildings,[2] similar to the townhouses I had restored in New York. The board of the association planned to tear down the four houses it had purchased in order to build a new building on the prominent corner of Elk and Eagle Streets. Alarm bells went off in my head, but I made no response. If I was hired, this would be my first institutional commission. There would be plenty of time to discuss the demolition of the old houses.

Our next meeting was in Albany. The day before the appointment I was given a tour of the existing headquarters, located in a nearby office building, and a brief on the program for the new project. As I walked down Elk Street, I noticed that on the uphill end of the block facing the park (our site was on the eastern,

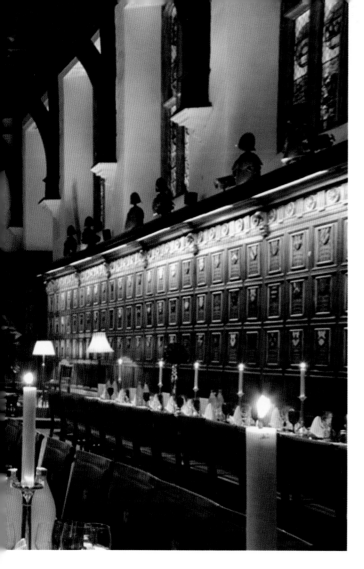

2   3

downhill end), several of the original townhouses had been bulldozed. One had been replaced by a banal and scaleless building, another paved for parking. My concern about replacing four historic townhouses with a modern building resurfaced. Empire State Plaza was already looming over the streetscape,[3] and I felt that the removal of any more houses would destroy forever the integrity of this block, not to mention the public outcry that was sure to emerge.

Along with Mike Seymour and Hazard Gillespie, the design committee included Hugh R. Jones and Stuart Scott—two more past presidents of the Bar Association—and John Berry, the executive director. We met at Warner Bouck's office on Columbia Street, just around the corner from the Bar Association's new plot. Bouck had been retained as outside counsel to the association to help identify and assemble the site and to draw up the contract between the architect and the association. Early in our discussion Mike Seymour mentioned the Inns of Court in London; he particularly admired the interior of Middle Temple.[1] I had visited these buildings on a trip to London, and the committee's enthusiasm made me wonder if they were hinting at a traditional design. I questioned the group rather candidly, and they assured me that the building should symbolize the "progressive" spirit of the Bar Association. But they also commented that they would prefer the new design not be "offensive" to the adjacent nineteenth-century buildings. I left the meeting enthusiastic about the challenge but still concerned about what the reaction might be to the razing of the four townhouses.

The subject of the next meeting was my contract. As soon as I entered Bouck's conference room, I noticed a document the size of the Manhattan telephone book on the long conference table. It finally dawned on me that having thousands of lawyers as a client was going to be a daunting and risky experience. I had not consulted an attorney of my own, and I had no experience with issues of liability, errors and omissions insurance, or other legal traps that might be awaiting. I had only my experience in Japan to guide me: there, a deep bow would have signified an agreement to proceed. Bouck motioned to the hefty contract and suggested that I take it back to New York to review with my lawyers. In front of the distinguished barristers, I said that I had no lawyer, no intention of leaving without a signed contract, and no interest in delaying the design. To my hosts' astonishment, I flicked through the document to the signature page, took out my pen, and signed. My new clients and I shook hands and I left for the city.

Not long afterward the association's intention to tear down the four townhouses was made public. Within days the decision was challenged. An article in the *Times-Union* [4] described the emerging controversy and stated that several members of the Albany Historic Sites Commission had expressed their distress. The following week the Hudson River Valley Commission (created, ironically, by Governor Rockefeller in 1966) held a public hearing. The result was a judicial order barring any demolition.

At the next meeting with the client, occasional snide comments referring to interveners, nosy neighbors, and little old ladies in tennis shoes were offered, but the disparagement soon ceased. The committee recognized that the Bar Association faced a serious reputation problem. For any architect, there are few situations worse than receiving an exciting commission and then having it disappear. The time had come to solve this conundrum by design and negotiation rather than by confrontation.

1

From the earliest days of my practice, I have used medical metaphors to describe design solutions. Whether or not this habit arose from my early education, I believed that the Bar Association had an opportunity to perform an act of "healing." Although contemporary additions to historic buildings were rare in the United States, Europe was rife with precedents. I was familiar with Pierre Chareau's Maison de Verre in Paris (1932), Gunnar Asplund's extension to the Law Courts in Göteborg (1937), [1] and Louis Kahn's Yale Art Gallery in New Haven (1953). [2] The last was especially significant because of my time at Yale and my studies with Kahn. Also, James Stirling's project for the Olivetti Training School in Surrey, England (1969), [3] had just been published in the United States. These inspirations, my own instincts, and the site's boundaries and historic context implied a radical solution—radical for the late 1960s, that is.

2

3

4

Era of 1830 Awaits Wrecker's Ball

By CHUCK MALLEY
Times-Union Staff Writer

Albany's Elk Street belongs to an era that has passed away, yet its spirit is very much with us today.

The houses along the street, standing shoulder-to-shoulder like men at attention, form an unbroken wall at the north end of Academy Park. Their tall, gaping windows have watched the park since the 1830s and 1840s.

Seeing the b u i l d i n g s from across the park, they look like a painting on canvas — perhaps something the street-scene painter, Utrillo, would have made a picture of. Their colors are red, green and white.

The Federal s t y l e buildings make a clear statement. They say "This is Old Albany." There is little doubt that the houses belong where they are; that they are an integral and necessary part of the square.

But some of them probably will not be there much longer. The houses at Nos. 2, 3 and 4 Elk have been strong enough to

The State Street building will be demolished and replaced by a 22-story office tower.

The l a w y e r s favor the Elk Street site because it is only a few steps away from the Court of Appeals and Hall of Justice and just a block from the Capitol. The architect for the proposed buiding hopes to have a model ready by June.

Folowing are comments from some people on the Elk Street situation:

Mason Tolman, member of the Historic S i t e s Commission: "I care very deeply about the buildings and will use what little influence I have to save them."

Albert Hartheimer, architect: "Unfortunately, the p r o b l e m does not lie with the Bar Association, but with the law. I think there could be an ordinance with teeth in it that would prevent people from doing this."

Continued Hartheimer, "If we feel stronlgy e n o u g h, we can p a s s such an ordinance. The mayor could do it if he wants to."

Henry Blatner, architect: "If

thing good, something appropriate. The buildings present a wonderful facade and the facade should be maintained, but not necessarily as it is."

Bernd Foerster, professor of architecture, RPI: "The significance of Elk Street far exceeds the importance of the separate structures. The buildings must be seen together in relation to their urban environment.

Added Foerster, "The city can ill afford the loss of these 19th Century houses. Out of the entire City of Albany, the Historic Sites Commission has set aside only a very small number of areas for a major preservation effort, and Elk Street has always been at the top of the list."

J o h n Mesick, architect: "In the case of Elk Street, it would be f e a s i b l e to impose design criteria so that the scale, height and material are controlled (in the case of a new structure by the Bar Association).

Mesick added, "It is possible to have a better wall on Academy Park if these conditions were imposed. The whol block should be one building with no setbacks, no piecemeal development."

Although a "save Elk Street" movement is u n d e r way, the man on the street — Mr. Public himself — has not yet made his influence felt. In favor of saving the buildings, however, are the Albany Historic Sites Commission, Mayor Corning and the

Hudson River Valley Commission.

In addition, the Schenectady Stockade Association has voted to launch a letter-writing campaign to try to head off the Bar Association's plans.

The Sites Commission, which has only advisory powers, was created by a city ordinance in 1966 to, among other t h i n g s "safeguard a n d preserve the historical, cultural and architectural heritage of the City of Albany."

The same ordinance designates the north side of Elk Street and Columbia Street from Hawk Street to Chapel as areas of special character or special historical or aesthetic interest or value.

THE
TIMES UNION

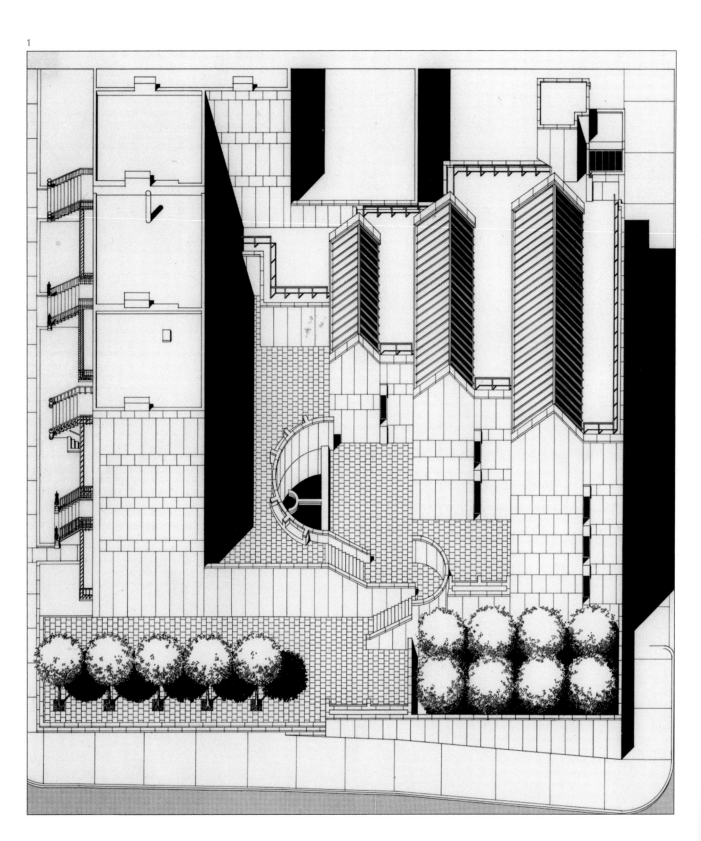

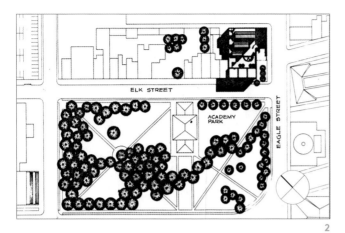

2

3

4 ↑   5 ↓

It occurred to me that we could remove the rear two-thirds of the existing houses (to the north) and restore the remaining portions, including the park facades. Then we could insert a new building on the remainder of the site, one that did not express itself on historic Elk Street. The old houses and the contemporary architecture would fuse. Most of the program would be accommodated in the new building. One of the preserved houses—4 Elk Street[4]—would provide the principal entry; otherwise, the interiors of what remained of the existing houses would be mothballed for future use.

We described the scheme, with drawings and a small model,[5] at our next meeting. A few days later, Mike Seymour called to say that the committee was pleased with the idea but concerned about added costs. And they were correct—there was a premium for grafting the new onto the old. But in the end, the completed complex would protect not only the integrity of this part of Albany but the attorneys' reputation as well.

The controversy over demolition/preservation/new construction had drawn attention outside of Albany, and *New York Times* architecture critic Ada Louise Huxtable covered the design in her column on July 21, 1968.[3] The Bar Association, she wrote:

is a demonstration project of how to use the past without turning it into a charade and how to extend its fabric functionally into the 20th century for the best kind of living environmental continuity. The philosophical and design lesson here is of national importance. So is the lesson for preservation.

1   2   3

The section through the complex demonstrates the simplicity of the scheme and the ease with which new could be attached to old.[4] A partially underground garage and delivery port opening to Columbia Street to the north forms the base of the new building. On top of the garage sits a courtyard looking east over Eagle Street. The courtyard is bookended on the south by the north sides of the old buildings—with new facades of Indiana limestone—and on the north by the three staggered volumes of the addition. The lowest contains the Hinman Law Library; entrance to the library is via 4 Elk Street and a connecting link. The library overlooks the fifty-foot-high Great Hall, the ceremonial room occupying the central volume. The third and highest space houses a grievance hearing room, the executive director's suite, and various offices. Each of the three volumes has a peaked roof with continuous skylights on the north-facing plane. The shape of the roofs recalls the residential roofscapes and scale of Columbia Street, which slopes down and east almost to the Hudson River.

Back in New York I was invited to attend a private salon—a group of young architects brought together by Philip Johnson.[1] At these informal meetings one or more of the architects was expected to show a current project; the other attendees criticized the project, not always constructively. I presented the Bar Association drawings with a certain amount of trepidation: some of the attendees (Richard Meier, Peter Eisenman)[2,3] were committed to a "theological" modernism and tended to look askance at historic restorations. However, the session proved to be valuable. Eisenman suggested some interesting, albeit minor, changes to the massing. He also explained the formal concept in terms that were, to me, intellectually convoluted but convincing sounding nonetheless.

4

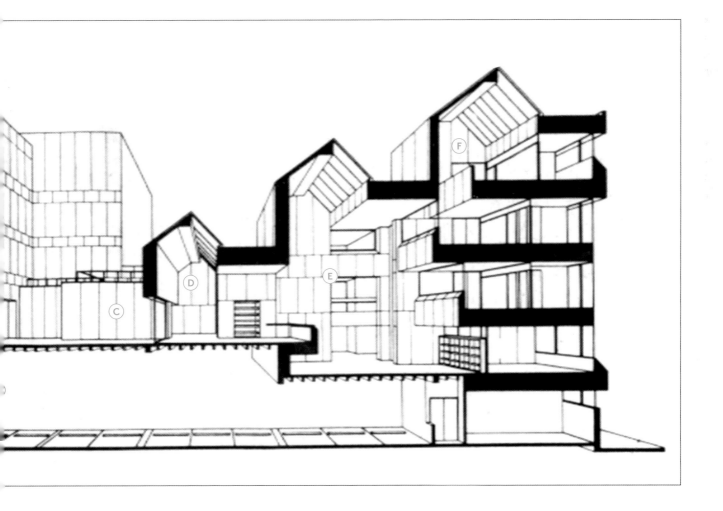

A. GARAGE
B. NEW COURTYARD FACADES
C. CONNECTING LINK
D. HINMAN LAW LIBRARY
E. GREAT HALL
F. GRIEVANCE HEARING ROOM

1

2

3

both in the judgments of the jury and in a great number of the submissions. One current is a coming of age of modern architects in terms of their leadership of responsible preservation efforts. This is quite a significant change from 20 years ago...Here, there is quite a different attitude, which is perhaps going too far in the maintenance of old facades in a kind of scenographic way. Another current is the semibrutalist aesthetic of the new buildings. In one direction, we're moving away from prettying up old buildings according to new aesthetic terms and in another direction we're moving away from prettying up our new buildings.

Fund-raising by the Bar Association had gone well, and it was not long before construction commenced under the excellent leadership and irascible Irish humor of John McManus, the head of one of Albany's largest contracting firms. The site preparation and foundations proved to be especially complex.[1] Almost immediately, the corner building developed structural cracks that were sufficiently serious to require its demolition.[2,3] There was one benefit: on this corner area we developed an open green space that related to Academy Park across the street. This small grassy area introduced some breathing room between the Bar Association and the courthouses across Eagle Street. The soil was a larger problem. The subsurface had, since the time of the Revolutionary War, been called "bull's liver": it was extremely unstable to begin with and, besides, was reportedly filled with cannon balls and bones of war horses. Additional structural reinforcement added $205,000 (over $1,500,000 today) to the overall budget, most of which was for foundation work.

Not too long after that the Bar Association received an award for unbuilt work from *Progressive Architecture* magazine. It was the first formal acknowledgment by our peers. The jury included Lewis Davis, Henry Cobb, Cesar Pelli, and Roger Montgomery.[4] Montgomery's published comment was particularly gratifying:

This project strikes me as possibly the most portentous of all the projects that we finally selected, in that it somehow draws together two of the currents reflected

1   2   3

As the builder and the consultants were addressing these engineering and financial hurdles, I was working with my colleague Pamela Babey[1] (now the senior partner of BAMO in San Francisco) on the interior design of the public spaces. We wanted the interiors to be as inventive and contemporary as the exterior envelope of the new building, yet we also wanted to connect them to the history of the law and to respect the relatively conservative tastes of the lawyers. We intended to express the dignity and progressive nature of the legal profession in a merger of old and new interior appointments, ones that would reflect the architectural design.

The Hinman Law Library[5] overlooks the spatial volume of the Great Hall, which was directly inspired by Middle Temple in London.[3,6] Forty feet wide by sixty-six feet long by fifty feet high and visible throughout the addition, this formal chamber was our greatest interior design challenge. One committee member suggested we contact the artist Norman Laliberté.[2] At that time, he was creating thematic tapestries using multicolored pieces of felt. Laliberté's work had been shown in the Vatican City pavilion at the 1964 World's Fair in New York; the same tapestries currently hang in the Rockefeller Memorial Chapel at the University of Chicago (also home to artist Hildreth Meière's exceptional glazed ceramic tile decoration).[4] I visited his studio in Brewster, New York, and found the work populist in spirit, extremely colorful, and intellectually rich. The marvelous tapestries he created for the Bar Association—a long banner that portrays the world's legal systems and eight smaller ones that depict the evolution of the seal of New York State—were hugely popular with members of the bar.

4

5 ↑

6 ↓

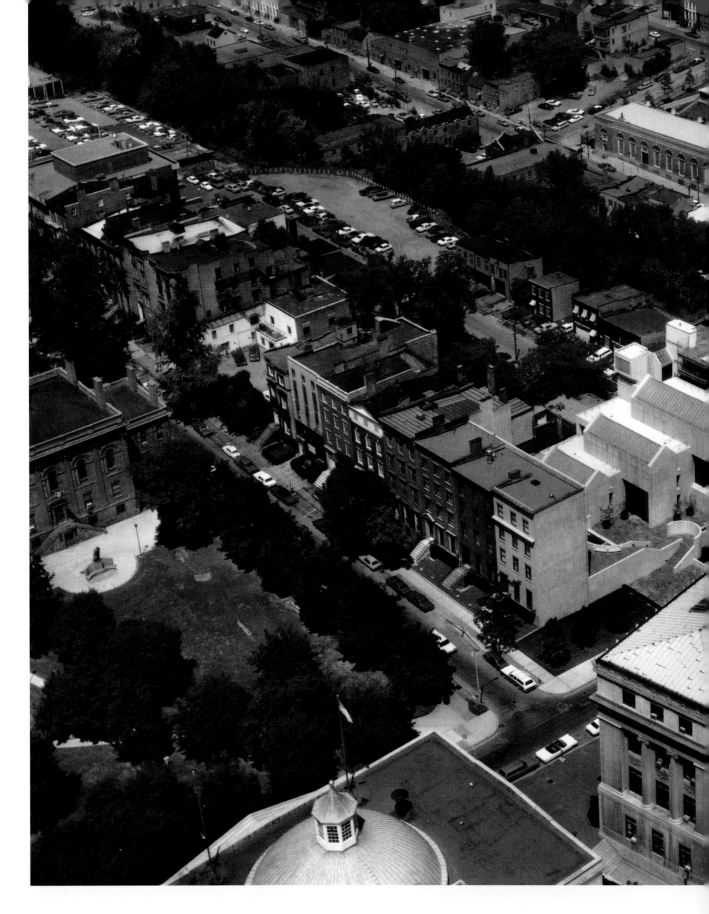

The association moved into its old/new home in 1971, and on September 24 of that year Governor Nelson Rockefeller delivered the dedicatory speech.[2] It was a beautiful fall day. The first thing I noticed was that hundreds of press people and a number of dignitaries and onlookers were milling about in the park across the street. I was flattered that this, our first public building, attracted so much attention. As the governor began to speak I heard a loud and insistent chant from the rear of the crowd. I finally realized that the new building was not the only focus of attention. The real reason for the excitement was a protest against the assault ordered by Governor Rockefeller that had ended the violent riot at Attica Prison just eleven days earlier.[3]

1

2

One rainy evening that winter, Ellyn and I were driving up Madison Avenue and I spotted Harry Cobb trying to hail a taxi. We stopped and he happily jumped in. Harry mentioned that he had been part of a recent jury in Washington. The AIA had bestowed on the New York State Bar Association a national Honor Award, the first AIA award given to an American building for combining historic and contemporary architecture.[1] Such hybrid buildings—500 Park Tower,[3] Seaman's Church Institute, the Rose Center at the American Museum of Natural History, the Brooklyn Museum— were to become something of a signature for our firm, both formally and ethically. But this early recognition was particularly gratifying because it was the first time that we had realized, in concrete form (in concrete, in fact), the abstract notion of architecture as a metaphor for healing.

3

Quinco Regional
Mental Health Center
Columbus, Indiana
1969–1973

The early 1960s represents an important turning point in mental health care. There were two predominant contributing factors—drugs and the law.

In the early part of the decade, antipsychotic drugs, primarily Thorazine, prompted a shift from housing the mentally ill in asylums to accommodating them in SROs (single-room occupancies). While this change would eventually increase the number of mentally ill living on the streets, it also had a more positive consequence: it rendered psychosurgery unnecessary. This fact might well have influenced one of President John F. Kennedy's New Frontier initiatives—the Community Mental Health Act of 1963.[2] The president had a personal interest in psychological well-being no doubt related to his oldest sister, Rosemary, who was permanently incapacitated at age twenty-three by a prefrontal lobotomy.

The Community Mental Health Act and the establishment of Medicare and Medicaid in 1965 led to explosive growth in private clinics, community mental health centers, and general hospitals. As a result, in the late 1960s and early 1970s, states greatly restricted long-term, full-care services in state mental institutions. The back-to-back assassinations of Martin Luther King and Robert F. Kennedy in 1968, following on JFK's, made mental health an ever more pressing, and immediate, concern. It was against this background that I designed a mental health facility in Columbus, Indiana.[1]

Early in 1969, the Cummins Engine Foundation wrote to us to ask whether we would be interested in being considered to design a community mental health center in Columbus sponsored by the Region 10 Mental Health Foundation. Quinco, its acronymic name, represents the southernmost five counties in Indiana. Ninety-seven Columbus residents, headed by Edgar Whitcomb (before he became governor of the state), had developed the plan for the community center, and Lowell Engelking,[3] chairman of the Region 10 Foundation, was responsible for building it.

1

2

3 ↑   4 ↓

5

6

The "Athens of the Prairie," Columbus was at the time a town of 27,000 (today it is closer to 45,000) in the southeastern part of the state. The nickname derives from the community's assemblage of exceptional contemporary architecture,[5,7] the brainchild of idealistic and generous J. Irwin Miller,[6] chairman of the Cummins Engine Company. The Cummins Foundation established a list of important architects of the day; the Cummins Company paid their fees for new public buildings in and around Columbus. Among the architects commissioned were the Saarinens, father Eliel[1,3] and son Eero;[2,4] Harry Weese; I. M. Pei; and Robert Venturi and Denise Scott Brown. To this day architects covet the opportunity to build in Columbus.

7   EDWARD CHARLES BASSETT/SOM, COLUMBUS CITY HALL
PAUL KENNON, SBC SWITCHING STATION
ROBERT VENTURI, FIRE STATION NO. 4
EERO SAARINEN, KEVIN ROCHE (ADDITION), IRWIN UNION BANK
I. M. PEI, CLEO ROGERS MEMORIAL LIBRARY
EERO SAARINEN, MILLER HOUSE
HARRY WEESE, FIRST BAPTIST CHURCH
JOHN CARL WARNECKE, MABEL MCDOWELL SCHOOL
GUNNAR BIRKERTS, ST. PETER'S LUTHERAN CHURCH

1

The project had meaning for me beyond the architectural. In the summer of 1949, before the use of antipsychotic medication, I had worked as a nurse assistant at Hawthornden State Hospital, a large public psychiatric institution. That hands-on experience, as well as consulting work on a children's psychiatric hospital in New York State[1] (a few years earlier I had designed a similar hospital as a school project), was the ideal qualification for this commission.

I flew out to Columbus for the interview—several other architects, including Gio Pasanella, a Yale graduate and friend, were on my flight; I assumed they were my competition—and the next morning I met Engelking at his office. A jovial Midwesterner, he spoke with a distinctive south Indiana accent.

Engelking escorted me to the interview with the director of Quinco, Dr. George C. Weinland, members of his staff, and several foundation trustees. The interview marked the first time I referred to my belief that architecture is a "healing art." Dr. Weinland explained how important it was to provide a physically and emotionally stable environment for twenty-five inpatients and numerous outpatients. Engelking stressed that the group wanted Columbus locals to see the center as a constructive addition to their community—Quinco was not to have facilities for psychotic or violent cases. The committee further emphasized that the architecture of the building must avoid creating any negative impression or stigma for outpatients. Mental health centers proved to be controversial in many towns more conservative than Columbus: the old myths concerning the mentally ill died slowly.

2

After the interview Engelking suggested that we drive over to the site. He casually mentioned that the location was in the flood plain of Haw Creek, a tributary of the White River, which frequently flooded.[2] We turned into the service drive of the Bartholomew County General Hospital and drove to the rear of the drab and shabby building. We passed the morgue, the hospital laundry, and several dumpsters filled with medical refuse. On a treeless field to one side were several residentially scaled one-story buildings that looked like a cheap motel but turned out to belong to a private nursing home.

A. PUBLIC SKATING RINK
B. PARK
C. GOLF COURSE
D. NURSING HOME
E. BARTHOLOMEW COUNTY GENERAL HOSPITAL
F. WATER TREATMENT PLANT
G. HAW CREEK

3

1

2

3

4

The other side of the creek offered a striking contrast. In Lincoln Park were located a row of hundred-year-old sycamore trees, a nine-hole public golf course, an ice skating rink by Harry Weese, and picnic areas. Engelking told me that the Army Corps of Engineers planned to realign the creek as part of a flood mitigation program. To my mind, this was a thoughtless act that would destroy most of the trees and eliminate a section of the recreation area. I recall reacting as I had a year earlier in Albany when I discovered that four townhouses were to be demolished to make way for the New York State Bar Center: what at first seemed to be a wonderful architectural opportunity was going to be problematic.

The Lincoln Park side of the creek was so attractive, and the proposed approach to the building was so unattractive, that I couldn't avoid the vision of a "bridge" building. I had visited the Château de Chenonceau in France,[1] which spans the Loire, and the Ponte Vecchio in Italy,[2] which crosses the Arno. Many other real and imagined occupied bridge structures, from the Rialto to John Soane's Triumphal Bridge, also came to mind.[3,4] The solution for Columbus would be to enter the new building through the park and to service it from the hospital drive. I was so persuaded by this notion that I shared it with Engelking at once.

I flew back to New York optimistic about our chances, and I was not to be disappointed. Engelking called to give me the good news. My colleague Jim McCullar and I began working on a site analysis and master plan—a series of studies that demonstrated how a bridge scheme might work. Three weeks later, on a beautiful autumn day, Jim and I went to Columbus for the initial presentation. We brought a diagrammatic sketch that illustrated how a dual-entry, bridgelike building might work. We also presented analytic drawings showing flood plain impact, creek alignment, and solar orientation. [2,3,4]

The building committee had done some homework as well. After broaching the idea of a bridge building with the city attorney and state officials, they determined that seven or eight public agencies would have to review whatever scheme the Region 10 board presented, including, of course, the Army Corps of Engineers. The corps was extremely skeptical of the concept of spanning the creek, but the agency did not veto the idea. It was made clear that any design would have to realign the creek to mitigate flooding. At a later meeting, the Army Corps of Engineers stated that any bridge building would have to utilize highway bridge construction; this method would have resulted in an awkward, ill-proportioned, and banal edifice.

Fortunately our structural engineers developed an alternative proposal. Pfisterer Tor & Associates of New Haven had been the engineer for Eero Saarinen's TWA Terminal at JFK Airport[1] and Louis Kahn's Yale Art Gallery. Together with Repp & Mundt, the local builder, the firm performed extensive soil and flow tests, conducted borings, and projected theoretical flooding scenarios. They concluded that widening the creek both to the north and to the south of the new building would solve the flood threat. And if this alteration was implemented as part of foundation work for the structure, it would be affordable. Eventually, the Corps of Engineers agreed to the design. As we moved forward, I began referring to the evolving center as "the bridge to mental health." This phrase became the project's motto and, in part, contributed to its approval and funding.

1

2   3   4

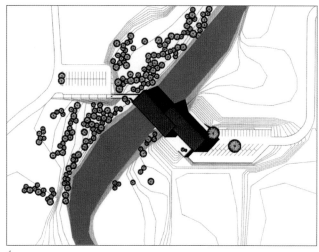

4

In spite of the regulatory, financial, engineering, and bureaucratic complexities, the actual design of the metaphoric bridge was surprisingly straightforward. One circulatory and one environmental objective guided the development. From a circulation standpoint, it would be advantageous to separate the public approach from the service and staff entrance, as I had deduced from my initial site visit. Lincoln Park became Quinco's "front yard." Environmentally, widening the creek for flood control preserved the trees and the park.

Daylight and transparency would be critical to the success of Quinco. Two precedents, one American and vernacular, the other European and contemporary, governed our thinking: the concrete grain silos of the Midwest[2] and James Stirling's Andrew Melville Hall at the University of St. Andrews in Scotland.[3] The multifaceted concrete facade of the latter was mediated by delicately detailed glazed openings.

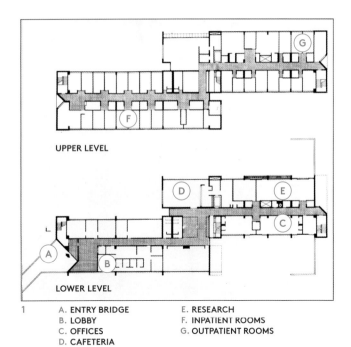

1
  A. ENTRY BRIDGE   E. RESEARCH
  B. LOBBY   F. INPATIENT ROOMS
  C. OFFICES   G. OUTPATIENT ROOMS
  D. CAFETERIA

UPPER LEVEL

LOWER LEVEL

2

The plan consists of two offset rectangular wings. These intersect at the eastern bank of Haw Creek. The building that spans the creek accommodates inpatient psychotherapy areas and examining rooms on the upper level and reception, offices, records, and patient screening on the lower level. Visitors and patients enter the facility via an elevated walkway.

The second wing has three floors; because of the topography of the riverbank, it is partially underground even though it is at the same level as the river wing.[2] The underground portion contains storage areas, mechanical equipment, a loading dock for trucks and ambulances, and an entry for employees and hospital staff. Above this is a floor of mental health research laboratories. The top floor is devoted to outpatient rooms.

At the intersection of the two wings is a two-story atrium.[3] A north-facing dining room with views of the creek and its tree-lined bank adjoins the atrium on the upper level;[4] below is a lounge for patients and staff. The sunshine that pours into the common areas and inpatient rooms[5] was a significant aspect of the curative mission of the center. The interior color palette is neutral except for yellow and vermilion supergraphics—so typical of the 1970s—in the atrium and lobby.

3

4

5

2

In 1980 a disastrous flood demonstrated that the "bridge" really worked. The complicated permitting, intricate public and private financing, and unique construction techniques came together in a benign "perfect storm." Slender planar supports rise out of the creek bed to engage the concrete superstructure.[1] The exposed concrete cradles precisely detailed glass infill. The quality of the formwork assured a concrete finish of exceptional quality. Only the narrow ends of the building are visible from the banks of the creek, allowing the center to merge subtly with its surroundings.[2]

The Region 10 Center was dedicated on December 17, 1972. I have always felt that it rationalized the conflict between process and art more than any of our other buildings. And while there was no way to know it at the time, twenty-five years later we designed another bridge building, the William J. Clinton Presidential Center, for a president whose campaign theme was the "bridge to the future."

The bridge metaphor is an example of how architecture can appeal to users and observers in ways both literal and figurative. The idea of bridging or connecting implies mending, restoring, healing. The optimism and generosity of this intention humanizes a built work, ultimately endearing it to its community.

Carnegie Hall
New York, New York
1978–2003

1   2   3

Who hasn't heard the question "How do you get to Carnegie Hall?"

There is a literal answer, and there is a capricious answer, and there are even several directional answers, because there are Carnegie Halls in Lewisburg, West Virginia; Pittsburgh, Pennsylvania; and Dunferlime, Scotland, Andrew Carnegie's hometown. But if you are trying to get to Carnegie Hall in New York City, the best response is "practice, practice, practice."

The idea for this iconic music venue was born in the mid-Atlantic in 1887 when Andrew Carnegie[1] met twenty-five-year-old Walter Damrosch[2] on a steamship heading from New York to London. While on board they became friends, and Carnegie and his new wife invited the young conductor to meet them in Scotland. It was there that Damrosch experienced his vision of a great hall for New York City. Carnegie was intrigued and decided to commit part of his fortune to the idea.

Carnegie retained William Burnet Tuthill,[3] a New York architect with musical inclinations. Tuthill engaged Dankmar Adler as an acoustical consultant. Adler had been Louis Sullivan's associate for the Auditorium Building in Chicago, which at the time was underway. Three years later, on May 13, 1890, Carnegie's wife, using a silver Tiffany towel, laid the cornerstone at West Fifty-seventh Street and Seventh Avenue. Carnegie Hall opened in 1891 with Tchaikovsky and Damrosch conducting.

1

2   3

4

5

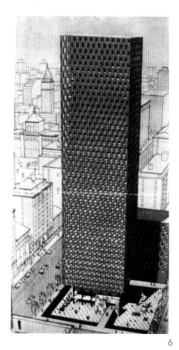

6

The hall was owned by the Carnegie family until 1925, when it was sold to Robert R. Simon. His son inherited it; by the mid-1950s he offered to sell it to the New York Philharmonic. My first visit to Carnegie Hall took place about this time. One day in the spring of 1953 my Yale classmate Walfredo Toscanini invited Ellyn and me to a concert his grandfather Arturo was conducting: the NBC Symphony.[3] Being seated in this historic hall was a thrilling experience, as was seeing the maestro conduct. The idea that we would one day create a master plan for the future of this American landmark was unimaginable.

The New York Philharmonic decided against buying Carnegie Hall, and it was put up for sale in 1960.[4] Sixty-nine years after its opening, New York's great "music box" was threatened with destruction to make way for a forty-four-story, fire-engine-red office building designed by Pomerance & Breines.[6] At the last minute the hall was saved by a combination of artistic celebrity, financial power, and public demonstrations by dancers and musicians.[5] The chief rescuers were Isaac Stern[1] and Jacob M. Kaplan.[2] Stern, of course, was one of the greatest violinists of the twentieth century. Jack Kaplan, a funny, curmudgeonly, but brilliant businessman, became one of New York City's few politically progressive philanthropists; his family follows in his footsteps to this day.

1

2

3

Over the next seventeen years the artistic reputation of the hall never ceased growing. Its physical fabric, however, was deteriorating. The public spaces and patron amenities had become shabby, and exit routes were unsafe. The floor above the primary auditorium, or main hall, was a catacomb of studios for artists.[5] Inevitably, water from overflowing water closets would seep into the main hall, sometimes causing musicians to abandon their performances.[4]

By 1978 the economy was coming alive after the oil drought of the early 1970s. Stern, board chair James Wolfensohn, managing director Norton Belknap, and other members of the executive committee decided that the time had come to plan for the future. Schuyler Chapin,[2] an elegant musical aristocrat, arranged for Wolfensohn and Belknap to visit Brooke Astor[1] with him. In this first of three visits they came away with a pledge of $25,000—enough to retain an architect. Chapin and Belknap were the last two patricians on the board. They had a gentle manner and puckish smiles that balanced the tough and often brusque manner of Wolfensohn, a financial executive.

Our invitation to be interviewed came about through Schuyler, then a fellow dean at Columbia University. Paul Byard, an associate in our office, joined me in the faded café at Carnegie.[6] Formerly general counsel to Ed Logue at the New York State Urban Development Corporation (VDC), Paul was familiar with the many anticipated legal and code issues. Our historic preservation experience, on the other hand, was limited, and our practical knowledge of concert halls was nonexistent.

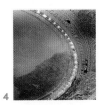
4

5

6

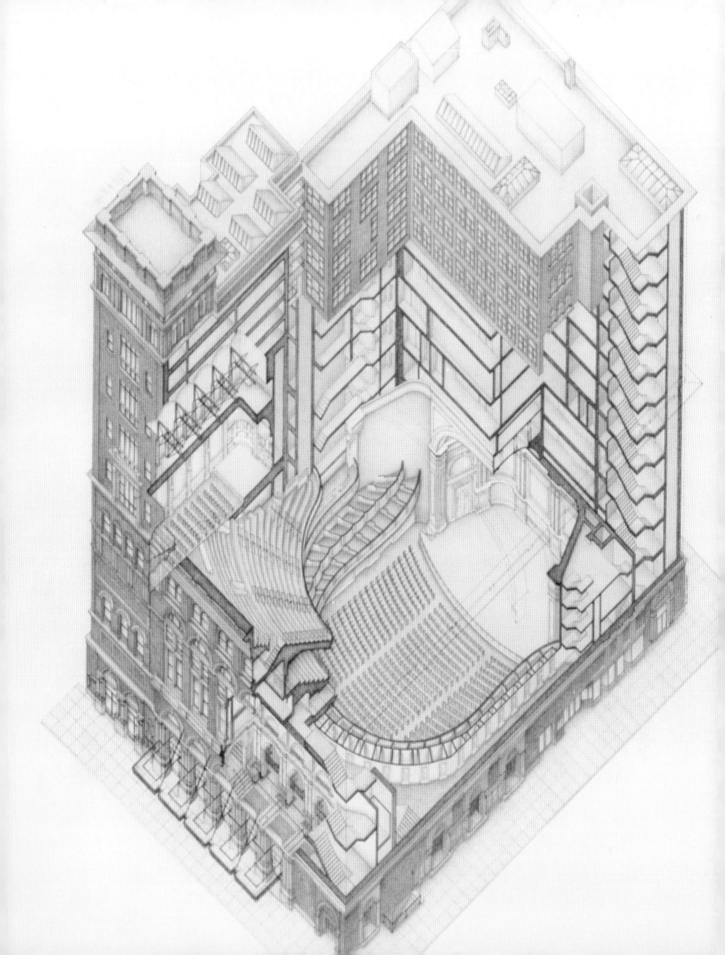

2

3

Before the interview, we toured the building, from the antique boilers and fans in the cellar to the open stairwells and incomprehensible corridors above. The term "rabbit warren," especially for the floor above the main hall, was inadequate. The general shoddiness made it clear that a plan was urgently required.

Among the projects we presented to Stern, Wolfensohn, Belknap, and Chapin were the Helen Carey Playhouse (now the Howard Gilman Opera House) at the Brooklyn Academy of Music [3] and Brotherhood Synagogue, [2] a former Quaker meeting house and, by coincidence, an early project of the J. M. Kaplan Fund. We had been suggested as the architect for the synagogue by Jack's daughter, Joan K. Davidson. At the conclusion of the presentation, we suggested a first step—an analysis of existing conditions.

Just before we began work on the building analysis, [4] Wolfensohn asked if we might suggest someone who could oversee the implementation of the master plan on behalf of the board of trustees. Other responsibilities would include dealing with public regulatory agencies, the construction manager, and all consultants except the acoustician, who was to report directly to the trustees. We suggested Larry Goldman, a Princeton graduate who was devoted to public service and had worked with Paul at the UDC. Larry had learned from Ed Logue the financial, social, and most important, cultural value of real estate development. His sense of humor and optimism allowed him to weather the thorny Jim Wolfensohn. He would guide the project through the opening of the renewed hall in 1986 and then go on to create the New Jersey Performing Arts Center in Newark.

Carnegie Hall
Master Plan

Phase 1
Building Analysis

James Stewart Polshek & Associates
Architects

4 ↑

5 ↓

Our master plan had five major elements: patron service and support spaces, which focused on the entry and service spaces on the Fifty-seventh Street side of the building; professional entry and performance support spaces, which addressed areas on the Fifty-sixth Street side; available development potential, which determined how to use the Rembrandt lot next door to meet functional needs and generate funds and revenues; internal systems upgrading, which centered on modernizing air conditioning, electrical, and other building systems; and music and recital hall interiors and other historic fabric restoration, which addressed protecting and restoring the performing spaces and other notable elements of the hall.

Although the stated first task was to improve patron services, the real first task was to understand the building. Carnegie Hall was actually three different volumes dating from 1889 to 1929,[1] including the campanile by Henry J. Hardenbergh, architect of the Dakota Apartments and the Plaza Hotel. None of the original Tuthill or Hardenbergh drawings could be found, and it was necessary to construct three-dimensional drawings in order to identify vertical cores, stairs, shafts, and entry/exit points. The horizontal and vertical circulation routes through the building were unimaginably complex; some of the stairways[2] were open for 160 feet from bottom to top. Their graphic representation resembled an M. C. Escher drawing.[3]

Once we and our consultants had a handle on the physical issues and the assignments before us, we began to detail the master plan. The first phase was the renovation and redesign of the lobby for the recital hall. (Along with the main hall and the rehearsal space, this was one of the three performance areas in the music hall.) Our re-creation of an original arch[4] transformed a shabby storefront back into Tuthill's graceful terra-cotta entranceway of 1891. Inside the renewed ground-floor lobby we created light fixtures within faux Corinthian capitals, a contrarian critique of postmodernism.

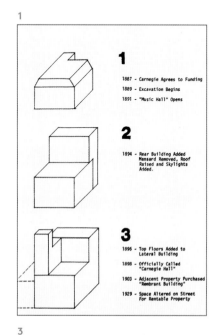

1

1887 - Carnegie Agrees to Funding
1889 - Excavation Begins
1891 - "Music Hall" Opens

2

1894 - Rear Building Added
Mansard Removed, Roof
Raised and Skylights
Added.

3

1896 - Top Floors Added to
Lateral Building
1898 - Officially Called
"Carnegie Hall"
1903 - Adjacent Property Purchased
"Rembrant Building"
1929 - Space Altered on Street
For Rentable Property

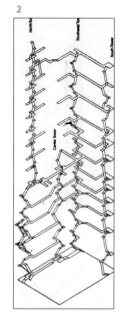

4

1

2

3

4

The second undertaking was the replacement of anti-quated building systems. Many future renovation plans would depend on new air conditioning and ventilation systems. Tishman Construction executed this hidden work in only ninety days in the summer of 1983 when the hall was dark. The company would go on to manage all further construction; its chair, John Tishman, [4] was a member of the Carnegie board.

The next phase saw our first physical design for Carnegie Hall, the Alice and Jacob M. Kaplan Rehearsal Space. [1] The space was originally the site of the old Chapter Room, the meeting place for Andrew Carnegie's chapter of the Masonic Order. We rede-signed it as an advanced rehearsal space and recording studio accommodating up to forty musicians. Exposed ducts and movable acoustic panels convey the multi-functional nature of the room. Mary Belknap, Norton's wife, suggested that we soften the room by painting it the peach color of her hairdresser's salon.

In the following stage of the project we turned to the exterior of the building. Nine decades of neglect, not to mention environmental factors, had taken a fearful toll on the twenty-six miles of mortar joints between the roman brickwork as well as on the balustrades, [2] cor-nices, masonry ornamentation, windows, and sky-lights. Commercial storefronts had been carved out of the Seventh Avenue facade, and the brick was filthy. We had to reverse these conditions and stabilize and seal the building envelope before major interior work could be undertaken. [3]

1

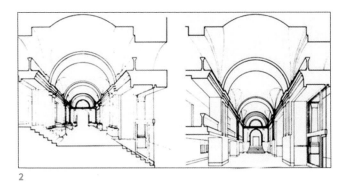

2

3   4

All of our work to this point had been, in a sense, pre-paratory. Phase four was the one that every historic preservationist in town was waiting for: the reconstruction of the main hall, recital hall, and main lobby. We entrusted the structural restoration of the lobby to engineer Robert Silman; he had previously handled the exterior structure. Ray Pepi of the Center for Building Conservation played a crucial role in the analysis of paint and other nineteenth-century building materials. Tishman hired Diane Kaese, who studied historic preservation at Columbia, to further safeguard the building fabric.

Arriving just in time for this period of work was Judith Arron,[1] Carnegie's new general manager and artistic director. She had been a creative force as manager of the Cincinnati Symphony, and with Norton Belknap, who became an effective co–managing director, she oversaw the renovation of the auditoriums and the creation of a new lobby on West Fifty-seventh Street. Brooke Astor's $1 million gift was a financial and emotional benefaction that allowed the lobby construction to proceed.

The most visible—and radical—change was the entry lobby. There had always been steps from the sloping sidewalk up to the entry level of the hall.[4] But between 1891 and 1986 the sidewalk rose and the number of steps diminished. Fewer steps created greater risk; it was not unusual for audience members to trip from the sidewalk into the shabby and dark lobby or to fall from the lobby out onto West Fifty-seventh Street.[3]

An early probe had discovered a ten-foot void beneath the existing entry level floor. In a series of sealed rooms were musical scores, electronic equipment, and other memorabilia. This was a gift not only to the archivists but to the architects—we were able to lower the lobby floor almost to street level by eliminating two sets of interior stairs.[2]

The new lobby offered, for the first time, an elegant gathering space for the hall.[5] Grand stairways to the east and west lead to an overlook that encourages the people-watching so indispensable to the world's great performance venues. Box offices were tucked in under the parquet promenade on the same level as the new lobby. A new elevator serving all seating levels, except the highest one, was installed.

1

2

3

4

5

6

The work of Charles Rennie Mackintosh[5,6] provided the formal precedent for the design details of the renovation. A Scot like Carnegie, born twenty years later, Mackintosh was strongly affected by the art and architecture of Japan, then newly accessible. (I had been similarly affected by two years in Japan in the early 1960s.) The gridded bronze marquee, lobby light fixtures and railings, café doors, and even the elevator interior reflect Mackintosh's influence.[1,2,3,4]

Other than in Las Vegas, gambling and architecture are usually not associated with one another. But the stakes could not have been higher as we embarked on the reconstruction of the 2,804-seat main hall, now known as Isaac Stern Auditorium. The soul of the Carnegie experience had always been the quality of the sound, and an acoustical modification of the space was paramount. Stern selected Abraham Melzer, an Israeli military jet navigator, as the acoustician. Abe was often AWOL from Carnegie, but never from his air force.

2

3

4

5

It had long been rumored around the music hall that in 1946 the makers of the inconsequential movie *Carnegie Hall*[3] had to cut a forty-five-by-fifteen-foot hole in the acoustic shell of the main hall in order to light the film. While there was indeed a hole, we were assured by Gino Francisconi,[4] Carnegie's archivist, that it had been made in 1898 after a fire temporarily closed the Metropolitan Opera House. The opera, which set up residence in Carnegie, needed the aperture to fly scenery from a loft suspended above the shell. The opening was never repaired but was disguised by a seven-ton "teaser" curtain.[1] We had to remove the old curtain and replace the punctured shell, restoring the grandeur of the full opening of the proscenium.

Abe,[5] with the encouragement of Tishman, specified a precast plaster system for the new shell. When the first pieces arrived, it was like fitting together the shards of a broken egg. Given the tight schedule, old-fashioned hand-troweled plaster was the only solution. Stage lighting, always a challenge in the original space, was solved by a "crown molding," which hangs from the new shell and contains all of the lighting.[2] New red seats and carpeting were installed. The seat color, as with every performance space, was a selection nightmare. After trying fifteen or twenty variations of red, nostalgia trumped innovation and we matched the original color. Wood-framed photographs of the great artists who performed at Carnegie over the years were mounted throughout the hall, and refurbished sconces were installed on the balcony fronts.

1

In the drab and acoustically challenged recital hall, Abe called for the addition of three enormous chandeliers, maintaining that they would assist in the fragmentation and redistribution of sound. Later, when these modifications proved to be excessive, sidewall drapes had to be hung as acoustical dampeners. We designed a new "Palladian" stage surround for the performance space.

The color of the fabric for the new seating in the recital hall was also much debated. At the end of one of our meetings, Isaac asked us to meet him in the luxurious Beresford apartment building. His studio was modest—a few chairs, a desk, and a grand cherry cabinet. He took out a key, opened the double doors of the cabinet, and retrieved a violin case, handling it as if it were a Torah on a high holy day. He placed the case on the desk and removed the violin—an instrument that must have been one of the most valuable in the world. But it was not the violin he wanted us to see—it was the blue-green velvet lining. It was clear that there would be no further discussion of the color of the seats in the performance space, now known as the Joan and Sanford I. Weill Recital Hall.[1]

The restoration was known as the "twenty-eight week miracle" because of the compressed timetable.[2,3,4] The schedule was audacious but necessary because of performer contracts. The budget—$2 million per week—was unprecedented. "Ground" was broken in May 1986 by Mayor Ed Koch, Isaac Stern, and Jim Wolfensohn. From that moment on, Tyler Donaldson, our project architect, rarely left the construction site.

2

3

4

The most indelible memory of those twenty-eight weeks was the "music" of the construction—harmony, syncopation, and rhythm—not to mention the energy and enthusiasm of the workers. Robert Dalrymple made a documentary of the restoration in which snippets of opera, jazz, swing, folk, classical orchestra and piano, show tunes, comedy, and political rants accompany the footage of the actual construction.

By Thanksgiving 1986 work on the main hall was complete. Before the grand opening a "hard hat" concert took place. More than 2,000 proud workers and family members attended. But opening night, with every music critic on the East Coast in attendance, would be the first real test.

On the clear and chilly evening of December 15, 1986, my wife and I arrived at Carnegie Hall in a horse-drawn carriage. [4] We were greeted by "footmen" and ushers, clad by Ralph Lauren in the red of the newly upholstered seats. Following this reception were several astonishing hours of music: Yo-Yo Ma, Marilyn Horne, Isaac Stern, Lena Horne, Jessye Norman, and of course, Isaac's old friend Frank Sinatra. [3] The celebration was not limited to the building restoration—we honored Isaac Stern, muse and leader.

1

2

Two years later, Judy Arron and I watched as a gigantic hole opened up in the four-foot-thick east wall of Tuthill's building. This was the start of the construction of sixty-story Carnegie Hall Tower, designed by Cesar Pelli on what had been known as the Rembrandt lot.[3] The office high-rise incorporates, on its lower floors, twenty-five thousand square feet of space for Carnegie programs; it also increased the endowment. Our team continued with the new areas of the Carnegie complex. In addition, we helped Pelli's office select a palette of materials for the tower that would be compatible with Tuthill's building.

The added space was used, in part, for a new backstage and facilities for the artists. This, in turn, allowed for an enlarged stage wing, more dressing rooms, a freight elevator, and a new backstage area for the recital hall. The recital hall was augmented with an enlarged lobby, a new elevator, and a renewed café. A new set of public spaces accessible from the main hall, christened the James D. Wolfensohn Wing, incorporated the Rose Museum,[6] the Carnegie Shop, and the Rohatyn Room[4] and Shorin Club Room reception areas. We also brought the café on the ground floor[1] into the twentieth century.[2]

The interior design of the spaces in the new wing is best characterized as "Carnegie comfort style." The materials included anigre wood paneling, brass trim, and Mackintosh-influenced lighting and detailing. We designed a blue-green carpet with multicolored borders inspired by Sonia Delaunay's drawings.[5]

3

4

5

6

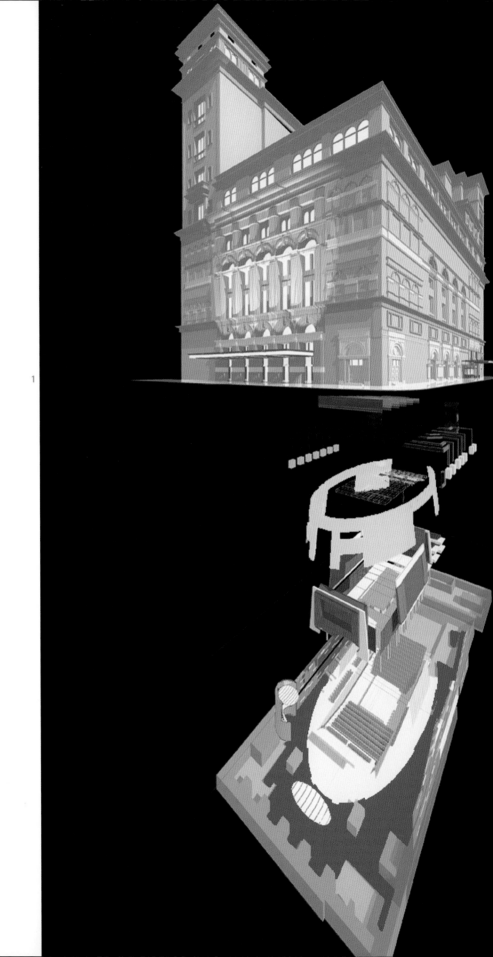

1

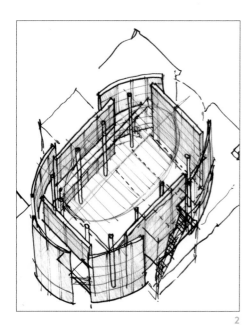

2

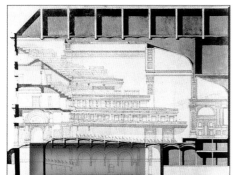

3

The end of the work for which we had been commissioned coincided, surprisingly, with a new project at Carnegie. Not long after the Shorin and Rohatyn Rooms were completed, I sat next to Judy at a preconcert dinner. She quietly told me that the lease of the cinema occupying the underground space where there had once been a recital hall would be up in June and that she wanted to develop a new midsize performance venue.[3] To me, this was an opportunity to create an architecturally modern hall, appropriate to music both modern and traditional. It was unclear how far we would get with the historic preservation contingent, which included a few influential trustees, but at the very least, we could remove the commercial presence from the Seventh Avenue facade and create a new entry. So began the creation of Carnegie's "third stage."[1,2]

1

2

3

4

In order to make a case for a true twenty-first-century hall, Richard Olcott, senior designer on the new project (and soon to be a partner), my wife, and I accompanied Isaac and Joan and Sandy Weill[1] to Paris. We wanted to see Christian de Portzamparc's Cité de la Musique[5]—comparable in dimension and form, the hall could be physically adapted to suit various types of music. We had to virtually sneak in with Pierre Boulez,[3] our tour guide, because of yet another Parisian *grève*. The elliptical concert hall was spatially interesting, but the detailing and construction had clearly suffered from the recession of the early 1990s.

Given the severe space constraints of the new hall, we too were looking at an elliptical insertion, but our auditorium would be rectilinear.[4] Richard and I presented this as a "baroque" figure, evoking images of early European chamber music venues, such as Sala Terrena, or House of Mozart.[6] We also suggested—shamelessly—that it was a metaphorical wooden violin case embracing a precious instrument.

Richard possessed both an understanding of historic architecture (he later served on the New York City Landmarks Preservation Commission) and an acute musical sensibility. He and acoustician Christopher Jaffe together shaped the hall, though it was Richard who was responsible for its visual warmth and intimacy. After several months of design development, we met with the executive committee. Board member Felix Rohatyn[2] asked me for an estimate of the costs. With little conviction, I mentioned a number between $12 and $15 million. Rohatyn shared his pointed rule of thumb for dealing with architects: double the higher number and then double it again as a contingency. This added up to $60 million (and the final cost was actually $72 million). Removing rock from under a century-old landmark doesn't come cheap.

5

6

2

In addition to the board, we had to satisfy the Landmarks Preservation Commission. The old recital hall[5] contained fragments from the original 1891 building. At the request of Jennifer Raab,[4] chair of the commission, we salvaged pieces of decorative plaster and ironwork. Those last relics are in the commission's warehouse in Brooklyn.

Aside from the budget, the principal obstacle was the available volume, delimited by granite below and the Stern Auditorium above. We had to convince the board that our scheme, including lobby spaces and patron amenities, would work inside the unforgiving enclosure. To bolster our argument, we used masking tape to create a full-scale plan in a TWA hanger at JFK Airport.[2]

The hall, named for Judy and Arthur Zankel,[3] was a far more complex undertaking than any of our earlier efforts at Carnegie. There were four notable risk areas: access, structure, sound, and flexibility. Getting audiences into the auditorium was relatively easy. An elephant-sized elevator and an escalator made ingress a breeze. But getting them out was another matter. Exiting the hall was slow. In bad weather the small street-level lobby filled quickly, and the surge of departing patrons then choked the escalator.

As for structure, we had to somehow figure out how to enlarge the space of the old recital hall. In 2000 David Dunlap quoted me in the New York Times: "If St. Peter's was out of space and had to build a chapel for 600 people, they wouldn't go across the Tiber. They'd excavate. The reason for the rock removal is that a performance hall has to have volume. The secret to any hall where unamplified music is played is volume. We couldn't go up. So we had to go down."

3

4

5

Digging twenty-two feet down required the removal of 6,300 cubic yards of Manhattan schist—enough to fill 363 New York City garbage trucks.[1] The excavation also routed hundreds of rats. The MTA denied our request to use subway freight cars at night, so the rock was carried out in canvas bags. Next came the bulldozer. With no "wiggle room" in this subterranean space, it was inevitable that there would be an accident. One day the twentieth-century steel blade of the machine cracked one of the nineteenth-century cast-iron columns below the main hall before the new steel structure was in place. There were many sweaty palms, but no real harm done.

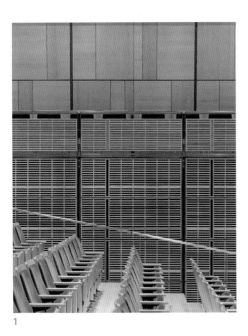

1

2

Christopher Jaffe was concerned with noise from the street and between the auditoriums. We isolated Zankel from the main hall just above with a new double ceiling. Extreme noise tests, carried out during performances upstairs, brought not a whisper of complaint. But the biggest concern was the subway, which practically abutted the hall. Three sets of east-west tracks start to change direction at Fifty-ninth Street, completing the turn at Fifty-seventh Street—metal wheels on metal tracks, twenty-four hours a day, exactly adjacent to Zankel Hall. It was impossible to completely eliminate the rumble of the trains, an unavoidable state of affairs in a late-nineteenth-century underground venue, but we came close.

Finally, the new performance space offered an opportunity to create a room where stage and seating arrangements could be varied.[4,5,6] Theatrical consultants Auerbach Pollock Friedlander and our design team, with occasional advice from stagehands, collaborated on a system that would allow for the reconfiguration of the room. The floor was made up of lifts that could be moved into a "garage" at one end. The lifts could be organized to form traditional end, thrust, in-the-round, and flat-floor stages.

James Levine[3] and the chamber orchestra of the Metropolitan Opera "test-drove" Zankel Hall before its public opening. At the end of the performance the musicians stood and applauded.

3

4

5

6

1 ↑

2 ↓

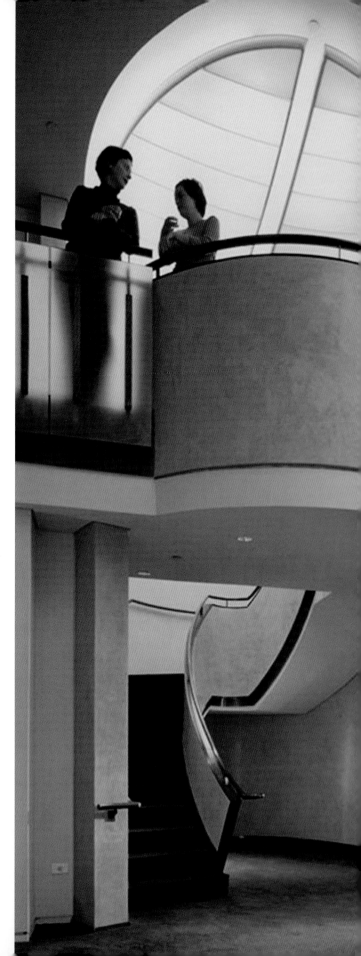

The opening of the hall on September 12, 2003, was as glamorous as that of Stern Auditorium, though on a smaller scale. Renee Fleming[1] performed with cellist Eric Jacobsen. After the performance Fleming praised the space, saying that she had never played in a warmer hall.

Tragically, the brilliant Judith Arron did not live to see the completion of Zankel Hall. The performance space was named in her honor.[2] Herbert Muschamp wrote an appreciation of Zankel in the *New York Times* on opening day:

The sense of enclosure within the earth actually enhances the brightness and clarity that the architects have brought to the design...The [urbane scent of Paris] lingers longest in the elliptical enclosure of polished Venetian plaster that surrounds the new auditorium like a cone of golden sunlight...A luxury version of a black-box theater, the hall has the feel of a broadcasting studio, which it partly is.

Zankel Hall was to be our last work at Carnegie. In 2009 Richard Malenka, the hall's longtime head of operations, asked us to submit a proposal for the floors above and around Stern Auditorium. A proposal? Since 1979 we had never submitted credentials or fee proposals. Malenka gently reminded me that Sandy Weill's son-in-law was an architect. That was that. As politely as I could, I responded with a phrase to the effect of "game over!"

But I have no regrets. It was a thrill to contribute to the revival of this seminal cultural institution. The Carnegie journey confirmed my belief that historic preservation is much more than preserving historic buildings. It is a way to recapture the more humane aspects of architecture—craft and collaboration. Collaboration is listening to all voices, to consultants and kibitzers, to historians, lawyers, conservation technicians, engineers, and public commissions. Craft is focusing on how things are made—materials, connections, function, and social importance. And Zankel perfectly represents both.

EXIT

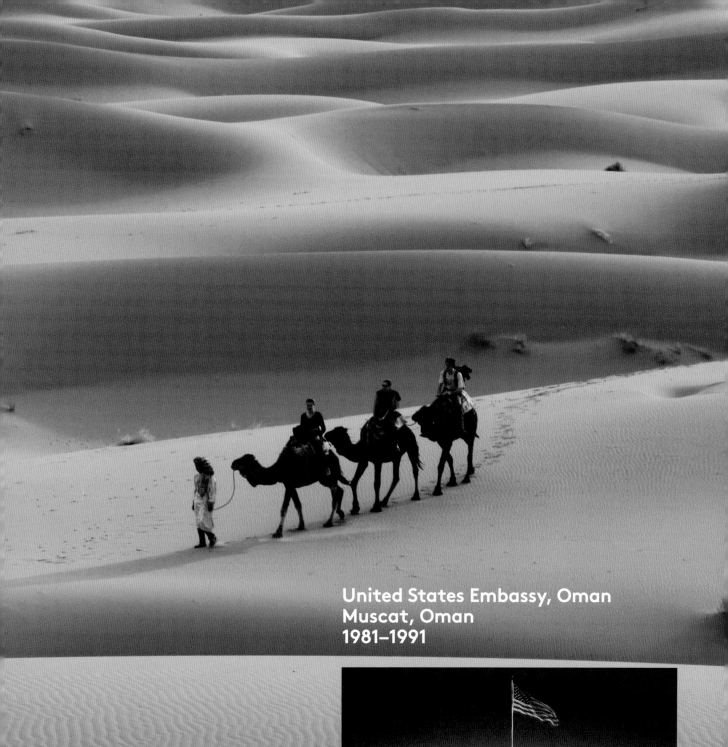

United States Embassy, Oman
Muscat, Oman
1981–1991

1

2

For decades the small arid nation of Oman was so isolated that it was called the "Tibet of the Middle East."

While it was the first Arab land to recognize the United States, sending an envoy in 1841, Oman was a closed country until well into the twentieth century. In 1968, with revolutions of one kind or another erupting throughout the world, the insular and backward-looking sultan of Oman was overthrown by his son, Qaboos bin Said,[1] in a palace coup. The new sultan began to liberalize Oman's government, upgrading health and educational facilities and creating modern highways, water system, and electric grids. With this came an increase in Westernized architecture—except for the Sultan Qaboos Grand Mosque.[2]

A geographical peculiarity gives Oman a vital strategic importance.[3,4] The Strait of Hormuz, a waterway about thirty miles wide that separates Oman from Iran, forms the entrance to the Persian Gulf from the Arabian Sea. A large proportion of the world's oil traverses the strait; trade routes between China, the Indies, and East Africa are linked in the bodies of water. Though few had heard of Oman until the oil embargo and the recession of the early 1970s, its history and location are an important part of the reason I became a participant in a real-life Arabian Nights story.

3

4

5

6

The tale begins in New Haven in 1954. My wife, Ellyn, and I decided to spend the summer before my graduation living and working in the Bay Area. I hoped to work for the San Francisco architect Joseph Esherick. I was particularly interested in his houses, which had a formal clarity and a special sensitivity to the landscape of Northern California.

At that time, George Howe[5] was the dean of the Yale School of Architecture. A charmingly aristocratic modernist from Philadelphia, he invariably carried a pint of bourbon in the pocket of his leather-lined tweed jacket. Before coming to Yale, Howe and William Lescaze had designed the iconic Philadelphia Saving Fund Society building.[6] Howe resembled FDR in politics, class, and religion and, like FDR, was considered a "traitor to his class." Howe was responsible for bringing Louis Kahn to Yale; Kahn taught while overseeing construction of the Yale Art Gallery.[1]

Howe wrote to Esherick on my behalf, and in May I received a letter from him inviting me to come out. We started our cross-country trip a month later. Our first stop was Akron, Ohio, where we visited my family. Then we were off to Chicago; Oskaloosa, Iowa; and Racine, Wisconsin, to see various Frank Lloyd Wright buildings.[2,3,4] We took the northern route through Glacier National Park and then drove down to Reno, Nevada, and Lake Tahoe.

1

2

3

4

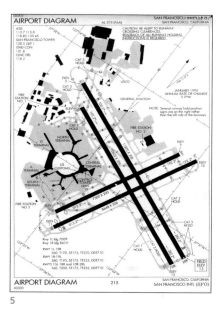

5

Our entrance into San Francisco, over the Bay Bridge, coincided not only with a torrential rain storm but with a stunning moment in American political history. We pulled off the road and parked, riveted by the car radio. This was the very moment during the Army-McCarthy hearings when Joseph Welch, the brilliant Boston attorney, confronted the nefarious Joseph McCarthy: "Have you no sense of decency, sir?"[1]

We found a Murphy-bedded apartment on Sacramento Street across from a public tennis court, and finally I made my way to the Esherick office.[2] I had glimpsed my first Esherick house in Berkeley, on our way into the city.[6] I expected to find a bustling atelier, but to my surprise, I found the architect alone, surrounded by empty drawing tables. He was deeply apologetic, explaining that the dire economy resulting from the end of the Korean War the previous year had stopped the projects he had anticipated I might be working on. So much for Northern California regionalism.

Disappointed but undaunted, I passed the summer working for the engineering firm DeLeuw Cather. They had subcontracted some work to William W. Wurster's firm, Wurster, Bernardi & Emmons,[3] and that was where I spent most of my time. The team leader from the Wurster office, Audrey Ksanda (later Audrey Emmons),[4] a flamboyant blonde, became my mentor. She taught me to draw on blue linen with India ink, and introduced me to martinis. Creating landing approach diagrams for the Strategic Air Command may have clashed with my politics, but it was work.[5]

Twenty-two years would pass before I met Esherick again. We spoke of our practices—how the increasing importance of nature and context was affecting our work, and how the idealism implicit in early modernism was on the wane. I was unaware that Esherick was a member of the Architectural Advisory Board of the State Department's Office of Foreign Buildings Operations (now the Bureau of Overseas Buildings Operations).

The agency's primary purpose was to ensure that American embassies would be models of architectural excellence. A further objective was to convey the optimism and values of the United States while still expressing a sensitivity to the design traditions of the host country. The AAB was made up of prominent American practitioners. This older group had an unstated obligation to recommend for these unique commissions the members of an emerging generation of architects.

1

2

3

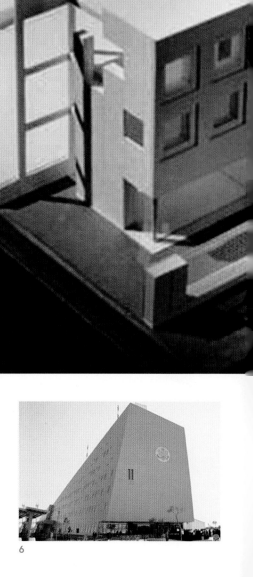

4

5

6

7

8

9

10

11

In 1980, four years after that second meeting with Esherick, I received a call from William Slayton, the deputy assistant secretary of state and director of the FBO.[8] Slayton invited me for lunch at the Yale Club. We spoke of his days, and mine, working for I. M. Pei; Pei's New York office, Webb & Knapp, was then part of the William Zeckendorf organization. We reminisced about Pei's principled work and his particular genius with clients. Pei had designed Slayton's house,[3] which was inspired by Le Corbusier's barrel-vaulted weekend house outside of Paris, built in 1935.[1] In a strange coincidence, our one previous experience working for the State Department, a new chancery in Lyon, France,[7] was also inspired by a Corbusier project, the Maisons Jaoul of 1956.[2] Our project was terminated by the recession brought about by the oil embargo of the early 1970s.

Slayton explained that a member of the AAB had recommended our firm for an embassy commission. I knew that it must have been my almost boss, Joseph Esherick. Bill identified the assignment as a new chancery and ambassador's residence in Oman. I wondered whether it would be a problem, for a project in the Arab world, that I was born Jewish. But Slayton informed me that Oman was one of only five Arab countries to recognize Israel. There would be no objection. I didn't realize at the time that I had just been selected for the commission. There was no formal interview, submission of documents, or security check. A far cry from the endless vettings architects endure today!

I flew down to Washington with my partners Paul Byard[9] and Jim Garrison[10] for our first meeting with Bill, his staff, and the project architect, Reid Herlihy.[11] We toured the FBO's offices with Bill and admired photos of some of the embassies that had been built (or were in progress) under his watch: Alan Y. Taniguchi's in Guyana;[4] William Caudill's in Saudi Arabia;[5] and Harry Wolf's in Abu Dhabi.[6]

1

2

We then received a two-hour briefing on the site (not inspiring) and the strategic importance of the location (unnerving). The program included an elaborate residence for the ambassador as well as the chancery (offices, consulate, etc.). Bill's team explained that we would need to appoint a "security officer" who would possess a dedicated safe for all papers related to the project.

We returned to New York to begin research into Oman's historic, geographic, and political circumstances. The nation, which occupies the southeastern corner of the Arabian Peninsula, is almost exactly the size of New Mexico. The population is close to 2.5 million—also equal to New Mexico's. Nicknamed the "magic kingdom," this country was the legendary home of Sinbad the Sailor[3] and the source of frankincense and myrrh prized by the Queen of Sheba.[4]

Oman had long been an important factor in commerce because of its location in the Arabian Sea. While culturally and politically a traditional Arab state, the nation has long-standing ties, political, military, and economic, with the United Kingdom.[1] Oman had comparatively little oil but was still rich enough to contemplate the ambitious modernization put forth by Sultan Qaboos bin Said after he replaced his father.

The climate of Oman is extreme, and this would significantly influence the design of the building. The site, about ten miles west of the capital city of Muscat on a beach facing north to the Arabian Sea, is located almost exactly on the Tropic of Cancer. At summer solstice the sun is directly overhead. Average temperatures are well over 100 degrees, and humidity levels are frequently 85 percent or more. In 1980, just before our first visit, a record temperature of 146 degrees was recorded on the roof of the British Embassy. On the coast there is no vegetation to provide shade or shelter. Only in oases, where date palms have been cultivated for over a hundred years, is there respite from the sun.

Initially a small post, the U.S. Embassy grew as the location of Oman—perfect for monitoring and controlling the sea distribution of crude oil—became more important. The Iranian hostage crisis of 1979–81 also required an increased American military presence in the Middle East.[2] Thanks to the long friendship between Queen Elizabeth and Sultan Qaboos bin Said—he had attended the Royal Military Academy Sandhurst—the United States was invited to use RAF bases in Oman.

3

4

1

2

In January 1981, Ellyn and I left for Paris, Athens, and Oman, where we were to meet Paul Byard and Reid Herlihy. At a stop in Abu Dhabi, I was curious to see the terrain. I peered through the aircraft door for just a moment before I was abruptly jerked back inside. A flight attendant indicated four machine pistols pointed at me.

Our home in Muscat was the Intercontinental Hotel— a luxurious early example of the modernization of the country.[1] There we had our first traditional Omani experience—we were offered tiny cups of very thick black Arabian coffee from a turbaned fellow sitting cross-legged on the lobby floor.

The next morning, Paul, Reid, and I were driven west on the impeccably manicured Qaboos Highway[2] to Medinat Qaboos. On the beach facing the Arabian Sea was the future Diplomatic City, a row of embassy sites. As a "city," it had a long way to go. Our plot was a barren stretch of sand covered with natural debris.[3,4] To the south were the dark and treeless Hajar Mountains, some as tall as 3,500 feet.

The sites staked out for the various embassies were identical, as if each would be one of dozens of RVs. The tracts were in three parallel rows and were oriented exactly north-south. Each was supplied with utilities. The embassies of Jordan, Egypt, and the UAE were already constructed in a faux Islamic style. The future U.S. Embassy was to occupy the third parcel from the east end of the beachfront row. The building would eventually be flanked by Pakistan and India—geopolitical common sense.

That evening our group had drinks at the hotel. The view from the upper-floor bar looked over the Arabian Sea. We thought we were looking through the darkness to a small town in the desert. What we were actually seeing were the lights of supertankers waiting in line to enter the Persian Gulf.[3] Maritime insurance companies wanted the tankers in and out as quickly as possible to minimize exposure.

The next day we walked through Muscat to view the sultan's "golf tee" palace.[2,4] Then we were presented to U.S. Ambassador Marshall W. Wiley. The embassy was in an eighteenth-century house built into a rock outcropping in the center of town.[1] The ambassador sat at a desk on the ground floor with his back to a window—proof that security was virtually nonexistent. He was enthusiastic about Oman and its people but understandably concerned about the Iran-Iraq war that had commenced a year earlier.

1   2   UNITED STATES EMBASSY AND AMBASSADOR'S RESIDENCE   James Stewart Polshek
    SULTANATE OF OMAN   Feasibility Report   & Partners · Architects

3   4

5

The following morning, armed with box lunches, Paul, Ellyn, and I took off on seemingly invisible roads into the vast Wahiba Sands. We did not go far before encountering the first of a number of small villages of traditional mud dwellings.[1] Each house merged with the earth and was indistinguishable from the next except for metal or wood doors: painted in primary colors, the portals defined the "personality" of the individual dwellings.

Walking through villages on spiderweb-like paths polished by a hundred years of use felt like time travel. Adjacent to the paths were water courses called *falaj*.[4] For thousands of years, falaj acted as irrigation systems. Drawn by gravity, water flowed down stone steps or shallow canals, with cleaner uses such as washing and bathing at the top and less sanitary functions at the lower levels.

Work began in earnest when we returned to New York.[2] The program we developed, totaling 45,000 square feet, included a chancery with offices and support spaces for approximately eighty people. We allowed space for public embassy functions, such as consular services and military, cultural, and commercial attachés. Parking for thirty-five to fifty cars, warehouse storage, and workshops were inserted below grade. The ambassador's residence would be semi-attached to the chancery; a driveway just inside the perimeter wall would provide access. Landscaping and a shaded swimming pool in a courtyard separated the two buildings. We also incorporated secure communications spaces for the CIA "spooks"—though we were not allowed to design them.

The classic Arabian courtyard was conceptually and spatially similar to that in a traditional dwelling. This design element, which offers shelter from the heat of the sun, has been integral to the region's architecture.[3] Here we enclosed it in the manner of a mini, air-conditioned shopping mall and used it to organize the quasi-public embassy spaces. The perimeter wall was made of a grid of lightweight fibercrete that provided shade and screened the glass behind.[5]

6

A. AMBASSADOR'S RESIDENCE
B. AMBASSADOR'S ENTRY COURT
C. POOL
D. CIA SECURE COMMUNICATIONS
E. INTERNAL COURTYARD
F. RAMP DOWN TO PARKING
G. PUBLIC ENTRY
H. FORECOURT
I. SECURITY
J. RESIDENCE GARDEN

1

Just before the Architectural Advisory Board was convened to review the design, we were notified that the project could not go forward. The domestic economy was in a severe recession, and violence was on the rise in the Middle East, made tragically evident by the October 23, 1983, terrorist bombing of the Marine barracks in Beirut.

Given the need for heightened security, many U.S. embassies were replaced or upgraded, and the FBO was expanded. It was not clear what effect this would have on the Oman embassy and on U.S. architecture overseas in general. We were worried about whether there would be a project at all and, if it were to proceed, whether the design quality would be compromised.

In 1985 we were authorized to proceed with a redesign of the embassy. New guidelines asked us to incorporate recently formulated structural standards and shielding strategies, including enhanced seismic guidelines that would respond to potential bombings, defensive thresholds, safe havens, and paths of retreat.

A modified program eliminated the ambassador's residence, underground parking, and delicate light-admitting screens. One of the changes that particularly disappointed the embassy staff was the relocation of the cafeteria from the light-filled ground floor to the cellar. But these were not the only hurdles we faced.

The sultan and his ministers had become concerned that the architectural direction of new construction in and around Muscat was favoring Western styles over Islamic influences. He commissioned an Australian planning firm to develop guidelines for all new buildings in the country. The study, turned over to us by the

2

FBO, was copiously illustrated with ogee arches, Islamic motifs, and other elements of the Islamic vocabulary. My only knowledge of "Islamic" architecture at the time was the Tangier Restaurant and Cabaret in Akron, Ohio,[1] and a faux mosque movie house in Helena, Montana.[2]

Our new design kept the rigorous orthogonal geometry of the first scheme, which allowed for planning flexibility. An eleven-meter-square "tartan" planning grid defined interior functions as well as a resulting central atrium. The parking, on grade on the approach side of the new building, enhances the security perimeter. We relocated the gardens to the area between the chancery and the wall of the compound on the side along the sea.

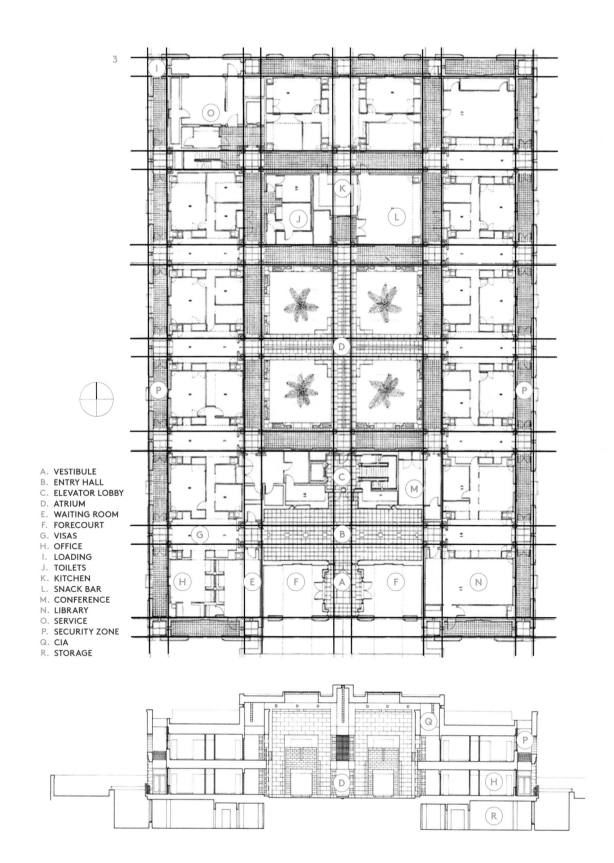

A. VESTIBULE
B. ENTRY HALL
C. ELEVATOR LOBBY
D. ATRIUM
E. WAITING ROOM
F. FORECOURT
G. VISAS
H. OFFICE
I. LOADING
J. TOILETS
K. KITCHEN
L. SNACK BAR
M. CONFERENCE
N. LIBRARY
O. SERVICE
P. SECURITY ZONE
Q. CIA
R. STORAGE

The FBO asked us to pay careful attention to the "public aspects" of the new embassy—the facades. Rather than adhering scrupulously to the Australian report—or to any specific existing structure—we looked to three precedents: Egyptian pylon temples,[2] the mosque of Córdoba,[1] and two unbuilt designs by Louis Kahn, the Angola Embassy of 1965[3] and the Meeting House at the Salk Institute of 1962.[4] All contained elements that were appropriate to a government building in a Muslim state, notably austere symmetry (the temples), polychrome arches (the mosque), and arches and concrete detailing (Kahn's schemes), and all influenced the expression of the facade.

The final scheme for the building would be presented at our long-delayed meeting with the FBO's advisory committee. At this time the AAB was composed of Ralph Rapson (dean of the School of Architecture at the University of Minnesota),[2] Donn Emmons (partner at Wurster, Bernardi & Emmons),[3] O'Neil Ford (partner at O'Neil Ford and Carson Architects),[4] and Edward Charles Bassett (senior design partner at Skidmore, Owings & Merrill in San Francisco).[5] My anticipation (or was it trepidation?) in advance of the meeting reminded me of the anxiety that preceded my final design review at Yale. Jim Garrison and Reid Herlihy mounted large renderings of the building and assisted me with the explanations.[1]

The first question did not bode well. Ford, generally known to be agreeable and droll, began in his South Texas drawl, "Are you one of them postmodern fellas like Michael Graves?" He was responding to the multicolored bands of stone on the arches of the facades. I answered with a simple "No, sir," too nervous to invoke the historic precedents that had inspired the polychromy. He then asked me about the rear garden, which I had referred to as an "outdoor room." "There is no such goddamn thang as an 'outdoor room'—where I come from, rooms are indoors!"

Nervous laughter broke out, then Ralph Rapson took over. He asked why the plan was so insistently symmetrical. Once again I mentioned our precedents—the Egyptian temples and Spanish mosque, in particular—and the sultanate's request to create an architectural expression that would incorporate a Muslim sensibility. I began to speak about the human body, using it to represent symmetry—until I looked up and realized Dean Rapson was missing his left arm. I hadn't thought it could get any worse.

Near the end of the rather abrasive meeting, Ford started another rant against postmodernism. Bassett, who until then had been quiet, defended our design eloquently, and finally, after a little good-humored face-saving, we received the board's approval.

1

1

2

3

4

5

We had originally planned to build the stone arches the same way they might have been constructed in the Middle Ages, with the weight of the stone blocks and the thrust that they exerted transferred to precast concrete blocks. However, new security standards trumped medieval intentions. Government engineers determined that our age-old technique would not withstand the explosive force they considered the primary threat to the stability of the outer wall. In the end we redesigned the arches so that they were hung rather than supported.[3] The exterior walls had reinforcing bars spaced three inches apart to resist blasts and also to prevent human entry if all the concrete was destroyed.[4] This is the same structural requirement used in building prisons.

The only other construction problem of any consequence was the stainless-steel alloy used in the exposed metal railings and trim. Neither our specification writers nor the FBO's engineers had recognized that the alloy selected could not stand up to the salt air, sand, and wind of the area. Six months later the metal was replaced by a salt-resistant alloy.

One of our few disagreements with the FBO concerned the State Department's "Buy American" policy. The issue was the stone for the facades. The polychromatic design was essential, and it had been approved by both the State Department and the sultanate.[1,2] For the buff stone we had identified Kasota stone from Minnesota. But there was no red stone available in the United States with a density and hardness that could withstand the harsh climate, and so we had specified the granite that had been used in India by Le Corbusier and in Bangladesh by Kahn. We were initially told that we could not use this material. What ultimately won the case was not aesthetics, persuasion, or a challenge to patriotism but the new blast-proofing requirements.

Diplomatic protocol requires an architect to personally present the plans of an embassy to its ambassador. I flew to Oman with large rolls of drawings. Groggy after the twenty-four-hour trip to Muscat, I left the documents in the overhead luggage compartment. By the time I realized my blunder, the plane had departed for Australia. Fortunately the drawing rolls were safely returned the next day. Ambassador John R. Countryman, who had replaced Ambassador Wiley, seemed to be pleased with the design. We chatted about the political volatility of the region as we drank Omani coffee.

The politically connected Texas conglomerate Brown & Root was awarded the contract. It was an appropriate choice given the symbolism of this isolated and heavily protected U.S. outpost, a kind of Wild West way station.[5] Brown & Root subcontracted to a UK construction company experienced in working in the Middle East. Because of the unstable nature of the region, the pressure on the schedule was extreme. Oman had no available workforce, so common laborers came across the water from Pakistan, skilled stonemasons flew in from Korea, and the general construction trades arrived from India.

1

In general the construction progressed well, and the quality of the work was superior to what could have been achieved in the United States. The tense politics of the Middle East removed bureaucratic obstacles, thereby expediting the schedule. The tight timing required extra visits by architects from our office and staff from the structural engineering firm. This resulted in both the beauty of the craftsmanship and the fulfillment of our mandate to create a building that would respect the design traditions of the host country.

Views of the completed building from within and without show the contrasts in the natural context of mountain and sea. The chancery garden with its long reflecting pool expands the site perceptually. The "outdoor room" that inflamed Ford, which faces the chancery garden, is used by the staff in all seasons.[2] The green spaces were partially covered by stretched Teflon fabrics to create a shaded outdoor gathering space inspired by covered souks.[1] Lining a series of reflecting pools are whimsical, oil-can-shaped fountains.[3] Even though there is less oil under Oman than under the other Gulf states, it is still the lifeblood of the country.

The blast-resistant stone walls that form the outermost layer of the building are arranged in bays. Each of the bays has an arched opening over a rectilinear opening. [4,5] These respond to both climate and security issues, and they also foster ever-changing patterns of shade and shadow that enrich the stone envelope.

2

3

4

5

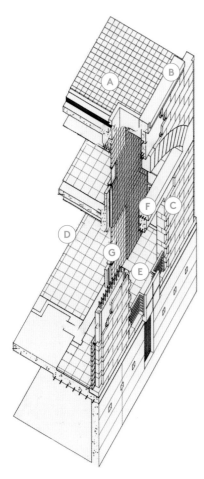

1
A. PRECAST ROOF PAVERS
B. PRECAST CONCRETE COPING
C. STONE CLADDING
D. REINFORCED CAST-IN-PLACE CONCRETE
E. CERAMIC TILE
F. PRECAST CONCRETE TIE BEAM
G. GLASS BLOCK

2

3   4   5

The interior details and finishes are consistent with the visual language of the exterior envelope.[3,4] The court is brilliantly lit by symmetrically placed openings reinforced to prevent potential attackers from dropping through the skylights.[2] We developed a water feature as a reference to the falaj, which reinforces the strict geometry of the floor.[5] Behind the windowless upper portion of the "prosceniums" that form the internal facades of each bay facing into the court is the secure communications section of the embassy.

1

2

Sunset on the Arabian Peninsula is an intense visual experience. One of my last memories of the newly completed building is its silhouette at twilight. We never knew if there was a formal dedication.

Several years later I went to Oman with O'Neil Ford for a postoccupancy report. He was as charming and witty as could be—and he loved the building! I did too, but I was never to see it again. The geopolitics of the turbulent region keep it shrouded in secrecy.

Brooklyn Museum
Brooklyn, New York
1986–2004

1 2

The populist spirit of the Brooklyn Museum is said to have been inspired by Walt Whitman's[1] inventiveness and humanistic values.

Although its roots go back to 1823, with the founding of the Brooklyn Apprentices' Library Association by Augustus Graham,[2] the institution that would become known as the Brooklyn Museum came to life in 1841 when the library moved into the Brooklyn Lyceum on Washington Street. Whitman, then sixteen years old, was the acting librarian.

In 1843 the library and the Lyceum merged to form the Brooklyn Institute, which was itself reorganized in 1890 as the Brooklyn Institute of Arts and Sciences. The institute presented fine arts exhibits, offered public lectures on topics as diverse as geology and abolitionism, and due in part to the City Beautiful movement that grew out of the 1893 World's Columbian Exposition in Chicago,[4] began planning a new museum. The last several decades of the nineteenth century were a time of explosive museum growth. Fine arts museums were founded or opened in Philadelphia, Hartford, Boston, Chicago, Pittsburgh, and Washington, D.C.

The new museum in Brooklyn, designed by McKim, Mead & White, was conceived as the focal point of Prospect Park, a cultural, educational, and recreational district developed by Frederick Law Olmsted and Calvert Vaux starting in 1865.[5] Intended to rival New York's Central Park, the park is a rough chevron in shape; not quite half a century later, Ebbets Field would arise close to its easternmost point. The almost-six-hundred-acre swath accommodates the Brooklyn Botanic Garden as well as the museum, which sits at the oblique intersection of Eastern Parkway—also a work of Olmsted and Vaux—and Washington Avenue.[3] Although most of Eastern Parkway is a tree-lined boulevard edged by pedestrian malls, the stretch in front of the museum is rather barren. The great landscape designers did not quite succeed in bringing the country into the city, but their template served and continues to serve the important organizations of the area as well as the larger region.

3 ↑

4 ↓

5 ↓

3

1 ↑

2 ↓

180 BUILD, MEMORY

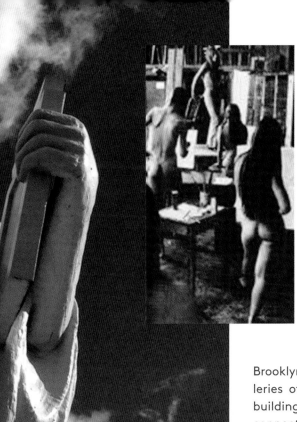

5

6

7

4

8

9

Brooklyn's unparalleled diversity has enlivened the galleries of the museum. In the parking lot behind the building, which was originally envisioned as a formal connection between the museum and the botanical garden, stands a replica of the Statue of Liberty, dating from about 1900, that welcomes the dozens of ethnic and religious groups of the borough.[3]

The Brooklyn Museum, the Brooklyn Academy of Music, the Brooklyn Botanic Garden, and the Brooklyn Children's Museum remained constituents of the Brooklyn Institute of Arts and Sciences until the 1970s. The Museum Art School[4] joined the roster from 1941 until 1985. Its faculty included William Baziotes, Max Beckmann, Ben Shahn, Jack Tworkov, Reuben Tam, Donald Judd, and Robert Smithson; most have work in the museum's collection.

Also represented in this great repository are Americans Gilbert Stuart, Winslow Homer, John Singer Sargent,[5] and Mary Cassatt[8] and Europeans Claude Monet, Gustave Courbet, and Henri de Toulouse-Lautrec.[9] The museum is particularly renowned for its Asian and Egyptian collections.[6,7] All recall the patrician patrons who created and continue to support the museum. Over the years, occasional controversies have fueled the vitality of the museum. The masterpieces of the collection, in fact, set the scene for the public disputes, reminding visitors that exhibits on hip-hop[2] and *Star Wars*[1] attract new audiences but do not take away from the importance of the institution.

1

2

3

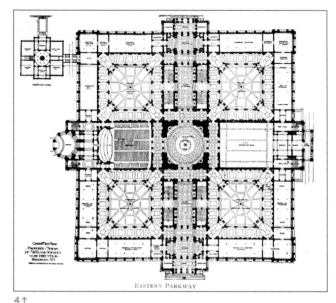

4 ↑

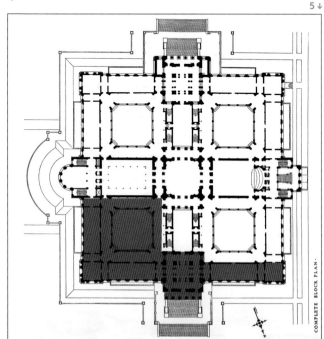

5 ↓

Construction on the museum began in 1895 to McKim, Mead & White's designs, [1,4] which resulted from an 1893 competition. In 1897, upon its completion, the initial built section was surrounded by farmland. [2] It resembled the lonely first portion of Calvert Vaux and Jacob Wrey Mould's American Museum of Natural History, erected twenty years earlier. Work on the center pavilion and its grand stairway was initiated in 1899; [3] at the last minute the trustees decided to tuck an auditorium under the stair. This decision stretched the construction of this part of the building to six years. It also required the architects to raise the main floor by five feet, sixty inches that would come to have enormous consequences. The museum grew in fits and starts until 1926, when the center pavilion, the northwestern and northeastern wings, a portion of the eastern wing, and the northeast interior court were completed. [5,6] Although just a fragment of McKim, Mead & White's original grandiose concept, this phased structure adequately served the museum for years.

6

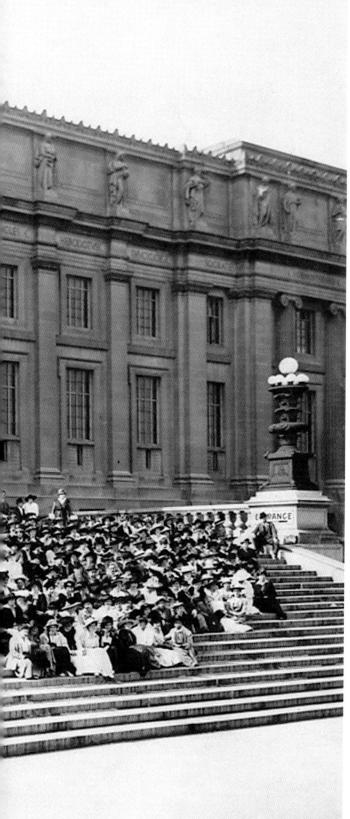

2

3

4

The middle of the Great Depression saw the appointment of a new director. Philip N. Youtz[2] is the only architect to have held that position. He was a "theological" modernist—note the eyewear—and was not entirely sympathetic to the decaying Beaux-Arts masterpiece on his hands. Soon after his 1934 appointment he consulted William Lescaze, even though the successor firm to McKim, Mead & White (the last of the firm's founding partners had died in 1928), represented by partner William Kendall, was still under contract. Lescaze and George Howe had, just a few years earlier, completed the Philadelphia Saving Fund Society building in Philadelphia, the first International Style skyscraper in the United States.

Youtz made little secret of the fact that he (and his soon-to-be architect) wanted the steps removed. The twenty-eight-foot-high granite stairway[1] had been neglected for decades, so it was not long before he got his wish. Water penetrating the joints of the steps had compromised the steel support structure, and there were no funds, emergency or otherwise, to pay for the repair. While Kendall was in Europe, Youtz submitted a proposal to the New York City Art Commission and quickly began demolition.[4] McKim, Mead & White soon resigned from the museum. Youtz's intervention resulted in a sheer masonry wall with five isolated apertures.[3]

1   2   3

In 1980 Joan Darragh [1] was appointed as the vice director for planning and architecture. She lamented the state of the building: "The north, main Eastern Parkway facade had been denuded by the removal of the stairs; the west elevation, although romantic and nostalgic, had been left unfinished in the manner of a Hollywood set; the East Wing had received a Modernist slap on the back; and the south elevation...had become an uninviting pastiche of the incomplete and the uninspired."

In 1986 the museum trustees held an international competition for a new master plan intended to provide a blueprint for the museum's growth into the twenty-first century. One of the fifty-seven firms that submitted qualifications to the invited competition was Arata Isozaki & Associates. My friend and colleague Ann Kaufman [3] had just completed a year in Isozaki's office as a Luce Scholar. She had studied at Columbia when I was dean at the School of Architecture, helped me establish the Buell Center for the Study of American Architecture, also at Columbia, and then came to our office. Isozaki contacted her to discuss the competition, and Ann suggested he consider collaborating with us.

Born one year after me, Iso [2] (as he was known) studied architecture at the University of Tokyo and worked for Kenzo Tange, Japan's master modernist. He emerged as an internationally known designer in the mid-1970s. In 1974 he completed the Museum of Modern Art in Gunma Prefecture. His most recognized project was the Tsukuba Center Building, [4] opened in 1983. Iso was deeply interested in contemporary art and concerned with inventive form making using the vocabulary of postmodernism. While I rejected this language, I did not believe that a little theoretical discord would be a bad thing.

The mid-1980s found the profession in yet another recession; in our office, Carnegie Hall was under construction but not much else was in the pipeline.

4

Neither I nor Joseph Fleischer, the managing partner, had ever been sympathetic to competitions. There was an art to winning them, I believed, an art that we didn't possess. Instead I preferred a face-to-face client interview. A few factors conspired to change our minds, in addition to the weak economy: my experiences in Japan, the firm's knowledge of building in New York City, respect for Isozaki (who did seem to know how to win competitions), and the composition of the jury (correctly analyzing the jury was crucial). The group included Klaus Herdeg, professor of architecture at Columbia; Phyllis Lambert, director of the Canadian Centre for Architecture; architect James Stirling; trustees Alastair B. Martin, Robert S. Rubin, and Jeffrey C. Keil; and Robert T. Buck, the director of the museum. [5]

Ann arranged for Iso and me to meet at the Carlyle Hotel in New York, Iso's home away from home. When we discussed the jury, Iso told me that he and Stirling constituted a "mutual admiration society"; I told him that I had recruited Herdeg for my faculty at Columbia and that I had done a house for Phyllis Lambert's brother, Edgar Bronfman. We also spoke of the museum culture in New York, the reputation of the Brooklyn Museum, and the complexities that we anticipated in working between New York and Tokyo.

186   BUILD, MEMORY

1

2

Then we turned to our separate roles in the project. I proposed that we share design responsibility equally, and Iso agreed. I also suggested that the staffs of both offices be responsible for different aspects of the drawings and models required by the brief. Iso's response was very Japanese—equivocal. He wanted his office to prepare the final models and presentation boards and our office to handle the New York issues—Landmarks Commission, community relations, press, and social obligations. One more factor played into our collaboration. An American/Japanese team could use the thirteen-hour time difference to its advantage. We would be able to turn one working day into two.

The jury selected ten of the fifty-seven teams that responded, including ours, for interviews and five teams, again including ours, to compete. Joan Darragh wrote the program with professional advisor Terrance R. Williams. Terry's office developed the site plans and base drawings for all participants. The five firms were invited to a three-day briefing; director Bob Buck was the final speaker. Despite Joan's protestations and under-the-table kicks, he issued one specific instruction—the grand stairway on Eastern Parkway must be returned in one form or another.

Iso and I agreed to meet in London in early July. He was heading west from Japan and I was heading east to Paris. Jim Garrison accompanied me to London. He shared my knee-jerk antipathy to postmodernism and feared that design disputes might have a negative effect on the outcome. I didn't agree. Shin Watanabe, [1] Iso's close associate, also joined us. Later he would work in our office in New York, coordinating east and west activities.

David Chipperfield offered us a meeting space. The four of us quickly agreed to certain principles. One was that the new plan must reflect the asymmetry of the Washington Avenue/Eastern Parkway intersection. [3] Another was that the center of the plan, where McKim, Mead & White would have built a great dome, must be reestablished—established, actually, since nothing was ever built in that position. [4] There was much doodling and little talk; Iso is very quiet. In the end we thought we had a conceptual framework for the design, and we agreed to meet in New York in about a month.

Before we left the country, Sir Richard Rogers gave us a tour of Lloyd's of London. At the base of the building Rogers had inserted a tiny piece of the facade of the insurance giant's former headquarters. [2] We thought the new structure was an extraordinary accomplishment. But the bespoke-suited brokers booed Rogers! It was an embarrassing occurrence, but serendipitous as well. The Brooklyn competition would also involve pastiche—a modern addition to a partially realized Beaux-Arts masterpiece.

Grid line from original Master Plan by McKim, Mead & White

Eastern Parkway

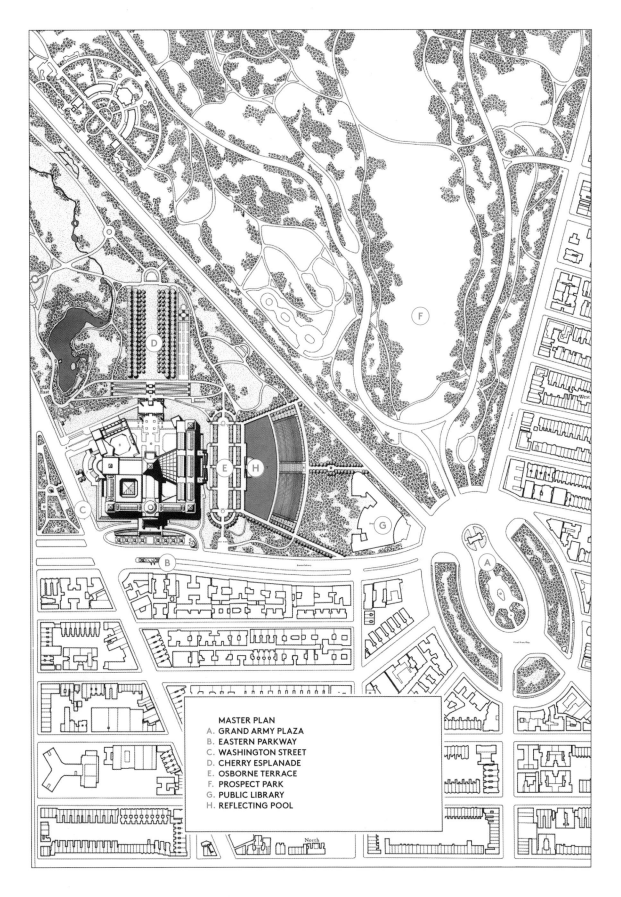

MASTER PLAN
A. GRAND ARMY PLAZA
B. EASTERN PARKWAY
C. WASHINGTON STREET
D. CHERRY ESPLANADE
E. OSBORNE TERRACE
F. PROSPECT PARK
G. PUBLIC LIBRARY
H. REFLECTING POOL

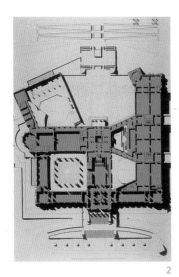

2

As we developed our scheme over the next few weeks, we had only a few substantive disagreements. Iso wished to include, in place of the missing dome at the center of the original plan, a 150-foot-high limestone-clad obelisk.[3] I thought it excessively dramatic and formally irrelevant to either the neighborhood or the fragmented building. We did, however, agree on the two functions we wished to associate with the center of the edifice: an entrance from the south (a second monumental entrance) and a hub for circulation routes within the museum.[4] In what was a kind of functional trade-off, I agreed to the obelisk but insisted on including a huge reflecting pool and stage inspired by Billy Rose's Aquacade in Flushing Meadows. This hybrid component would sit to the west of the Osborne Garden at the Brooklyn Botanic Garden, activating the stolid west facade of the museum. The water feature seemed appropriate since the area was once home to the Mount Prospect Reservoir, which served the city of Brooklyn. In the end, neither the obelisk nor the reflecting pool would see the light of day.

Silk-screened presentation drawings were emerging as Iso's trademark. Well aware that the museum planned an exhibit of all five submissions, he insisted that the screening be done in Tokyo. I had some doubts about the intensely vivid fuchsia and gray color scheme, but I couldn't deny that the boards were eye-catching.[2]

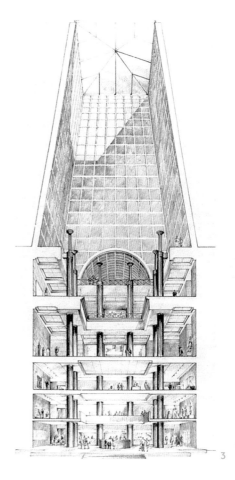

3

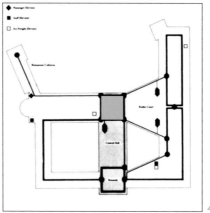

4

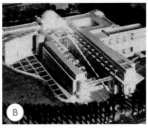

1
    A. KOHN PEDERSEN FOX
    B. VOORSANGER & MILLS ASSOCIATES
    C. SKIDMORE, OWINGS & MERRILL
    D. ATKIN, VOITH & ASSOCIATES

2

3

The jury met in October 1986 to review the entries.[1,2] Our joint venture was unanimously selected as the winning team.[3] The Art Commission and the Landmarks Preservation Commission rarely meet, but in this case, the two groups asked the museum for a joint, nonbinding review of the winning scheme. Their common interest was the impact of the plan on the landmark building and on the urban design of its historic precinct.

A year and a half later, the museum organized an exhibition of the five competition entries. Said Paul Goldberger in the *New York Times,* "The winner...rather deftly managed to embrace classicism and go far beyond it at the same time."

1

2

3

4

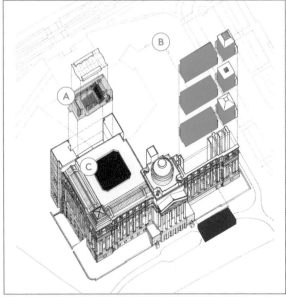

5   A. IRIS AND B. GERALD CANTOR AUDITORIUM, 1991
     B. MORRIS A. AND MEYER SCHAPIRO WING, 1993
     C. BEAUX-ARTS COURT, 2001

Our success did not mean that our master plan would be realized in its entirety or at one time. Each element was considered separately, from architectural and financial as well as other stances. Duncan Hazard, an associate partner at the time, would coordinate the design and construction of each phase. The auditorium, named for Iris and B. Gerald Cantor,[3] a 460-seat hall with acoustics appropriate for film, lectures, and chamber music, was the first joint design undertaking.[2] The new auditorium replaced a 1919 hall under the main stairs.[1]

In the 1970s Prentice & Chan, Olhausen had developed a windowless service volume on the unfinished south facade.[4] In addition to mechanical systems, the limestone-sheathed "bustle" had allocated space for the auditorium. Our office was responsible for most aspects of the interior of the room—wall material, stainless-steel details, marble trim, seating. Iso applied his signature Marilyn Monroe curves to the sconces that uplit the ceiling. He wanted Minoru Nagata as the acoustician; the two had collaborated on Casals Hall in Tokyo. Nagata created a three-dimensional plaster "wave" form on the ceiling. It was marvelous both visually and acoustically, but it had a quirk—conversations that could not be heard from an adjacent seat were sometimes audible fifteen rows away. The auditorium was dedicated in 1991.

In 1993 we began work on the Morris A. and Meyer Schapiro Wing. Meyer[6] was a venerated professor of art history at Columbia; his brother Morris,[7] a successful investment banker. They were an unbeatable Brooklyn-born partnership. The northwestern wing was the first portion of the museum to be built, and its three primary galleries had hardly been touched in the intervening ninety-plus years. We transformed the forty-by-one-hundred-foot spaces into twenty-first-century display areas for different collections.[8] Each featured individual ceiling forms and illumination strategies. The most dramatic is the third-floor gallery; the gently vaulted ceiling softens the installation of the museum's exceptional collection of ancient Egyptian art. On the fourth and fifth floors are exhibition galleries adaptable to all media; the fifth floor has a vast skylight with a lay-light ceiling and, again, Iso's signature Marilyn Monroe curve.

6

7

8

1

2

3

Arnold Lehman[3] succeeded Bob Buck as director of the museum in 1997. Two years later Iso left the master plan team. His wife, Aiko Miyawaki, one of Japan's most important contemporary artists, was ill, and he could no longer actively participate. Arnold's ideas were often radically inventive, though not always realistic, and he always encouraged us to explore new strategies. He was involved in every detail of the design, including work that was already in progress, and was intent on making his increasingly respectable but still tattered Beaux-Arts beauty "dressed to kill."

His influence was first felt in the renovation of the Beaux-Arts Court,[1] the only one of McKim, Mead & White's four interior courts to be realized. Used for galas and community events since its completion in the 1920s, it had, like many parts of the museum, suffered from deferred maintenance. The sound and lighting systems were antique, and the glass-block floor that filtered light to the gallery below was in urgent need of repair. The support system for the floor had failed in a number of locations. We did not want to replace it with a modern system, since New York City fire codes would have required a strict separation between floors. So we devised a scheme that raised the floor with inset laminated-glass panels; these would meet the code and also allow light from above or below to create the magic aura of the old days.[2] In addition, we had to rebuild a vast leaking skylight. James Gainfort, an alumnus of our office, oversaw the restoration of the skylight. The renewed court opened in 2001.

The glass technology we used for the Beaux-Arts Court would inspire the next architectural venture. The objective—the sole objective—in the redesign of the Eastern Parkway plaza was to put a new "nose" on the building. The days of the dark, windy, and bland public space were numbered.

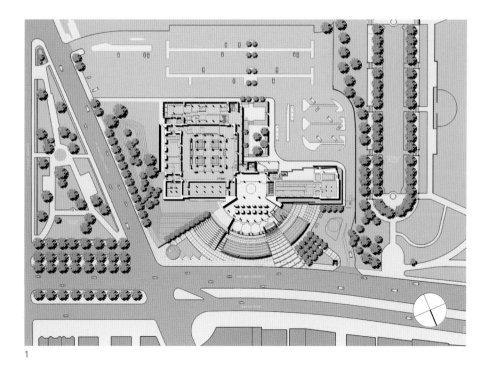

1

Arnold had a vision for an entry experience that would merge indoor and outdoor spaces. He wanted the approach to be a destination for visitors of all ages, whether or not they were planning to enter the museum—a place for people watching, gathering, and contemplation; an environment where spontaneous entertainments might erupt. Water and trees were integral to his concept. He also wanted to provide a graceful way for vehicles to deliver their passengers and to call out the museum entrance for those arriving by subway. A generous welcome for visitors with strollers or walkers was mandatory. He wanted the new entrance plaza to literally embrace the community. Last on the director's wish list was a distinct if slightly mysterious declaration: "I want people to return even before they enter."

The obvious first thought—though not an idea we were truly committed to—was to reconstruct the original stair in a modernist manner. But analysis of the approach, entry sequence, urban context, and institutional goals made it clear that this proposition was not feasible. The height of the stair—any height, actually—worked against federal requirements regarding access for the disabled. Moreover, a formal stairway would contradict the twenty-first-century sensibilities and democratic vision of the museum, principles that dated to its founding. Finally, restoration of the

stair would not resolve issues of internal circulation or improve the relationship to the surrounding context.

As we continued, two complementary desires came to define our scheme: maintaining the classical symmetry of the original plan, or at least the appearance of classical symmetry, and responding to Arnold's contemporary vision. Our studies of the precinct of the museum uncovered hemicyclic forms in a variety of places: in the museum, in McKim, Mead & White's original auditorium entry on the eastern side of the building; in the Brooklyn Botanic Garden, at both ends of the Osborne Garden and at the southern end of the Cherry Esplanade. That geometrical figure became our governing metaphor.

The building presented us with Philip Youtz's thirty-foot-high masonry wall. We wanted to transform this into a singular, immediately identifiable entry. The McKim, Mead & White design featured large areas of glass only in the skylights. Guided by the Beaux-Arts original, along with recollections of greenhouses, European train stations,[2] and gallerias, we devised a semicircular, glass-roofed and -walled entry pavilion. The light and reflectivity would contrast with the stone facade, softening its mausoleumesque grandeur.

5

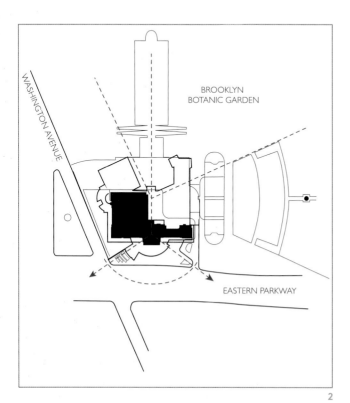

WASHINGTON AVENUE

BROOKLYN
BOTANIC GARDEN

EASTERN PARKWAY

2

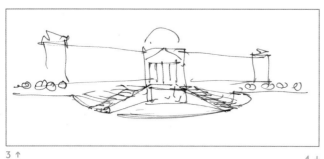

3 ↑   4 ↓

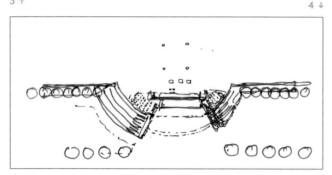

We adapted the curvilinear form to the building by aligning north-south axes. But then we redirected the energy of the axis of the glass enclosure to the corners of the site, acknowledging the oblique approaches.[2] The arc terminates in a new amphitheater to the east and a vehicular drop-off to the west. In between is a generous entry plaza. A glass canopy marked with white steel masts and a portion of the plaza gesture toward the subway.[1] The sophisticated structural design required the kind of detailed connections more commonly found on racing sloops. Robert Young, who had previously worked for Bernard Tschumi, had a unique understanding of French glass technology and was largely responsible for the detailing.

Early sketches of curvilinear entry schemes featured two stairways flanking a flat, on-grade entry.[3,4] Eventually, under modest pressure from Brooklyn Borough President Howard Golden, the east stair disappeared. When we crafted a wood model showing bermed earth in its place, Joan mistook the layered contours for steps—and there arose the idea for the amphitheater. The west stair would also vanish from the design.

Along with the hemicycle, the idea of steps became a governing metaphor for the project.[5] As a whole, the scheme hints at the sixty-eight steps of the long-revered McKim, Mead & White stairway. Four major components are stepped: the roof of the glass pavilion; the grass seating facing the pavilion; the amphitheater facing the street, which descends to a computer-animated fountain; and the cable-supported glass entry canopy. The glass roof of the pavilion is the most striking—its five curved steps consist of "treads" of patterned glass and "risers" of clear glass. These semicircular planes cascade down to an elevated walkway, or *passerelle* (a French term meaning "skyway" or "fast bridge").

1

2

3

The walkway connects one side of the arc to the other, allowing visitors to peer down into the pavilion. A free-standing stair that springs from a shallow pool at the western side of the plaza offers access to the passerelle.[1]

The passerelle was one of only two significant design conflicts with the client. Some members of the building committee thought it a folly, one that the city administration would view as frivolous. Fortunately Arnold supported our intention. The other dispute was with Joan. She was particularly concerned with maintenance of the plaza and insisted on plant material that would keep people from sitting on the grass. In this case, we were aided by the budget: sod was cheaper than thorny bushes.

The local community board was not happy with the glass "welcome mat." They preferred stone, and they wanted stairs. A negative assessment from the board had the potential to derail the project, so Joan piled the members into a bus and drove to Eighty-first Street and Central Park West. She pointed to the Rose Center and explained that the new pavilion would be similarly welcoming. On the way back to Brooklyn, all we saw were smiles.

That was not to say that there were no further obstacles. As we entered the regulatory process, it was no surprise that historic preservationists demanded that the original grand stairway be restored. The near-hysterical reaction to the exhibit "Sensation: Young British Artists from the Saatchi Collection" on the part of Mayor Rudolph Giuliani's office was less expected.[2] The show was on display between October 1999 and January 2000, just before the new pavilion was to be presented to the Landmarks Preservation Commission. The mayor threatened to cut off city funding for the museum; the uproar itself threatened approval of the design. In the end, the mayor backed down, and Jennifer Raab, chair of the LPC, deftly steered her commissioners to a near-unanimous decision to grant a certificate of appropriateness.

A. SKYLIGHT
B. ROOF TERRACE
C. PORTICO
D. SECOND-FLOOR TERRACE
E. STOOP
F. ELEVATED PROMENADE
G. EXTERIOR STAIR
H. STATUES
I. ENTRY
J. STEPPED LAWN
K. CHERRY GROVE
L. FOUNTAIN
M. VEHICULAR DROP-OFF
N. REAR ENTRY
O. SUBWAY STATION

1

2

3

The construction of the pavilion involved risks not normally encountered, though they had something in common with our work on Zankel Hall at Carnegie Hall, which was taking place at roughly the same time. Both parent institutions remained open during construction, and the foundations of both buildings required special protection. The security of visitors was the first priority for both organizations; for the museum, safeguarding art was of almost equal import.

After we removed Youtz's "Berlin Wall," we were left with the brick piers supporting the Doric columns of the original portico. We stripped them of plaster and cleaned them. Arnold's first thought was to paint them white—a reasonable modernist impulse. But they were such a powerful reminder of the past—specifically ancient Rome—that we convinced him to leave them as they were. They stand in the pavilion as a portal between past and future. [3]

The curvilinear form of the pavilion was reinforced by two classical sculptures by Daniel Chester French, *Manhattan* and *Brooklyn*. [2] Each stands, facing her borough, on a pedestal disposed in relation to the arc. The installation of the statues, each roughly twenty tons, could have put the artworks in the museum above at risk. The workmen guided the sculptures into position at an extremely slow pace and monitored vibration hour by hour. Nervous curators didn't relax until the "patient" was "closed up."

1

2

The Martha A. and Robert S. Rubin Pavilion is the most notable consequence of the removal of the grand stairway in 1934. Bob Rubin led the board of trustees for seventeen years, guiding his beloved museum through New York's financial and political shoals. Visitors to the museum enter the grand structure directly from the street via the crystal pavilion. When the museum is closed, the glass hemicycle provides a focal point nevertheless. Bursts of sunlight reflect off its glass facets, and its radial vectors reach out to visitors from Brooklyn and beyond. In the early evening, the entry glows like a giant welcoming lantern.

Herbert Muschamp[1] commented on the relationship between our pavilion and the museum building that preceded it in the *New York Times:*

Mr. Polshek adheres to the view that architecture is best spoken in a vernacular dialect...The McKim, Mead & White museum itself, opened in 1897, embodies the Beaux Arts conception of classicism as a common tongue. Mr. Polshek gives form to that idea's 20th-century descendant, the adoption of engineering as the basis of a vernacular style.

2

3

4

Since its opening on April 17, 2004, four million visitors have passed through, around, and over the pavilion.[1,2,3,4] Public esteem can be measured in bodies lolling on the grass steps, visitors perching on the amphitheater, children frolicking in the fountain, museumgoers traversing the skywalk, and individuals young and old pressing their noses to the glass of the new lobby. Neighbors across Eastern Parkway look out to a renewed New York City landmark. Walt Whitman is smiling from above.

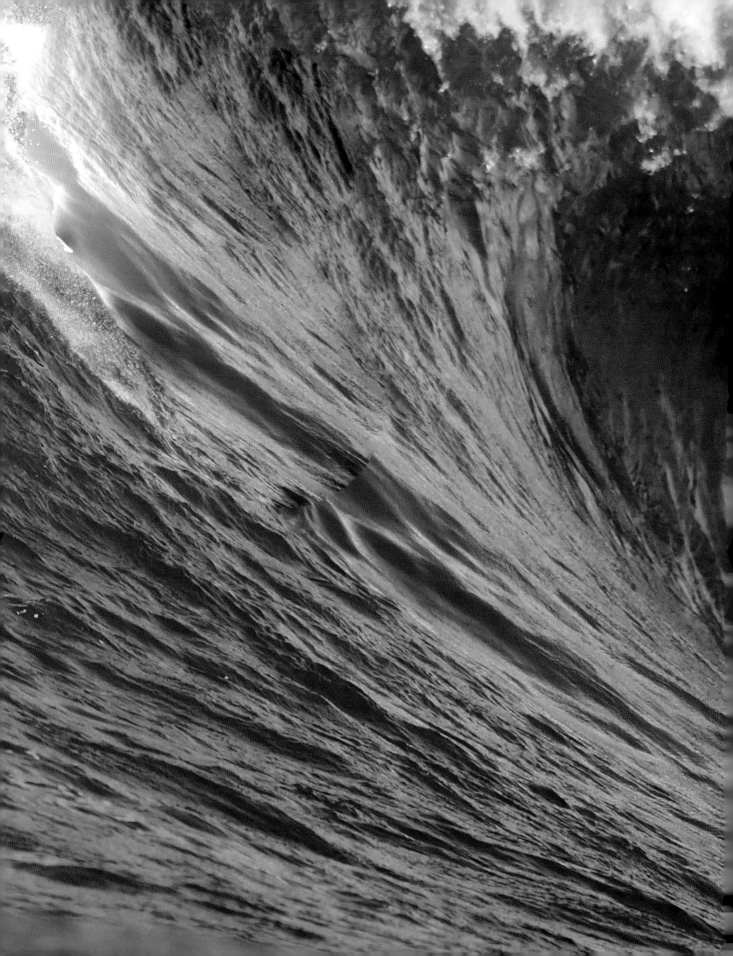

Seamen's Church Institute
New York, New York
1988–1991

Water, water, every where;
And all the boards did shrink;
Water, water every where;
Nor any drop to drink.
—Samuel Taylor Coleridge,
 "The Rime of the Ancient Mariner"

The U.S. Merchant Marine consists of private and government-owned merchant vessels. In times of peace, the fleet transports cargo and passengers. In times of war, the Merchant Marine can be called upon to deliver troops and supplies for the military.

The life of a merchant seaman is not easy. Weather, wars, piracy, privation, and fire have, since ancient times, made seafaring a dangerous occupation. The pre-1915 history of labor at sea is a series of cautionary tales involving flogging and many other crimes. The legislation outlawing such inhumane acts, the Seamen's Act of 1915, was supported by the International Seamen's Union; this organization, after a period of turmoil, was incorporated into the American Federation of Labor as the Seafarers International Union.

During World War II submarines and mines resulted in the loss of 733 cargo ships. The casualty rate in the Merchant Marine was the highest of any of the services. The Merchant Mariners' Memorial[1] at the southern tip of Manhattan, designed by Marisol, is a haunting tribute to the seamen who lost their lives in a U-boat attack in World War II. Storms, conflict, buccaneering, and war still plague the high seas.

The Seamen's Church Institute, an ecumenical organization, was founded in 1834 to protect the rights of merchant seamen. Today, the institute is the largest and most comprehensive mariner's agency in North America. President Franklin Delano Roosevelt,[2] an "ancient mariner" himself, served on the institute's board from 1908 until his death in 1945. The maritime attorneys of the SCI are the country's leading advocates for merchant seamen.

1

2

3

A gentler activity of the institute is Christmas at Sea.[3] Since 1898, the year of the Spanish-American War, groups of volunteers have knitted caps, scarves, and socks to be sent to thousands of seamen. In addition, SCI's chaplains visit more than 4,000 vessels in the Port of New York and New Jersey, in the Port of Oakland, and along American inland waterways.

The permanence of most architecture would appear to be the antithesis of transient seafaring, just as the generosity and profound humanism of the institute would appear to be the opposite of rough-and-tumble life at sea. However, all merged in the new headquarters building we created for the institute.

1

2

3

4

5

The earliest institute buildings were floating chapels—small church buildings on barges—that clearly communicated SCI's mission. [5] In the early years of the twentieth century, the distinguished New York firm Warren and Wetmore designed the institute's first home at 25 South Street in Lower Manhattan. [2] This twelve-story building was capable of boarding 580 seamen. Only hours before the construction began on April 15, 1912, news arrived of the sinking of *Titanic*. [1] The Seamen's Church Institute honored the victims in a lighthouse on the roof of the new building. [4]

In 1968 the institute moved to new headquarters in a brick tower at 15 State Street, designed by Eggers and Higgins. [3] The lighthouse memorial was moved to the South Street Seaport Museum complex. Over the next twenty years, the number of merchant mariners laying over in New York dramatically decreased, and in 1985 the building was sold.

1

2

3

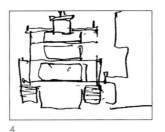

4

5

Our involvement with a new headquarters for the SCI began in a rather circuitous manner. In 1988 the firm was retained for a feasibility study of a site made up of two midblock properties on Water Street in the South Street Seaport Historic District. The client was an aggressive young developer who, as they used to say in the movies, "packed heat." On the southern property was an uninteresting two-story industrial building. On the northern tract had been the Schermerhorn Ship Chandlery. Although the building had been altered dramatically, it retained its brick facade with a cast-iron and granite storefront and also a quoined service entrance leading to a rear yard.[6] In the designation report for the historic district, the Landmarks Preservation Commission called this portal "one of the finest and most unusual details of the Historic District."

The aggressive developer failed to pay his bills, and soon the two properties were up for sale. Richard Berry,[2] an attorney and a board member of the SCI, encouraged his colleagues to buy the site for a new headquarters building. While the SCI had no obligation to continue working with us, there were a few points in our favor. Since we had secured city approvals for the earlier development of the parcel, we understood the zoning and landmarks restrictions. We had experience in both historic preservation and new construction. And we were familiar with the challenges of building on landfill from our earlier Bar Association building in Albany.

This was the first time we collaborated with Frank Sciame,[1] a young builder who studied architecture at City College and was uncommonly knowledgeable about both design and landmark issues. My associate Richard Olcott was especially interested in working on this project: his grandfather, Alfred V. S. Olcott, was president of the Hudson River Day Line,[3] and serendipitously, one of Richard's student projects at Cornell had a program eerily similar to that of the institute.[4]

One of the first challenges we had to deal with was the condemnation of most of the chandlery. Although we were planning to integrate the historic edifice into our structure, the substrate was composed of ancient layers of refuse and soils, and the building's foundations were supported on three layers of eighteenth-century timber cribbing. The New York City Department of Buildings deemed the masonry side walls unsafe: they would have to be demolished. We saved the facade and reconstructed it in the original location, and we replicated the footprint and floor plan of the chandlery.

6   7

4   5

The client had no preconceptions with respect to the design. The identity of the institute depended upon its mission, not its visual presentation, and its previous homes were either traditional or banal—or both. For us, however, the project offered an opportunity to express the image of the SCI in a contemporary vocabulary within the context of Manhattan's oldest commercial district. We invented a narrative in which a new brick facade on the south would merge with the historic Schermerhorn building face.[3] Together the two would form a metaphoric pier permanently connected to the shore. This entity represented the past—stable and predictable. Floating atop the brick pier would be a composition of white enameled steel panels calling to mind a ship at sea. This composition symbolized the future—dynamic and uncertain.

We broke ground in July 1989. The Schermerhorn facade was reconstructed, as planned, and on the street facade of the southern extension, we interpreted in steel I-beams and plate glass the granite-columned base of the older building. A white porcelain-enamel entryway, alluding to the iconography of the nautical roofscape, unambiguously identifies the main entrance.[1]

The new brick front suggests the regular Georgian grid of the chandlery yet interrupts the rhythm to satisfy internal functions. The vertical dimensions of the apertures are derived from the historic building. On the fourth floor the windows are extended horizontally, conjuring the upper decks of a ship,[2] and the large vertical opening above the entry corresponds to the building's vertical circulation core and signals the transition between old and new structures. New window openings have marine-influenced riveted steel surrounds. The curvilinear forms of the nautical roofscape owe a debt to Le Corbusier's Villa Savoye:[4,5] we are far from the first architects to be fascinated by the sculptural shapes and logical organization of ocean liners.

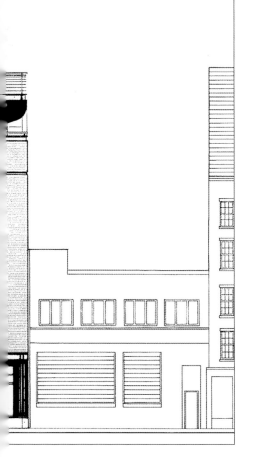

A. ENTRY/LOBBY
B. SEAFARERS CLUB
C. CHAPEL
D. TERRACE
E. OFFICES
F. OPEN WORKSPACE
G. MULTIPURPOSE ROOM

1

2

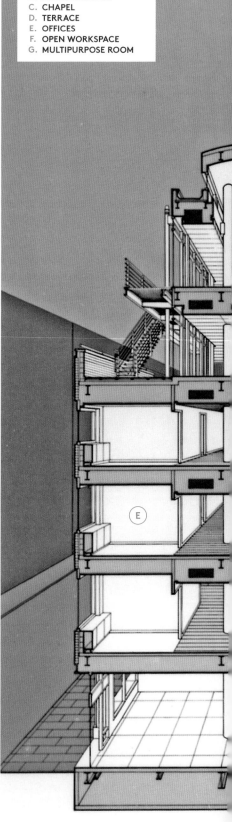

E

Since we were building on ancient landfill, we needed a lightweight steel structural system. A grid of columns supports the building and defines interior zones. The core is articulated as a ship's funnel that rises the full height of the building and beyond. Its sculptural presence is especially evident in double-height volumes on the first and second floors and the sixth floor. The volume on the first and second floors encloses the lobby,[7] where the building's principal spatial, structural, and iconographic themes are introduced. The curtain wall facing the rear yard was inspired by Pierre Chareau's iconic Maison de Verre of 1932.[2] We had wanted to use glass block to filter light into the interior, but the cost was prohibitive; instead we settled on a translucent fiberglass-panel system.[1]

The second, third, and fourth floors contain private offices facing Water Street; at the rear of the building are the Seafarers Club[5] on the second floor and open-plan work areas on the third and fourth floors. Circulation corridors that double as galleries run down the center of the floor plates. Stainless-steel pedestals supporting glass vitrines contain a captivating collection of model ships.[6] Nautical artifacts, from *Normandie*'s bell to rope macramé, tattoo designs, and sea nymph figureheads, adorn the walls.[4]

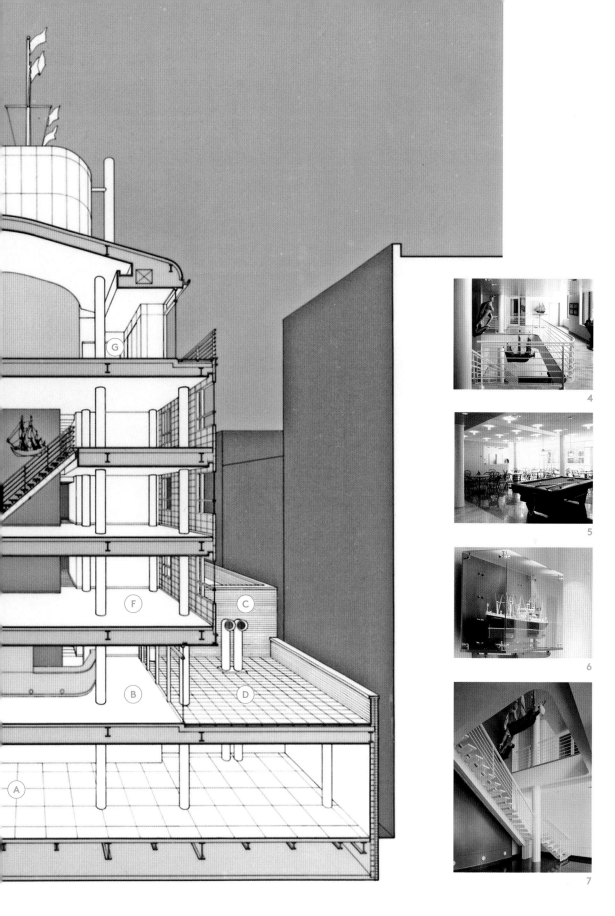

1

2

On the fifth floor, a wood-floored gallery along the north side of the building is separated by a glass wall from an exterior terrace.[2] An outdoor stair connects the terrace to the deck of the sixth floor, a multipurpose room with panoramic views of Lower Manhattan.[1]

Navigation has been taught by the SCI as far back as 1899, though its school was not established until 1914. At 25 South Street, the institute created a seventy-four-foot-long pilothouse and flying bridge 212 feet above the ground.[4] The new building accommodates, on the third floor, what is believed to be the largest maritime training center in the United States.[3] A darkened chamber represents the bridge of the supertanker *Exxon Charleston*. An elaborate simulation screen reproduces, among other locations, Prince William Sound, where, in real life, a navigational deviation precipitated the *Exxon Valdez* environmental disaster. Throughout the building, furnishings and fittings, as well as materials and a color palette that allude to shipboard life, emphasize the institute's commitment to seafarers.

1

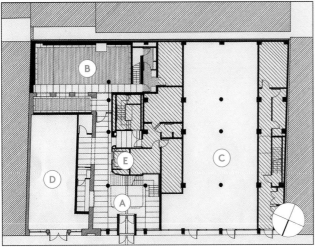

2   GROUND FLOOR
    A. LOBBY
    B. CHAPEL
    C. GALLERY
    D. SHOP
    E. SERVICE CORE

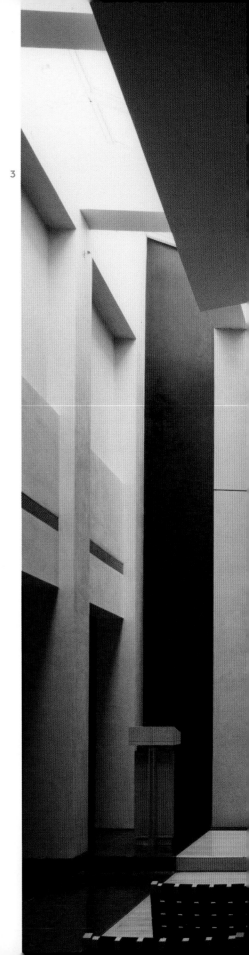

3

Inserted into what had been the rear yard of the old ship chandlery is a nondenominational chapel.[3] The entry door focuses on the baptismal font.[5] Sunlight floods the room through a clerestory. Holly Ross, an architect and artist, created the nautical motif on the blue-tinted clerestory glass.[4] The chapel incorporates objects from the institute's collection: a blue-clad figurehead in the shape of a woman (the "Mystery Maiden"), a votive ship suspended over the altar. The model was inspired by a description in *Moby-Dick* of a seamen's chapel in New Bedford, Massachusetts. There is a small balcony with an organ.

On the upper levels of the historic structure are the Center for Seafarers' Rights, the world's only full-time, free legal-aid service for merchant mariners, and the Joseph Conrad Memorial Library,[1] which is furnished with documents and photographs of the young Polish writer who shipped out under the British merchant flag.

4

5

In October 1990 the SCI organized a luncheon hosted by Tony Marshall, the son of Brooke Astor. The guest of honor, Princess Anne, attended with Alfred Lee Loomis III, chairman of the board.[2] The building was not yet finished; the elevator, not yet working. Mrs. Astor, arriving a bit late, walked up the glass-enclosed fire stair but missed the top floor and ended up trapped on the roof of the building. A policeman on the street saw her waving a hankie and came to her rescue.

Once it was finally completed, the headquarters for the Seamen's Church Institute was dedicated on May 1, 1991. The ceremony replicated that of a ship's launching. Brooke Shields[3] wielded a champagne bottle to the sound of bells and whistles. The Reverend James R. Whittemore, director of the SCI, said:

At the beginning of the century, it was the exploitation of seamen ashore that was the problem. Now it is the problem of exploitation of seamen aboard ship. We used to cater to Americans, for whom the union has since done a very good job. Three-quarters of the seafarers who come to port are from third-world countries, and marginal operators take advantage of them.

1

In 2010 the Seamen's Church Institute relocated to Port Newark. New York City was no longer the destination of choice, and increasingly, ships arriving in Manhattan in the morning would leave that same day. The Sea-Land Container Terminal constructed at Port Newark in 1958 gradually rendered most of the traditional port facilities in New York Harbor obsolete. The South Street Seaport area, home to the SCI, had become primarily a tourist attraction. The institute decided that the value of the building would better serve to bolster its endowment.

In stepped the successful avant-garde performers Blue Man Group. The Blue Men and their wives created an informal play group that over time morphed into an education program. The Blue School[1] purchased the building in 2010, and by September 2012, two hundred students replaced the thousands of seamen who had used the facility during the previous twenty years. The nautical imagery perfectly suited the needs of the school. Most notable was the conversion of the chapel into a meeting hall and gymnasium. Even though the tenancy has changed, the social value of the historic envelope and the physical space within has not. After all, blue is the color of the sea.

Santa Fe Opera
Santa Fe, New Mexico
1988–1998

1

What do the history of grand opera and the history of the atomic bomb have in common?

In the first half of the twentieth century, two young men left New York and arrived in the high mountain air of New Mexico. Both John Crosby,[2] founder and director of the Santa Fe Opera, and J. Robert Oppenheimer, director of the Manhattan Project,[3] were born into wealthy Manhattan families. Both had childhood illnesses—Crosby had asthma and Oppenheimer had colitis—and were sent to the Sangre de Cristo Mountains in northern New Mexico for recuperation. One would grow up to be a great scientist, the other a renowned figure in the world of opera.

Oppenheimer went west in the early 1920s, where he camped and rode in the mesas and arroyos not far from the village of Los Alamos. Crosby attended the Los Alamos Ranch School in the early 1940s. Both young men were captivated by the spirit and physicality of the place. Oppenheimer returned to purchase the Los Alamos Ranch School (which had closed in 1942) as a residence for the dozens of scientists who were to build the atomic bomb. Crosby returned to create the Santa Fe Opera.

2

3

1

2   3

On August 1, 1988, the second month of the Santa Fe Opera's short season was about to begin. I was looking up at a twilight star through the split roof of the audience chamber as I waited for Maestro John Crosby to conduct Penderecki's *Black Mask,* one of the avant-garde operas Crosby insisted on including each season.[2] It was already cool at 9:00 p.m., and I was exhausted from the long trip and high altitude. But the evening breeze and distant lightning kept me alert.

Six weeks earlier I had received a call from Brad Woolbright, assistant to Maestro Crosby, the famed director of the opera. Brad explained that the thirty-one-year-old company was considering architects to execute a long-range planning study of its complex outside Santa Fe. As a first stage in the selection process, four members of the committee had visited our office. They described the opera's history and its current state, operationally and financially. It was not necessary for them to speak of its impeccable artistic reputation. It had long been a musical icon in America.

For the next step I flew to Santa Fe to meet John Crosby on the opera grounds. The site is in the high desert of northern New Mexico—7,000 feet high and deprived of oxygen.[1] Dan Duro, then technical manager, took me down to meet the maestro at his modest ranch home just below the opera complex. His associates had described him as both taciturn and courtly. But they also let me know that he was passionate in his defense of artistic integrity and considerate of everyone in the opera family, from stagehands to divas. Dan ushered me into a small office at the rear of the house. As I had been warned, conversation was awkward. John rarely looked up to engage my eyes.

He began, almost mumbling, by noting that Schuyler Chapin[3] had recommended our firm. They had been friends since Schuyler was deputy general manager of the Metropolitan Opera. Later Schuyler was dean of the School of the Arts at Columbia, at the same time I was dean of the School of Architecture. Schuyler was also a member of the board of Carnegie Hall, and my renovation of the historic hall had been completed only a year before this visit to Santa Fe. I spoke to John of that experience in some detail, making special mention of issues of patron circulation and comfort, acoustics, and collaboration with the hall's leadership.

1   2

My early work in Japan also seemed to interest the conductor, especially my reaction to the Japanese design sensibility and the almost religious importance of landscape.[1] For John, New Mexico's landscape and natural world were very much part of this opera's experience. He described how the site for the opera house was chosen. He spent the summers of 1954 and 1955 recording nighttime temperatures, rainfall, prevailing winds, sound patterns, and echoes on the 199-acre property his parents had purchased years before. The next year he asked Jack Purcell,[2] an acoustician with Leo Beranek in Los Angeles, to help identify a site for the new opera theater. The two men hiked through the arroyos and mesas of the property. Jack carried a small yachting regatta cannon, and when the pair reached a place that he thought might be appropriate, he would fire it in different directions to test reverberation times.

The original theater, created in a natural amphitheater in 1957, was built for $115,000 and seated 480 patrons on wooden benches. At that time it was the only uncovered outdoor theater in America designed exclusively for opera. It was also the only company to offer training for young singers. The Santa Fe Opera's inaugural performance, on July 3, 1957, was *Madama Butterfly*, and the company was almost immediately acclaimed for its anticipated contributions to the country's cultural life.

In 1965 a mezzanine was added, but two years later, four weeks into the season, a fire demolished the theater, destroying hundreds of instruments, costumes, and scores. A new theater, built for $4 million, was completed for the start of the 1967 season.[3,4] This new house seated 1,889 and, like the first theater, opened with *Madama Butterfly*. The theater had an orchestra and a balcony with real seats. A roof covered the front of the orchestra, pit, stage, and backstage; the balcony and rear seats were sheltered as well. Between the two roofs was a gap that allowed audiences to appreciate the evening sky as the 9:00 curtain drew near.

3

4

1

2

3

4

John had asked me to arrange a presentation. To prepare, we researched the climate, geography, and history of northern New Mexico. We also looked at other outdoor music venues: Red Rocks Amphitheatre in Red Rocks Park, Colorado[1]; Benedict Music Tent in Aspen[2]; Blossom Music Center in Cuyahoga Falls, Ohio[3]; and Wolf Trap in Vienna, Virginia. [4] And of course, we studied the existing campus and its operations. We planned to discuss Carnegie Hall and also assembled materials on vernacular architecture and landscape that were relevant to the opera's dramatic site.

On the appointed day John and his senior staff appeared. I offered a personal travelogue on indigenous architecture around the world that was in some way related to the Santa Fe Opera site. Examples included a Swedish stone hut,[8] a Moroccan village,[9] Zen gardens in Kyoto, a lookout at Mohonk Mountain House in New York State,[10] Four Corners National Park, a doorway in the Middle East, Katsura Palace, and Le Thoronet, the Cistercian abbey in France.[11]

I left Santa Fe without a clue to Maestro Crosby's opinion of our time together. But the marriage of vernacular architecture, Native American folk art, and the refined culture of opera made this an incredibly desirable project. Back in New York I gathered a team for the project: Blake Middleton,[7] Sarah "Pinky" Caples,[6] and Tim Hartung.[5] Blake was a talented young designer who had won a Prix de Rome. Pinky was a perceptive Smith College and Yale architecture school graduate. Tim would manage the project.

1

2

The questions afterward concerned Carnegie's master plan, patron amenities, working with two different acousticians, and box office issues. The entire visit was a little over ninety minutes long. Several days later Brad Woolbright called, asked us to prepare a contract, and invited us to return to Santa Fe in July. This second visit would provide an opportunity to study backstage operations, meet the technical and administrative staff, and most important, see an opera with John Crosby.

Nancy Zeckendorf[2] was chair of the opera board and had been, for nine years, a dancer in the company. She could not attend the interview, but her later involvement turned out to be critical. For ten years, she was our muse, interpreter, and protector. She had an innate sensitivity to and interest in architecture. Her husband, developer William Zeckendorf Jr., was the son of the fabled real estate tycoon William Zeckendorf Sr.;[1] earlier generations of Zeckendorfs had come to live in New Mexico in the 1860s. William Jr.'s understanding of real estate and finance were also vital components in the realization of the project.

During our visit Pinky and I attended Wagner's *Der Fliegende Hollander (The Flying Dutchman)*.[4] Our seats were in the orchestra under the gap in the roof. It was a starless night, and suddenly, as the operatic tension built onstage, a flash of lightning followed by a thunderous clap brought on a deluge.[3]

Even Wagner could not have invented such a sensational device. Operagoers near us grabbed their rain gear or took cover. Members of the orchestra frantically attempted to protect their instruments. Small pieces of red silk held by the cast blew into the audience. It was a striking instance of an increasingly common weather event, due in no small part to the geography of the site.

3

July and August in Santa Fe are characterized by afternoon thunderstorms. Late-day thermal winds rise from the surrounding mesas, at 7,300 feet, increasing the intensity of the storms. Wind-driven rain would become a major factor in the redesign of the opera's roof structure. However, the drama of the spectacular location, with its sunsets and its natural acoustic properties, not to mention cost factors, ruled out even the mention of creating a new hall on a different part of the property.

4

1

2

3

Another unique aspect of the Santa Fe Opera that goes back to the 1957 theater was the absence of a traditional fly tower: audiences could look through the stage and out the sides at the surrounding panorama.[1] The "tower" was and is underground, and the stage is served by a giant elevator.[2] Scene shops and costume storage fit into the hillside under the stage; the opera house has a modest profile against the Sangre de Cristo Mountains.[3]

The *Flying Dutchman* debacle alone justified an examination of the opera theater's future. But even before 1988 John had recognized the need for a comprehensive plan for the full 199 acres of the site that would cover maintenance, physical development, and economic stabilization. Such a plan was sought for many reasons. Aside from changing weather patterns and audience members growing weary of being poured on during performances, patrons had come to expect a greater level of comfort as the national economy expanded and the acquisition of personal wealth increased. Also at that time, the development of a more culturally aware audience coincided with increasingly affordable travel: more of those comfortable seats were needed. Other motives included landscape issues such as erosion, confused wayfinding, noise from traffic on the Taos Highway, expansion of rehearsal space, more parking, and easier access from the lots to the theater.

1

John approached Jane and Arthur Stieren for help.[1] They came to the opera each year from San Antonio, and when they came they brought with them favorite old masters from their collection. The Stierens made a gift that was specifically targeted to the long-range plan. Underlying the master plan and its three primary objectives was a commitment to maintain the general relationship of the orchestra and balcony seating to the stage and backstage support spaces.

The first goal was to create a hierarchy of needs for maintenance and improvement of the physical plant. These would come to include parking, site drainage, patron amenities, particularly the women's restrooms, lounge space, opera club, gift shop, ticket services, and security. The second was to organize those needs in a way that would act as a catalyst for financial planning. This would include the creation of naming opportunities and also increased income from added seating. The third aim was to synthesize existing and potential new structures into an overall plan with a single cohesive image.

Our final plan was organized around four components: the theater complex, support spaces, including a pool, housing for performers and crew,[4] and an inn for visitors.[3] We also addressed wayfinding.[5] Within the master plan were various roof designs that were more than ordinarily challenging. At the same time that we sought to minimize the impact of climate, we needed to increase the number of seats.

2

A. APPRENTICE HOUSING
B. INN AT THE OPERA
C. TAOS HIGHWAY
D. OPERA THEATER
E. POOL, CAFÉ, REHEARSAL

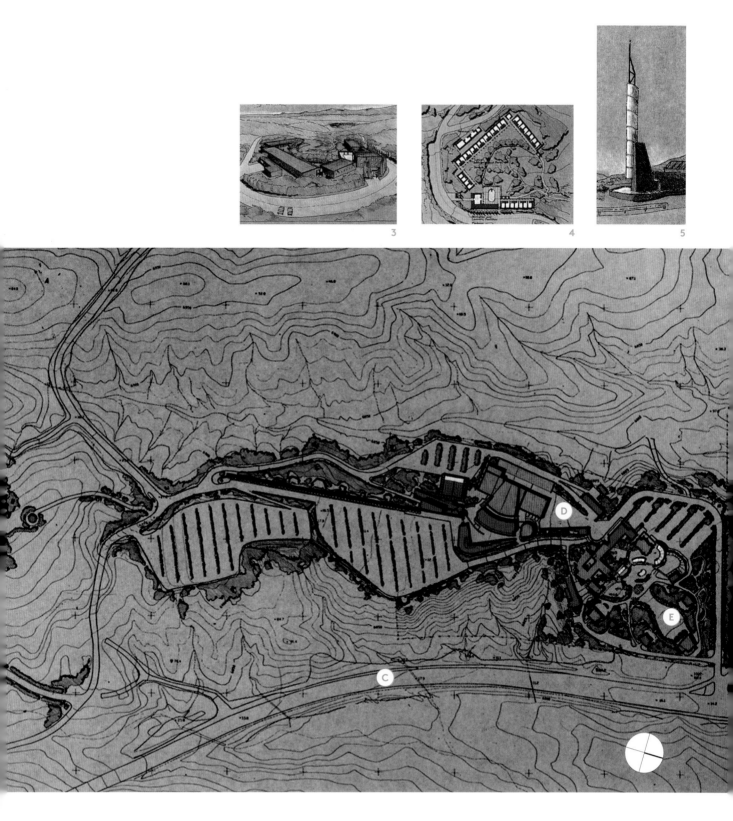

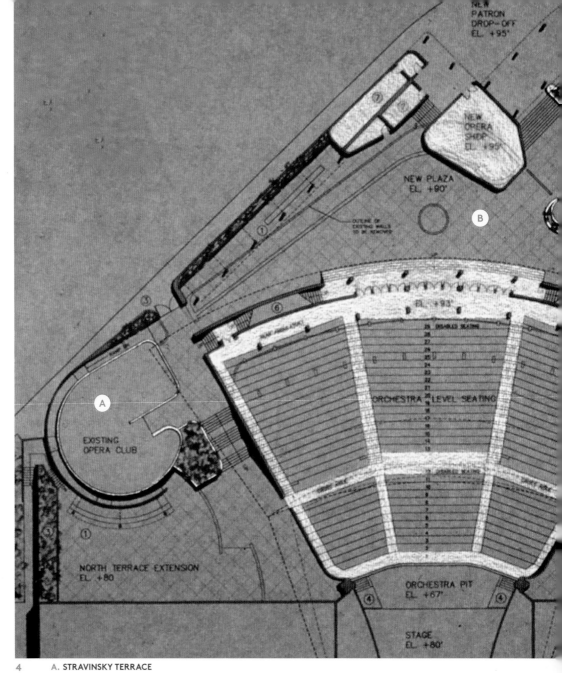

1

2

3

4

A. STRAVINSKY TERRACE
B. CROSBY TERRACE
C. LOLLIPOP TERRACE

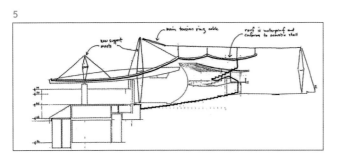

5

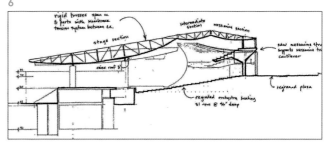

6

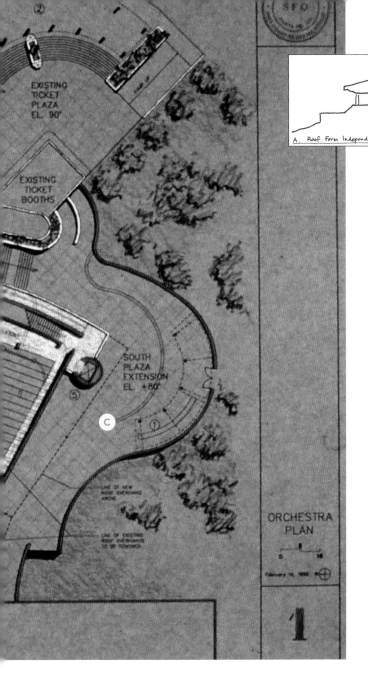

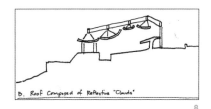

A. Roof Form Independent of Acoustic "Shell"

B. Roof Composed of Reflective "Clouds"

7

8

EXISTING
TICKET
PLAZA
EL. 90'

EXISTING
TICKET
BOOTHS

SOUTH
PLAZA
EXTENSION
EL +80'

C

ORCHESTRA
PLAN

1

While some elements of the master plan were aspirational, the one we never doubted was a new theater. By this time, Nancy Zeckendorf was attending all meetings. Patrick Markle[1] had replaced Dan Duro as the opera's technical director. With Guy Nordenson,[2] our structural engineer, we studied techniques to diminish the disruption of rain and wind. Simultaneously, Len Auerbach,[3] our theater consultant, explored ways to expand the seating without affecting the acoustics, sight lines to the stage, or views to the landscape.

The increased capacity of the theater required the expansion of three different preperformance and intermission areas: Stravinsky Terrace to the north, the "Lollipop" Terrace to the south, and Crosby Terrace to the east. The primary audience entrance was at Crosby Terrace.[4]

The "giant prairie dog" was still in the room: the twenty-eight-foot gap between the roof over the balcony and the roof over the front of the orchestra. Both the client and the design team wanted to acknowledge the old theater by admitting daylight at this break. We could not move ahead until an agreement was reached as to whether to leave the roof open or closed.

We embarked on another, more detailed study, examining alternate roof and mezzanine structures.[5,6] Jack Purcell—still involved more than thirty years after he first hiked the site with Crosby—developed, in sketch form, ideas for both an acoustic "shell" and reflective "clouds."[7,8] We also looked into ways to deflect the rain that was penetrating into the covered portion of the theater. I had sided with those old-timers who believed in "toughing out" the weather. To these patrons being seated under a starry sky compensated for getting drenched a few times each summer. Finally, however, John settled the issue in favor of the future rather than a nostalgic past. Even so, the sides of the audience chamber would remain open.

Blake, Guy, and I went back to work, and before long we came up with a solution. We connected the roofs of the balcony and the orchestra with a translucent, Teflon-covered clerestory.[2] This construction allowed light in and kept rain out. Although the concept was simple, the technical reality was not. We had to confront issues of wind, waterproofing, cost of cladding material, acoustics (cars and rain), and long-term maintenance. A laboratory in Ontario conducted wind tunnel tests, and Guy carried out dozens of calculations and extensive computer modeling.

We had to test not only the clerestory idea but also the uplift for both sections of the roof as well as the interaction between them. The light steel support structure would transfer loads to existing concrete "star" columns.[3] Reusing these columns was economical; it would also allow a little of the opera's history to remain.

The support assemblage for the roofs had to accommodate both existing and new conditions. The weight of the new roof was restricted, because the star columns had load limitations. It is supported by a system of steel masts and tension rods that minimizes deflection while carrying a dead load of 435 tons. The solution resulted in a relatively thin roof profile that provides an inconspicuous nine-foot-high technical penthouse. A grid of uninterrupted catwalks allows free access to lighting positions.

1
A. CABLE/MAST STRUCTURE
B. BALCONY TRUSS
C. CLERESTORY
D. TECHNICAL PENTHOUSE
E. STAR COLUMNS
F. STAGE
G. ORCHESTRA PIT
H. LIFT
I. SET/COSTUME STORAGE
J. BALCONY LOBBY OVERLOOK
K. OPERA CLUB
L. STRAVINSKY TERRACE
M. STANDING ROOM
N. CONTROL BOOTH
O. CROSBY TERRACE

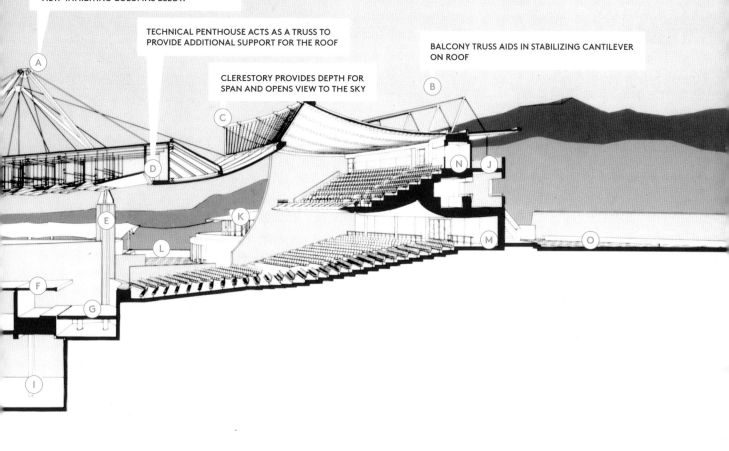

CABLE/MAST STRUCTURE REDUCES NEED FOR VIEW-INHIBITING COLUMNS BELOW

TECHNICAL PENTHOUSE ACTS AS A TRUSS TO PROVIDE ADDITIONAL SUPPORT FOR THE ROOF

CLERESTORY PROVIDES DEPTH FOR SPAN AND OPENS VIEW TO THE SKY

BALCONY TRUSS AIDS IN STABILIZING CANTILEVER ON ROOF

2

3

1

2

3

Another year passed as we tested the plan. The economy soured once again, affecting fund-raising that had become more ambitious along with the scope of the project. At a certain point we stopped working entirely. When we recommenced work, a new regulatory issue cropped up: we needed a variance to build forty feet higher than was allowed by local building codes. Patrick and his crew hoisted a long section of PVC pipe with an American flag attached to its top to the proposed elevation. The neighbors with a view of the opera were alerted and asked to respond. No complaints were received within a week, and the authorities signed off on the new height. The way was cleared for us to pursue the structural design with Guy and the acoustic specifications with Purcell, and then to proceed with construction documents.

We finally sent the drawings out for bid, and as is often the case, the estimates were too high. We all made an effort to find savings and shortcuts, and the board agreed to a ten-month construction schedule. Finally, on September 1, 1998, moments after the final curtain of the season, Manhattan Construction Company of Dallas initiated demolition of the existing balcony and enclosure.

On construction projects where an addition is to be grafted onto an existing structure, the timing of the delivery of different structural elements is critical; there is little margin for error. Operation Desert Storm caused delays in the fabrication of the custom-made steel for the roofs, which was taking place in Germany. Various trustees pulled diplomatic strings and the problem was solved. Even more problems were addressed by four patient but tenacious women who were responsible for the success of the construction schedule: Dierdre Burns, Ann Quarels, Damu Radheshwar, and Chrystalla Kartambi.[3]

We presented the "Santa Fe Opera Master Plan: An Architectural Development Concept" on August 11, 1989, almost exactly a year after we visited Santa Fe for the first time. The scheme was inspired by both the ancient dwellings at the Puye Cliffs[2] and the sophisticated research at Los Alamos. The union of past and future was intended to represent permanence and change, stability and mobility, memory and aspirations.

1

2

3

4

John was not fully satisfied that the orchestra pit would be safe from wind-driven rain. We designed, with guidance from engineer Nick Isyumov, a thirty-six-foot-high pole with a model airplane–like wing attached to it. Eight of these vertical wind baffles, almost immediately nicknamed "lollipops," were installed along the south side of the theater.[3] The wind baffles were meant to redirect precipitation, but their weakness became apparent during a rehearsal. A sudden shower and a gust of wind caused orchestra members to throw coats over their instruments and run for cover. John was on the stage in a few short minutes, and he was not happy about the money spent on a less than perfect invention.

More successful in countering the exposure to wind and rain are sixteen-foot-wide overhangs on the north and south. These expand the openness of the theater and offer long views to the south. The six-inch tongue-and-groove wood planking for the undersides of the new roof assured that the noise of rain was diminished, as was the ever-increasing sound of cars from Taos Highway. Steel splitter rails projecting from the roof edges reduce the effects of the rain and harmonize with the white-painted structure above.[2]

The white roof structure also had metaphoric weight to carry. We wanted to express the future—the spirit of innovation—and also the Native philosophy of Mother Earth and Father Sky. The delicate rods would be seen against Father Sky, while the stucco base of the building emerged from Mother Earth. Unlike the white steel of the roof structure, the walls that form the balcony and enclose the support buildings (gift shop, ticket booths, and opera club) belong to the vernacular language of northern New Mexico.[5]

A favorite preperformance site was the upper parking area, an overlook with a spectacular view to the west.[4] It was very popular with "tailgaters" in black tie or cowboy regalia who gathered for drinks and supper before performances. The lower parking levels required adjustments to their drainage systems and the lighting of paths to the opera's new entrance portal. That "ceremonial" gateway, which leads to the commodious east terrace, is a simple wood-plank-covered loggia.[1]

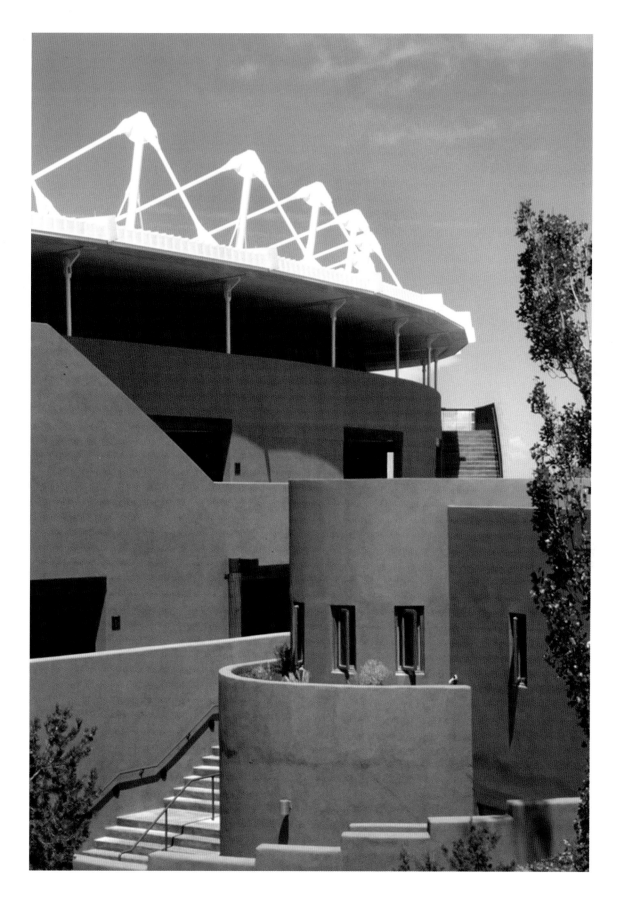

1

2

3

Finally opening night arrived: July 3, 1998. For forty-one years, the opera had maintained its unique cultural traditions in the same enchanted place. The weather was ideal. Tuxedos and long gowns are even more glamorous set against this rough high desert mesa dotted with piñons and eroded by arroyos.[3] The new entry portal and loggia were particularly welcoming in the glow of the setting sun.[1] Just before 9:00 p.m. we took our seats, and for the third time at a Santa Fe Opera theater inauguration, *Madama Butterfly*'s great faux moon shone for the opening notes.[2]

Just after the overture ended I felt a tap on my shoulder and turned to see John motioning for me to follow him. Together we moved from one position to another to listen to the sounds of voices and music. It was always hard to read John, but his body language and occasional tight-lipped smiles gave me confidence that all was going well. When the first act ended, we entered the opera club and John raised a flute of champagne in a toast.

During the next intermission Ellyn and I made our way to the Stravinsky Terrace. And at the end of the performance, after extremely long standing ovations, we attended a postperformance party. The full moon was high in the sky when the magical evening ended.

While John Crosby died in 2002, Nancy Zeckendorf remains active in the cultural life of this artistic city. She will always represent, for me, the spirit of the Santa Fe Opera.

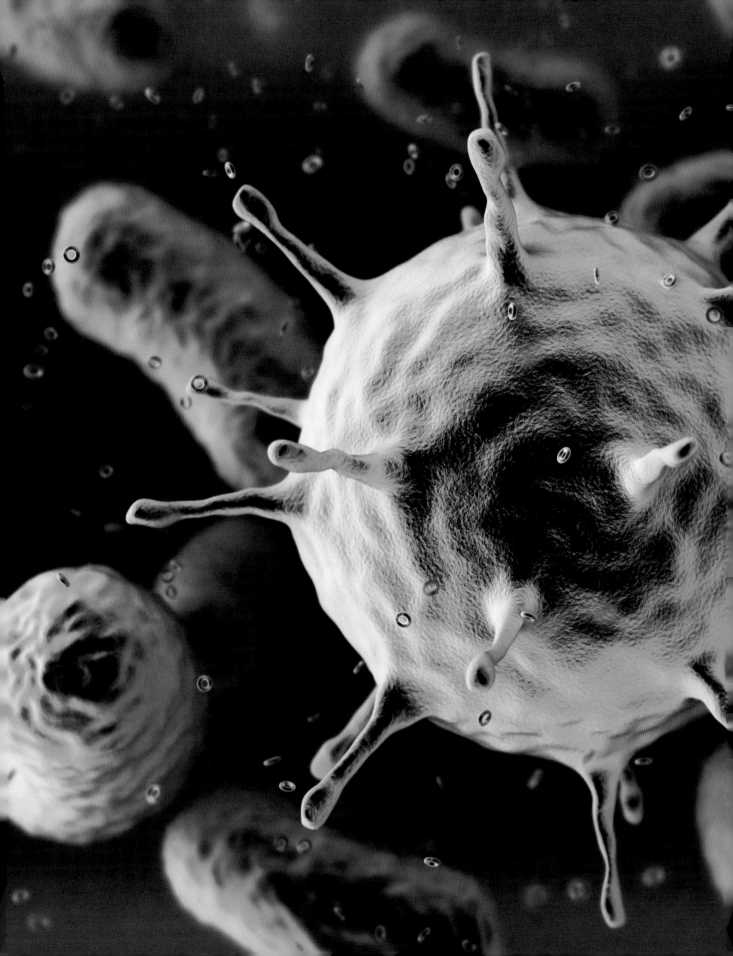

Newtown Creek Wastewater
Treatment Plant
Brooklyn, New York
1990–2014

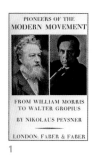

1   2   3   4

Industrial buildings of the nineteenth and twentieth centuries were much in vogue in schools of architecture during the 1950s and early 1960s.

The interest in factories, bridges, power stations, grain elevators, earthworks, and waterworks was not arbitrary. In those days, three historians dominated the chatter at architecture schools: Sigfried Giedion, Nikolaus Pevsner, and Reyner Banham. Their books—Giedion's *Mechanization Takes Command,* Pevsner's *Pioneers of the Modern Movement,* and Banham's *Theory and Design in the First Machine Age,* among others—indicate a shared belief in functionalism and an undiluted modernism. [1,2,3]

Pevsner once wrote, "A bicycle shed is a building; Lincoln Cathedral is a piece of architecture," emphasizing his belief in the value of both the functional and the aesthetic. At the time my preference was for the functional. I was drawn to the powerful constructions of American public utilities, such as the Fairmount Water Works in Philadelphia; [8] the structures of the Croton and Catskill water systems, which serve New York City; [9] and the great dams of the American West. I was also captivated by the pioneering works of Antonio Sant'Elia and Tony Garnier. And I was moved by the directness and honesty of English functionalism, the abstractions of Russian constructivism, the romantic minimalism of Italian futurism, and the pure engineering of Pier Luigi Nervi, [7] Robert Maillart, [5] and Buckminster Fuller. [6] In 1964 Arthur Drexler, director of MoMA's Department of Architecture and Design, curated an exhibit entitled "Twentieth Century Engineering." In the catalog he wrote, "In the twentieth century the art of architecture has sought to emulate [engineering's] rigorous efficiency and the boldness of its forms."

5

6

7

8 ↑

9 ↓

1

2

Historic examples include Walter Gropius's Fagus factory in Alfeld, Germany,[3] and Brinkman & Van der Vlugt's Van Nelle factory in Rotterdam.[4] In contemporary times, increasingly complex building types, typically brought into being to handle the effects of climate change and planetary instability, often manifest mechanistic forms that hark back to the early days of functionalism: the Maeslantkering storm barrier in Rotterdam,[2] the flood control gates on the Thames River,[1] and the Three Gorges Dam in China. This list might include the Newtown Creek Wastewater Treatment Plant in Greenpoint, Brooklyn. All of these creations demonstrate that complex feats of engineering can also be significant works of architecture, mergers of bicycle shed and cathedral.

3 ↑

4 ↓

The Newtown Creek plant opened in 1967 in Greenpoint, the northernmost neighborhood in Brooklyn. Forming part of the border between Brooklyn and Queens, the waterway for which it is named empties into the East River opposite the Bellevue and New York University Medical Centers.[2] Two bridges over Newtown Creek, the Pulaski and the Kosciuszko, bear witness to the Polish heritage of the area. Not far is Roosevelt Island, where Louis Kahn's recently completed Four Freedoms Park[1] perches on the southern tip. Though designed in the early 1970s, the masterful work of landscape and architecture was finally completed in 2012. I served on the board of the park, helping to safeguard Kahn's intentions.

The Newtown Creek complex is conspicuous from the Long Island Expressway and the Brooklyn-Queens Expressway as well as from most flight paths into LaGuardia Airport. From its inauguration the plant was regarded as a bad neighbor. In the late 1980s, a series of malodorous releases spurred local citizens to form GASP (Greenpointers Against Smell Pollution). By this time, discarded toxins, thirty million gallons of spilled oil, and raw sewage had made the creek one of the most polluted industrial sites in America. The fifteen-foot layer of congealed sludge at the bottom of Newtown Creek is termed, unappetizingly, "black mayonnaise."

Greenpoint's grassroots mission was bolstered by the Federal Clean Water Act of 1972 and later revisions; by 1990 the aging of the complex itself—its deteriorating buildings, peeling ducts and vent stacks, and quantities of industrial waste could pass for the set of a dystopian film—was the most persuasive argument for its complete upgrading. It was at this point that the New York City Art Commission (now the Public Design Commission) entered the picture.

The Art Commission was created in 1898 and owes a debt of gratitude to the City Beautiful movement exemplified by the architecture and planning of the 1893 World's Columbian Exposition in Chicago. Since 1914 the commission has met on the third floor of City Hall.[3] This relatively secret location contributes to the mystery surrounding its deliberations. The commission

1

is officially charged with reviewing designs for public art and architecture; in its early years the group was primarily concerned with public artifacts such as equestrian statues, murals, fountains, and parks. But by the 1960s, due to the increasing number and the increasing size of structures in New York City, the commission expanded its scope to cover the exterior design of buildings on city-owned land as well as sidewalks, playgrounds, lampposts, and large-scale public works, including, of course, the Newtown Creek Sewage Treatment Plant, as it was then called.

2

3

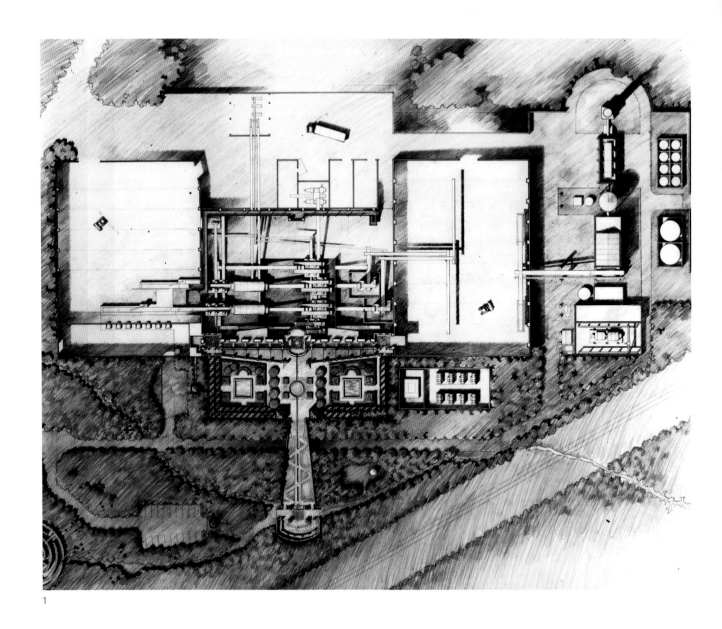

1

2

3

4

5

6

plan. The memo summarizing the review notes that the group "felt that the overall architectural character of the designs did not correspond well with the simple, industrial forms of the site and its existing facilities." Among the issues raised were attention to the general characteristics of industrial architecture, notably horizontality and repetition. The commission also stressed the importance of landscaping and, most important, guidance from an architect.

At the time the chief architect of the DEP was Michael Cetera.[6] A graduate of Pratt Institute, he was to shepherd the project over the next decade. Now in private practice, Michael frequently acts as a special advisor to the Public Design Commission. It was he who agreed to assist in the process of finding an architect, and it was he who ultimately recommended our office.

After our first meeting with Michael, we were introduced to representatives from the Triventure. I expected them to be unhappy with the idea of a shotgun marriage, but I was convinced by prior cross-disciplinary collaborations—a prototype manufacturing facility for the Westinghouse Corporation,[2] the North County Refuse Recycling Plant in San Marcos, California,[1] and the Jerome Park Reservoir in New York City[3]—that the process would benefit all parties. Steve Gyory, representing the Triventure, agreed that our mutual objective was to weave together a set of often contradictory concerns: the needs of the community and its anxieties about a large and expanding facility in its midst; the twenty-four-hour operation of the existing plant, which could not cease during the upgrade; the natural features of the site, especially along the waterfront; the facility's needs, particularly for flexibility in the face of ever-changing technology; the environmental and regulatory requirements; and the desire of the DEP and the Art Commission to achieve the highest standard of site planning and architectural design possible.

The original plan for the facility was approved by the Art Commission in 1943.[4,5] The new master plan for the plant, produced starting in 1990, would be the largest project, in size and in dollars, ever approved by the commission. David Dinkins was the mayor, Patti Harris was the commission's executive director, and Nanette Smith was assistant director. The Department of Environmental Protection, which manages the city's water supply, selected three large engineering firms to prepare the master plan. The Triventure—as the group formed by Greeley and Hansen, Hazen and Sawyer, and Malcolm Pirnie became known—presented a conceptual master plan to the commission on August 1, 1990. The commission proposed a thorough rethinking of the

1

Although our primary responsibility was to address the appearance of the buildings, it was important to thoroughly understand the various technical components of the plant. Our enclosure systems would accommodate scientifically simple but mechanically complex industrial processes involving heavy machinery, long spans, toxic materials, corrosive environments, and stringent safety and security standards. Between the outside perimeter of the fifty-two-acre site, fixed by the DEP, and the technical elements within the structures, there was almost no room in which to maneuver.

Water treatment plants use physical and biological processes that closely duplicate the way in which wetlands, rivers, streams, and lakes purify water.[2] In the natural environment, this operation can take weeks; at pollution control plants, it takes as little as seven hours. Generally a treatment plant divides its procedures into two: 90 percent for liquids and 10 percent for solids. The constituent parts of the plant are controlled from the main building. All incoming wastewater passes through a screening box, which removes large pieces of detritus, or residuals (garbage, socks, cigarette butts, grit and sand). The wastewater continues to three covered aeration tanks, where it is injected with bacteria (informally known as "bugs"[1]) that consume impurities. A small amount of sludge (the primary by-product of water treatment) and a large quantity of hot air serve as starters for the bacteria. After three hours the wastewater flows into open sedimentation tanks for another two hours; here bacteria and solids settle to the bottom. This sludge is removed for further processing. At this point, the almost pollutant-free water enters the disinfection facility, where it is treated with sodium hypochlorite (the chemical found in household bleach) and released into the East River. The total time in the plant is less than the time it takes to fly to Paris.

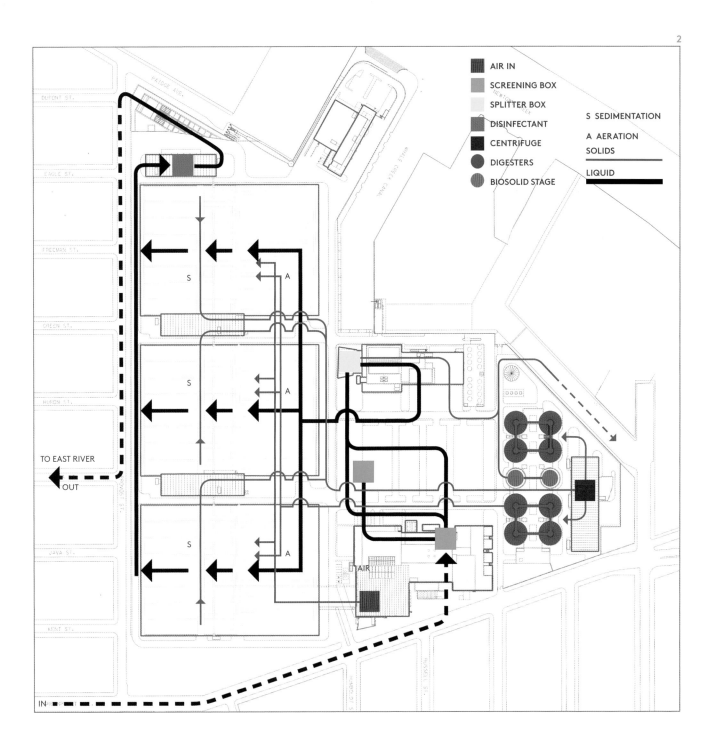

AIR IN

SCREENING BOX

SPLITTER BOX

DISINFECTANT

CENTRIFUGE

DIGESTERS

BIOSOLID STAGE

S SEDIMENTATION

A AERATION

SOLIDS

LIQUID

S

A

S

A

TO EAST RIVER

OUT

S

A

AIR

IN

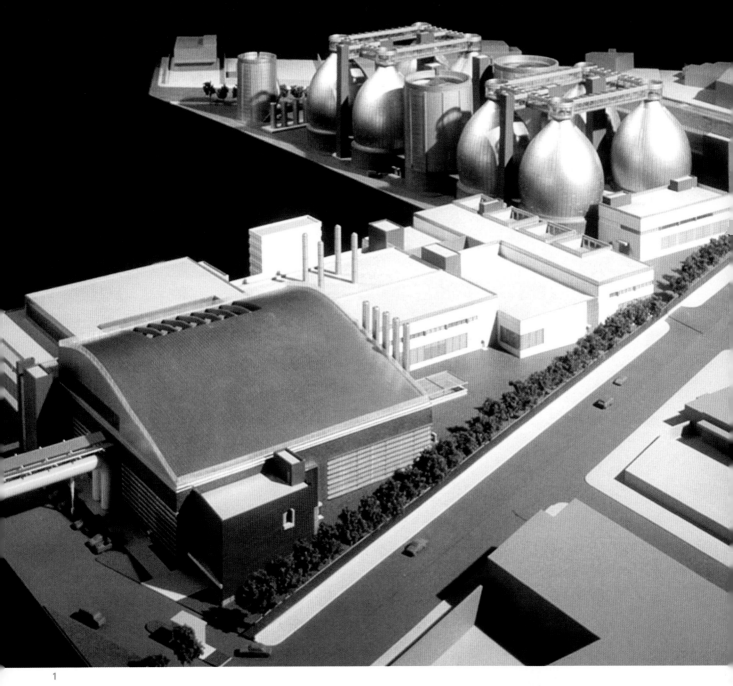

1

2

3

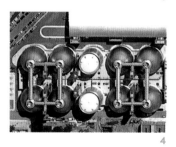

4

5

The solid treatment process starts as the sludge from the sedimentation tanks and from other processes is transferred to the digester tanks—better known as Greenpoint's eight "eggs."[1,2] The 130-foot-high and 80-foot-diameter ovoid forms facilitate the maintenance of the temperature at that of the human body— the optimal temperature for bacteria—and the circulation of fluid. Only part of the eggs is visible from the exterior, but inside and disguised within the "egg cups" and below grade, the entirety of the figure appears.[3] Liquid from the digester tanks is transferred into the adjacent centrifuge building. Water is separated from the sludge, and the biosolids, destined for fertilizer, are stored in flat-top tanks between the egg clusters.[4] Just north of the clusters are flares to burn off gases from the digester tanks.[5] The flames are disguised by stainless-steel cylinders. In the future it will not be necessary to burn the methane; the gases will enter the city grid for domestic and industrial uses.

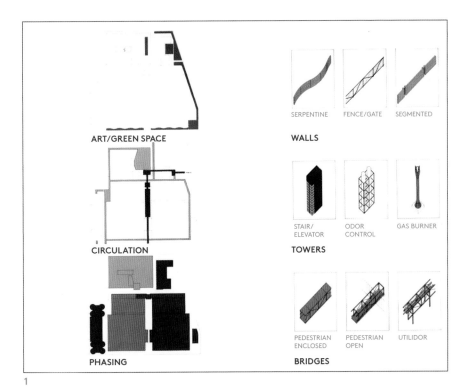

ART/GREEN SPACE

WALLS

SERPENTINE FENCE/GATE SEGMENTED

CIRCULATION

TOWERS

STAIR/
ELEVATOR

ODOR
CONTROL

GAS BURNER

PHASING

BRIDGES

PEDESTRIAN
ENCLOSED

PEDESTRIAN
OPEN

UTILIDOR

1

2

A. STAINLESS-STEEL-CLAD SLUDGE STORAGE TANK ON BRICK BASE
B. STAINLESS-STEEL EXHAUST STACKS
C. STAINLESS-STEEL-CLAD DIGESTER ON BRICK BASE
D. STRUCTURALLY GLAZED CURTAIN WALL FOR SUPPORT BUILDING
E. GREEN-BRICK STAIR/ELEVATOR TOWER
F. GLASS AND STAINLESS-STEEL SERVICE CATWALK
G. PROCESS AIR DUCT AND SUPPORT PYLONS
H. STAINLESS-STEEL LOUVERS
I. STAINLESS-STEEL ROOF AND CURTAIN WALL FOR TANK BATTERY BUILDINGS
J. TYPICAL STAINLESS-STEEL MAIN AND OVERHEAD DOORS AND CANOPIES
K. TYPICAL WHITE-BRICK AND STAINLESS-STEEL WINDOW WALLS
L. STAINLESS-STEEL ROOF AND PENTHOUSE OVER EQUIPMENT BAY BUILDINGS
M. TYPICAL BLUE-BRICK AND STAINLESS-STEEL CURTAIN WALL ON EQUIPMENT BAY BUILDINGS
N. ORANGE-BRICK ACCENT BUILDINGS

3

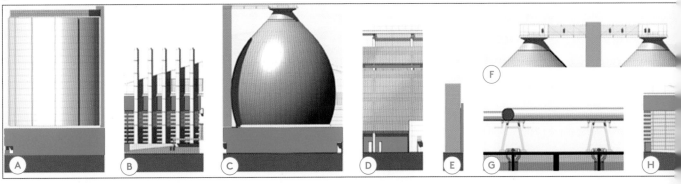

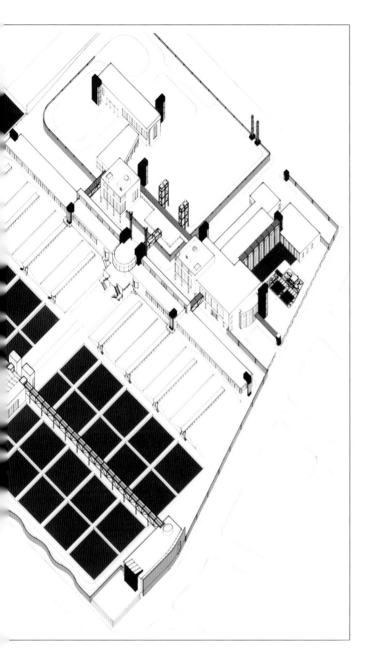

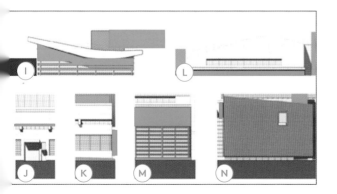

As our work began we focused on technical clarity, formal integrity, and functional efficiency. We wanted to make the diverse set of structures visually engaging from local streets, from distant freeways, and even from the air, and we wanted to do so without compromising utility or increasing costs. Redesigning the mechanical components and deodorizing the air in the plant's precinct were key objectives.

Our informal name for the master plan design strategy was the "kit of parts."[1,2,3] The first iteration was produced in 1990; by 1996 a "final" and more complex version was developed. This framework, as much conceptual as physical, organizes the appearance of the site. Scale, color, material, and shape are applied consistently yet singularly, as indicated by building function. The language evolves to suit changes in the techniques used at the plant as well as an extended period of design and construction. Color was a critical element of the overall strategy: the components are rendered in bright primary tones, resembling something of a Lego set for grown-ups. Since we could not shut down any part of the plant for even a day, we conceived a "musical chairs" scenario for adding and removing the plant's treatment buildings.

The Art Commission reconsidered the Newtown Creek master plan on the last day of October 1990. This time the group's assessment was rather different: "The committee felt," the memo summarizing the meeting recorded, "that the direction of the design and plan of this facility was appropriate." Concerns were raised nonetheless: the flexibility of the overall proposal; the design of the perimeter fencing (commissioner James Ingo Freed recommended an open angle to receive the community); landscaping (once again); incorporation of public art through the Percent for Art Program; and especially maintaining an open and public attitude through design and construction.

THE POOP PROJECT
A CULTURAL MOVEMENT

1

We embarked on minor revisions to the plan and, in the early 1990s, the first actual building. The small electrical substation exemplifies the transitory nature of our work.[6] It was used as a material and systems mock-up that would influence future decisions for the complex as a whole. After it was completed, the project went on hold for almost three years as the engineering team reviewed emerging waste technologies. The treatment process that was adopted rendered our small substation obsolete. Its facades were removed, and its function was absorbed into the main building.

We presented models of the updated version of the master plan to the Art Commission in 1997. The same submission was put through a trying but necessary review by the community board. The acronym for the review committee was "NickMick" (Newtown Creek Monitor Committee). Irene Klementowicz[5] and Christine Holowacz[4] in particular were well-intentioned but formidable adversaries. The Polshek/Triventure team spent many evenings in a gloomy meeting room near the plant eating lukewarm lasagna and listening to interminable commentary. Finally we gained the trust of NickMick and reached a consensus. The community organization that grew out of these efforts is now part of the aptly named POOP (People's Own Organic Power) Project.[1]

Once the master plan was approved, our role expanded to include schematic design for all building exteriors as well as the main physical features of the site. We were also responsible for collaborating with the Percent for Art Program, integrating the work of the selected artists. In addition, Greg Clawson[3] of our office, along with the Triventure engineers, supervised the work of the engineering team throughout the

2

years of documentation and construction. Greg's gentle personal manner and rigorous attention to detail were instrumental in managing restive locals, the DEP, and most important, Jimmy Pynn, the longtime superintendent of Newtown Creek.

In addition to the main building, the disinfection facility, and treatment tanks, the site accommodates the highly visible orange-tile-covered visitor center,[2] which is appended to the main building and is accessible from Greenpoint Avenue, and the support building, which contains offices, laboratories, personnel facilities, repair and maintenance shops, and equipment storage areas.

3 ↑
↓ 4

5

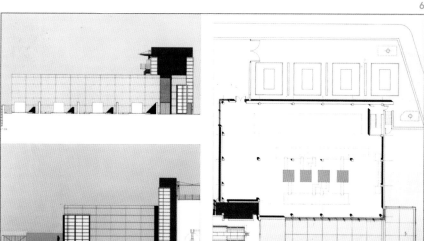

6

1

2

3

4

5

During the construction phase we were on the receiving end of various objections from the DEP. For instance, the DEP opposed the exterior color tiles we specified. We intended to use vivid earth, sky, and water tones to identify different functions of the plant. The DEP had experienced failures with a similar material in the past; once we ran another set of tests and requested more explicit references from the manufacturers, as well as on-site mock-ups, the agency came to agree with us. Two years later I noticed new tile samples at the site—samples that did not match the colors we had specified. A DEP architect had imposed on the team a depressingly dull color range. Instead of cobalt blues, forest greens, and vibrant oranges,[2,3] we had muddy earth, overcast sky, and murky water. With the support of NickMick we rushed to resubmit the original palette, which was eventually installed.

Almost from the beginning, our social objectives were not as easily defined or carried out as our physical objectives, though certainly they were inextricably connected. We wanted to make this environmental machine accessible to the public, particularly school-children, both physically and intellectually. Visitors would journey through, around, and over the plant, coming away with a renewed sense of the importance of clean air and water. We developed glass connectors, or "utilidors,"[1] that link the tops of the digester eggs and connect to the ground through green-tile emergency stairs. Fortunately there was a practical rationale for these pieces: they would aid service and maintenance. The aerial view of the plant made its functions easier to explain; spectacular views of Manhattan were a bonus.[4] The walkways have been closed to the public since 9/11; similar public ways at other utilities, such as footpaths over the dams at Ashokan Reservoir in the Catskill Watershed,[5] were closed and then reopened, and perhaps the utilidors will welcome visitors once again.

Our work with the Percent for Art Program was another element in the social/cultural aspirations of the treatment plant. Performance artist and self-anointed "architect" Vito Acconci was the first artist nominated by the selection panel. His contribution, *The Edge of the Plant/The Edge of the Neighborhood,* [1] required the removal of a lower corner of the cubic, bright orange visitor center on Greenpoint Avenue. The gash is meant to suggest a connection between the plant and the neighborhood. The piece also features a series of curvilinear water channels that run from inside the building to the outdoors. [2]

George Trakas created the second artwork, *Waterfront Nature Walk,* [4,5] an environmental sculpture that provides waterfront access for the people of Greenpoint and plant employees. An instant hit with neighbors and visitors, it emphasizes the intersection of nature and industry. It is set to be expanded farther along the edge of the creek.

Night lighting was another area through which we wanted to engage the community. The Percent for Art Program could not bear the cost of the installation, but fortunately Joel Miele, then commissioner of the DEP, stepped in. Hervé Descottes, a French artist and founder of the lighting firm L'Observatoire International, has created imaginative designs for the Museum of the Moving Image in Queens, the High Line on the West Side of Manhattan, and Alice Tully Hall at Lincoln Center. Descottes's night lighting transforms the shimmering silver digester eggs with a mysterious blue glow. [3] These magical objects attract attention from near and far.

1

2

Our odyssey at Newtown Creek, indeed the complete rehabilitation of the plant, would not have been possible without Jimmy Pynn.[2] A Cagney-esque figure (as a dancer, not a gangster), Jimmy is an effervescent and tireless leader who started with the Department of Public Works as a sewage treatment worker after his senior year at Brooklyn Tech high school. Currently he oversees both the plant's reconstruction and its operations. Many water treatment experts possess Jimmy's knowledge of the technical aspects of the process, but none can explain them as exquisitely (and endlessly) as he does. In tours of the plant, visitors (including, in 2009, members of the Design Commission) hang on his every word for a grueling two and a half hours; even so, their plaintive requests for "just a little more" recall a child's eagerness for one last bedtime story.

The construction schedule has been prolonged numerous times; currently, the residuals building is expected to be completed in late 2014. At that time the entire facility will have been replaced, in situ, at a cost of 4.2 billion federal, state, and local dollars. The Newtown Creek plant is now the largest of fourteen such facilities in New York City,[3] serving 1.5 million people in twenty-five square miles of Manhattan, Brooklyn, and Queens. The facility purifies more than 300 million gallons of wastewater every day—equal to the volume of a full-block, twenty-seven-story Manhattan tower.

1

And the SEWAGE?

Ah, the SEWAGE.

The 53-ACRE NEWTOWN CREEK
SEWAGE PLANT in
GREENPOINT, BROOKLYN,
is A REVELATION.

I GO there EARLY ONE MORNING.
OH MAMA.

2

CHRISTINE HOLOWACZ is WATERING THE LITTLE GARDEN
in FRONT of the VISITOR CENTER.

she
WORKS
with the
city to ADDRESS
the Needs and CONCERNS
of the Community.

INSIDE the VISITOR
CENTER is an ART
INSTALLATION by
VITO ACCONCI.

3

4

As the unique shapes of Newtown Creek's new components began to materialize, a kind of sewage treatment cult came into being. At first the plant was celebrated in blogs and among the city's design cognoscenti. It was cast in Jell-O for a local competition.[1] The marvelously inventive artist Maira Kalman took note of it in her *New York Times* blog "And the Pursuit of Happiness."[2,3] Such observers recognize that this unusual project does more than clean up the environment. It is simultaneously a gargantuan three-dimensional jigsaw puzzle more than twenty-five years in the assembling and a tribute to government and the common good it serves.

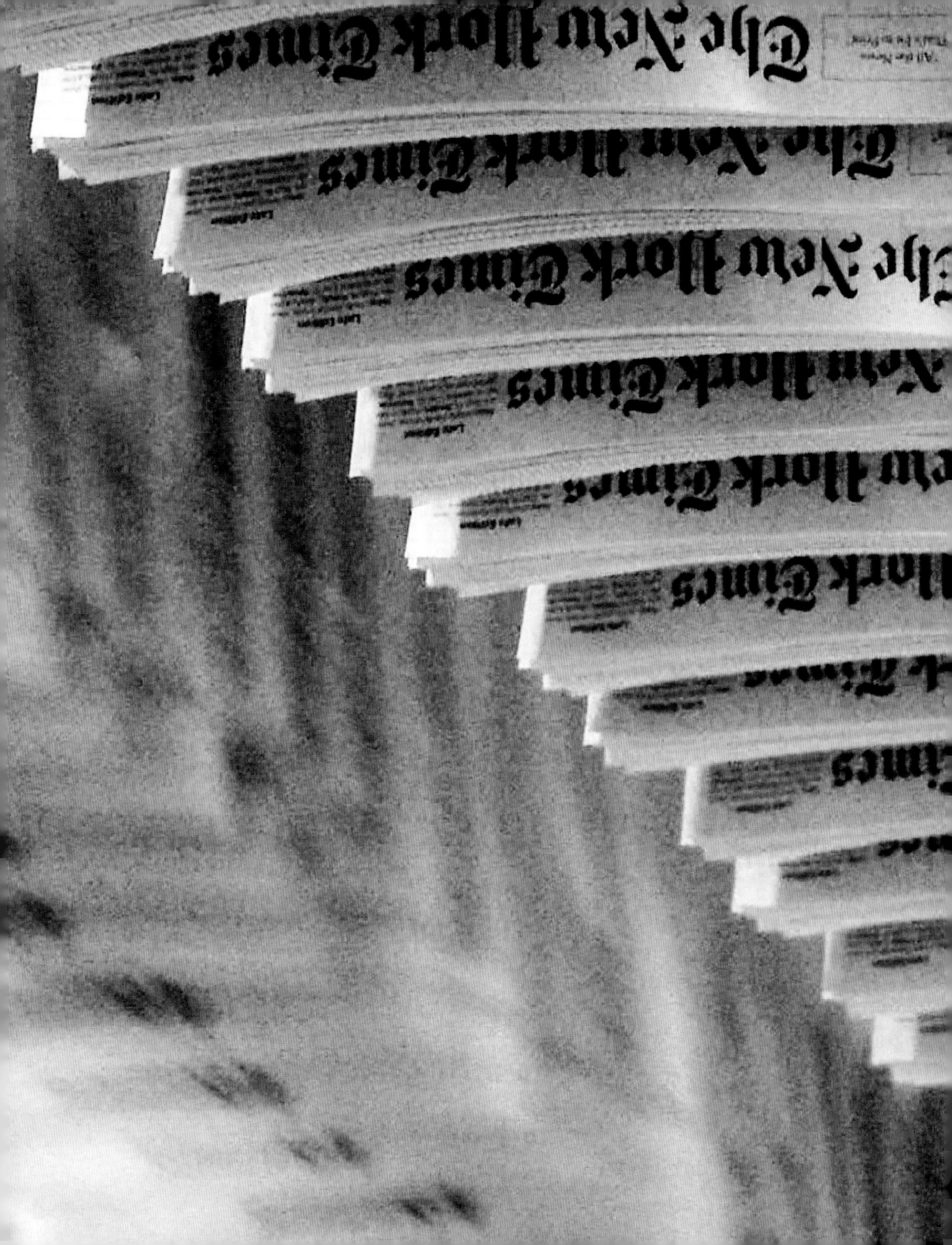
The New York Times

New York Times Printing Plant
College Point, New York
1993–1997

Newspapers became part of my life when I was fifteen. That year, 1945, witnessed three momentous news stories: the death of FDR,[1] the dropping of the atomic bomb,[2] and the end of World War II.[3]

1

2

A newspaper at the breakfast table was as ubiquitous as a paperboy shouting headlines from the street corner. In 1993 newspapers became part of my life in a different way. We were selected by the New York Times Company as architects for a new printing plant, an event that instigated a study of the history of newspapers, from the use of wood blocks in China in 200 AD[7] to the beginnings of digital printing in the late twentieth century.

As is widely known, Johannes Gutenberg's innovation was not the first printing press, but it was the first practical, economically viable printing mechanism.[6] His printing technology was responsible for a huge increase in the production of European books and leaflets, including the world's first newspaper, printed in Strasbourg in 1605. Numerous other newspapers followed, in Holland, England, France, Portugal, and Spain.

The term "newspaper" became common in the United States in the eighteenth century. *The Boston News-Letter*,[4] founded in 1704, served the thirteen colonies of North America. From that time on, daily and weekly papers were established throughout the United States. For three centuries they were both profitable and politically influential. Starting in the 1950s, however, television gradually eroded readership and financial yields. Then the end of the century saw the growth of the Internet, which accelerated the decline of daily papers. Between 2005 and 2012, advertising revenues fell by more than half.

3 ↑

4 ↓

1

2

A. I. M. PEI & PARTNERS, 1964
B. SKIDMORE, OWINGS & MERRILL, 1974
C. POLSHEK PARTNERSHIP, 2007

3

5

4

6

7

A small number of families presided over the American newspaper business from the mid-nineteenth century through the first half of the twentieth century. Publishing was a civic responsibility, and newspapers (as well as radio and television stations) became part of local culture. Among these extended families were the Pattersons of Chicago, the Pulitzers of St. Louis, the Binghams of Louisville, the Knights of Akron, the Grahams of Washington, D.C., the de Youngs of San Francisco, and the Chandlers of Los Angeles. Most of these families are no longer associated with the papers they founded: conglomerates such as Bertelsmann, News Corp., Gannett, and McClatchy dominate newspaper ownership.

Nevertheless, newspapers, like sports franchises, are still seen as "trophy" acquisitions. In 1993 Mort Zuckerman purchased the New York Daily News (founded by Joseph Medill Patterson in 1919); in 2007 Sam Zell obtained the Chicago Tribune Company (founded in 1847) via a buyout; and in 2009 Carlos Slim Helú invested $250 million in the New York Times (published since 1851). These "new age" investors are a far cry from the old families. But in New York, close by one another in Times Square, are the headquarters of two enduring newspaper dynasties—the Newhouses and the Ochs-Sulzbergers.

Samuel I. Newhouse Sr. was born in 1895 and purchased the cornerstone of the Newhouse media empire, the Staten Island Advance, in 1922. In 1964 he provided the founding gift for the Newhouse School of Communications at Syracuse University.[2] I. M. Pei designed the school's first building, and President Lyndon Johnson[7] delivered his Gulf of Tonkin speech as part of the opening ceremonies. Newhouse II, a banal addition by Skidmore, Owings & Merrill, followed in 1974. In 2003 our firm designed Newhouse III, a curvilinear, multifloored glass structure that unified the school.[1] The building was a gift from Donald Newhouse[3] and S. I. Newhouse Jr.;[5] Si's wife, Victoria,[4] represented the family. Judge John Roberts,[6] soon to be Chief Justice of the Supreme Court, gave the keynote address when the building opened in 2007. Johnson's and Roberts's visits to Syracuse attest to the political power of journalism.

1

2

3

Adolph Ochs[1] acquired the *New York Times* in 1896. The next year he coined the motto "all the news that's fit to print." This innocent phrase set the *Times* apart from its competitors—specifically Joseph Pulitzer's *New York World* and William Randolph Hearst's *New York Journal*. The exaggerated headlines and lurid photographs on the front page of today's *New York Post*[3] represent the traditions of the *World* and *Journal*. The *Times*, on the other hand, is known as the "old gray lady." The expression refers not only to the front page (the *Times* was one of the last daily newspapers to adopt color photography) but to its seriousness, even stodginess.

From 1913 to 1997 the *New York Times* was printed at the paper's headquarters on West Forty-third Street in Manhattan[4,5] and at a plant in Edison, New Jersey. In the early 1990s the publication undertook a billion-dollar, decade-long capital improvement program. David Thurm,[2] who oversaw the effort, seemed an unorthodox choice. Forty years old, he was not a newspaper man but a Harvard- and NYU-educated lawyer and film buff. (Before law school he worked briefly for Otto Preminger and 20th Century Fox.) His principal qualifications were his organizational skills, his impeccable taste, and his sense of humor, which enabled him to deal with labor and management, understand finance and aesthetics, and mediate among dozens of often-conflicting consultants.

Part of the capital program was a restructuring of production—computerized four-color presses, robotic delivery systems, high-speed automated folding and insert machinery—which would allow the paper to better compete with other national and local publications.[7] David called the firm to ask for materials relevant to the design of an industrial printing facility. Several days later he visited the office to explain the corporate structure of the paper, the functions of the building, and the site.

6

4 ↑

5 ↓

1

2

3

4 ↑   5 ↓

1 The Architecture of Production:
Precedents and Inspiration

2 Typological Analysis:
Circulation and Process

3 Site Investigation:
Connections and Opportunities

4 Building Systems Definition:
Structural and Mechanical

5 Enclosure System Selection:
Environmental Control, Light, Maintenance

6 Public and Private Space:
Employee and Visitor Amenities

7 Conclusion:
Image and Implementation

Soon thereafter, I entered the lobby of 229 West Forty-third Street with my partners Joseph Fleischer and Richard Olcott. David escorted us to the fourteenth floor to meet *Times* executives. The walls of the boardroom were intimidating, covered with photographs of world dignitaries: the Dalai Lama, Jawaharlal Nehru, Haile Selassie, Indira Gandhi, Golda Meir, Charles de Gaulle, Winston Churchill, and all United States presidents since 1869.

Sitting around a conference table were publisher Arthur ("Punch") Ochs Sulzberger;[2] his son (soon to be publisher) Arthur Sulzberger Jr.; president of the paper Russell Lewis; and president of the Times Company Lance Primus. I had met the elder Sulzberger first in 1969, when I presented our design for the exhibition "The Rise of an American Architecture"[1] to a Metropolitan Museum board committee he served on (the exhibit was part of a celebration of the museum's centennial), and then again in 1991 at the dedication of Barnard College's Sulzberger Hall,[3] named for his mother, Iphigene.

For the interview we had prepared a twenty-foot-long document entitled "The Architecture of Production."[5] It included five topics—typological analysis, site investigation, building systems definition, enclosure system selection, and public and private space—plus an introduction and conclusion. One image commanded special attention: a photomontage showing Nicholas Grimshaw's *Financial Times* plant in the UK[4] inserted into the *Times*'s site, which was beside the Whitestone Expressway in College Point, Queens. We ended by stating that we would endeavor to create a building that would symbolize the merger of the power of communications with the humane application of advanced printing technology.

1

2

David called a few days later and in his cheerfully direct manner made an appointment to discuss a contract. At our meeting he restated the paper's production objectives as well as its corporate goals—to improve labor relations and business practices. He had convinced *Times* executives that a well-designed building would benefit not only the employees but also the public face of the newspaper—and that it would cost little more than hiring a routine designer. David also described an unusually collaborative approach to the design. He was convinced that productivity levels would rise if machines could somehow work in partnership with employees.

The first step was a series of carefully choreographed partnering exercises that brought together architects, engineers, printing specialists, senior newspaper administrators, and the construction manager, Lehrer McGovern. A Midtown hotel provided the setting. Teams drawn from each of the groups arranged blocks into "designs" for a hypothetical new town. [1]

After the "therapy" we all went to see the thirty-one-acre site in College Point. [2,3] As we drove through the gates, I recognized it as a former NYPD car pound—one that I had visited several times in the past, unfortunately. Adjacent to it was a protected wetland. The ground was the consistency of pudding—similar to what we had encountered in Albany for the New York State Bar Center and in Lower Manhattan for the Seamen's Church Institute. The soil and the weight of the machinery and the paper rolls—each roll weighed a ton—would dictate the structural system of the 540,000-square-foot plant.

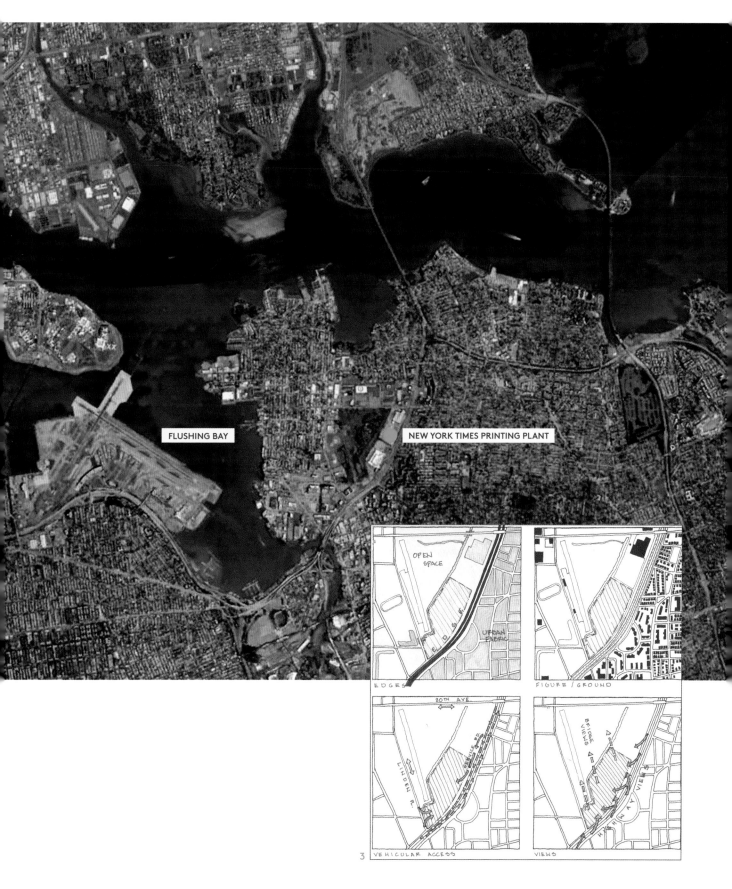

FLUSHING BAY

NEW YORK TIMES PRINTING PLANT

OPEN
SPACE

URBAN
FABRIC

EDGES

FIGURE / GROUND

20TH AVE.

LINDEN PL.

VEHICULAR ACCESS

BRIDGE
VIEWS

VIEWS

1

2   3

A. RECEPTION
B. ADMINISTRATIVE ENTRY
C. PAPER STORAGE
D. PRESS HALL
E. TRANSFORMERS
F. MAILROOM
G. DISTRIBUTION DOCKS
H. DISPATCH

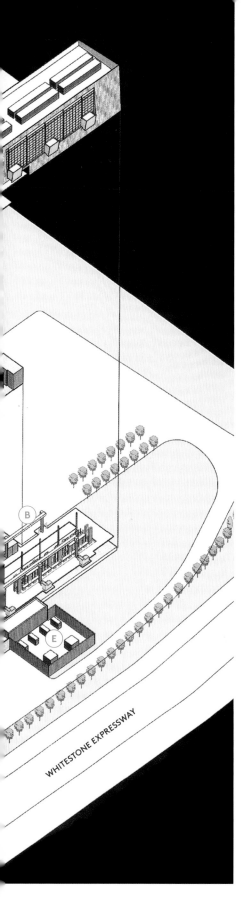

WHITESTONE EXPRESSWAY

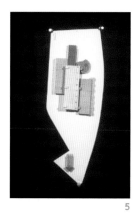

4   5

Printing is a linear process both physically and conceptually. Newsprint is delivered, then printed; the printed
papers are sorted and collated, bundled, and loaded.
The *Times* press hall called for four presses, each 150
feet long and 60 feet high. Other program requirements included employee lockers, food service, a
lounge, workshops, computer control stations, a mailroom, administrative spaces, loading docks, and paper
storage. In addition, we needed to build in a strategy
for expansion—in fact, management decided to add
two presses before we even began construction.

Within the building, the printing process is ordered
from front to back. The paper storage facility contains
2,230 giant rolls of paper; robotic forklifts deliver them
to the presses as needed.[1] Pressmen operate computerized printing controls from sealed "quiet rooms"
between the presses.[2] Overhead conveyors connect the
machinery to a double-height mailroom, where printed
sheets are fed into folding and insert machines. The
process culminates with the loading docks along the
west side of the plant. From there, millions of daily and
Sunday papers are delivered to front doors and news-
stands throughout the city.

While our first idea was one large, column-free space,
early massing models[4,5] suggested that distributing
the program elements into a series of discrete, identifiable, but interrelated volumes was a better solution.
Together with our engineers, Ove Arup, we developed
a grid of columns thirty feet on center. The columns
would also serve as vertical conduits for the complex
electrical and mechanical services that would support
plant operations.

1

The site for this enormous new "machine" was just fifty feet away from the Whitestone Expressway; each day, 150,000 cars sped by. Visually revealing the printing process to these motorists, and to a larger public, had emerged as a primary goal of the design. Prompted by the color printing process (four colors of ink—cyan, magenta, yellow, and black—combine in different proportions in every word and image), we devised a palette of saturated colors, visible from the highway and from the air, to complement our massing strategy. [1] The press hall is a corrugated-metal volume with a silver finish. Two smaller blocks, paper roll storage (cobalt blue) and the administrative wing (reflective glass), are connected to the press hall at the south end. Red corrugated-metal panels wrap the switchgear equipment in a block immediately to the east of the principal facade. An electric green stair tower marks the employee entrance, and signal yellow metal boxes, which protrude through the skin of the press hall, filter the fine ink mist produced there. [3]

Robotic equipment, which requires a perfectly flat slab, would be used extensively throughout the facility. But the load-bearing capacity of the ground (or lack thereof) was extremely problematic. The Arup structural team and printing plant specialists from the Charles T. Main Company offset the challenges of the soil with 100,000 cubic yards of fill and 1,100 friction piles, some sunk as deep as 240 feet. There would be no risk of uneven floor slabs. [2]

2

3

1

2

3

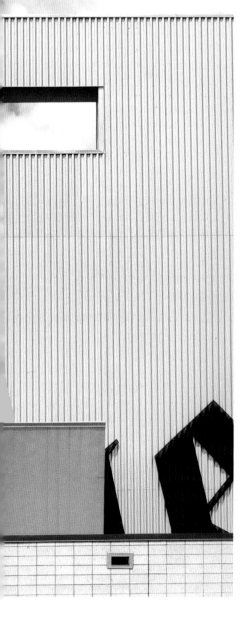

4

Large glazed cutouts in the east and north facades flood the press hall with light and reveal the presses to the hundreds of thousands of eyes that pass by. We used elements of the *Times*'s visual culture—typography, color, patterns, and so forth—to augment the public profile of the building.[1] The iconic Gothic logo is emblazoned at an angle across the facade, as it is on the company's delivery trucks.[2,4] We planned to wrap the logo onto the roof, so that it would be seen by the thousands of aircraft landing at nearby LaGuardia Airport, but budget constraints put an end to this idea. The reception hall announces the color palette,[3] and the plaza outside is paved in a black-and-white crossword puzzle pattern; the late Eugene Maleska, the paper's revered crossword editor, vetted the arrangement. Even the cobalt blue of the rollhouse was drawn from the *Times*'s ubiquitous vending boxes.

We broke ground in October 1994. Ironically, it wasn't until June 2007, when the *Times* moved into a new skyscraper designed by Renzo Piano, that David Dunlap, a longtime reporter focusing on architecture and urban design, wrote a piece that eloquently describes the end of the old way of producing newspapers. [4]

Listen. The sound is muffled by wall-to-wall carpet tiles and fabric-lined cubicles. But it's still there, embedded in the concrete and steel sinews of the old factory at 229 West 43rd Street, where The New York Times *was written and edited yesterday for the last time.*

It is the sound of news, dispatched to and from the third-floor newsroom since 1913, the first year of Woodrow Wilson's presidency. It is the noise of physical exertion: the staccato rapping of manual typewriters, hundreds of them; the insistent chatter of newsagency teleprinters, marshaled by the dozens. It is bells and loudspeakers, the cry of "Copy!"...

When the order was given to "Let go," a seemingly endless web of newsprint began rolling up from the subbasement to stream through the presses at such roaring speed that the whole 15-story building trembled and—it was said—The Times's ordinarily fearless mouse population grew deeply agitated...

The era of Underwoods and Linotypes ended in 1978, when The Times converted to computerized typesetting. And the presses on 43rd Street last thundered almost exactly a decade ago, on June 15, 1997.

The plant was completed in June 1997, and the first color edition of Adolph Ochs's creation came off the presses on October 16, 1997. The "old lady" was gray no longer. [3] Nor was the building. Cars driving at sixty miles per hour take a full ten seconds to pass. The three-dimensional assemblage of irregular volumes, intense colors, vivid graphics, and common materials dramatizes a new era in the newspaper's history.

3

4

Rose Center for Earth and Space
American Museum of Natural History
New York, New York
1994–2000

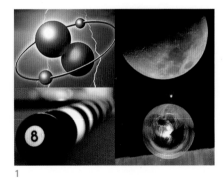

1

2

Spherical shapes, from atoms to moons, from cue balls to soap bubbles, have enthralled children and adults from the beginning of time.[1]

Nor are architects immune to the allure of the orb. In 1784 French architect and engineer Etienne-Louis Boullée, just one of the many architects consumed by spheres, designed a globe-shaped cenotaph, or funeral monument, honoring Isaac Newton.[3,4,5] Boullée intended to illuminate the Newton sarcophagus with starlight admitted through small holes in the dome—perhaps an early idea of a "planetarium."

Boullée fascinates architects of our time for his abstract style; in spite of its neoclassicism, his work is characterized by the removal of all unnecessary ornament. His belief that architecture must be expressive of its purpose further reinforces a connection to early modernism. Richard Etlin, in his book *Symbolic Space,* discusses Boullée's definition of character, which "involves three components: metaphorical character, which is achieved through the narrative organization of forms and spaces; expressive character, which relies on the emotional impact on the viewer of simple geometric forms; and symbolic character, which utilizes temple-like spaces dedicated to high ideals in order to make them, in a manner of speaking, present, palpable." Boullée's powerful imagery, not to mention his meditations on metaphor, expression, and symbolism, provided vital formal and conceptual precedents for our new planetarium at the American Museum of Natural History.

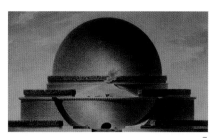

3

4 ↑   5 ↓

3

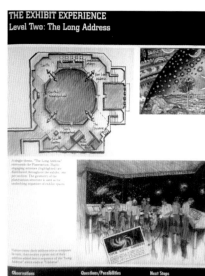

4

The intergalactic adventure began early in 1994 when I received a phone call from Jeff Kennedy, an exhibition designer in Boston. The Museum of Natural History had issued a request for proposals for the renovation of the Hayden Planetarium.[2] The RFP stressed new interpretive material and exhibit redesign; some of the installations had not been touched since the Hayden opened in 1935.[1] Jeff asked if we would team with him, even if our role involved only deferred maintenance (leaks, masonry pointing, air-conditioning, and modest upgrading of the building). Both our preservation credentials and the desire to be of service to this august institution spoke to our interest. Also, I had worked with the museum's chief executive, Ellen Futter,[3] a few years earlier. Initially an attorney at Milbank, Tweed, Hadley & McCloy and then the president of Barnard College for thirteen years, Ellen had been my client for Sulzberger Hall, a new dormitory.

Jeff and I put together a document known as a "leporello."[4] The firm often used this accordion-like format to present relevant work, design philosophy, and project approach. We agreed that I would open the interview with building upgrade issues, and Jeff would follow with exhibition concepts.

1

Not long afterward, Bill Gooch, the director of the planetarium, gave us a tour of the historic building. It was a
square brick Art Deco box surmounted by a copper-
covered concrete dome about seventy-four feet in
diameter. The primary facade faced West Eighty-first
Street. From the street the building appeared to be
freestanding, although it was connected to the main
museum complex on its south and east.

The planetarium was an addition to the unfinished
north side of the museum. The master plan for the
institution was a rectangle approximately 650 by 850
feet,[3] similar in size to McKim, Mead & White's
scheme for the Brooklyn Museum (1893)[4] and James
Renwick's Smithsonian Institution Building, or Castle,
on the National Mall (1855).[5] The first building, by
Calvert Vaux and Jacob Wrey Mould, dates from 1877.[1]
The south and east ranges, along with large portions
of the middle of the rectangle, were completed by the
1920s. But only small portions of the west and north
ranges were ever built.

Trowbridge & Livingston designed the planetarium.
This early-twentieth-century firm was known for the
B. Altman store and the St. Regis Hotel, both on Fifth
Avenue, and Engine Company No. 7 in Lower Manhattan. In 1939 the WPA *Guide to New York City,* co-edited
by John Cheever, called the Hayden Planetarium
"among the most interesting examples of modern
functional architecture."

2

But by the early 1990s, the planetarium was neither
attractive nor functional. The romantic mood conveyed
in early representations of the Hayden was far from
the reality offered by the dark north front. Theodore
Roosevelt Park, unkempt and overgrown, camouflaged
the main entry on West Eighty-first Street. Bordering
the building on the west was a chain-link-fenced parking lot. Every day exhaust-spewing school buses would
drop off their students at a series of fences leading to a
rear service door—a sequence the warden of Sing Sing
would have admired. As the buses idled, their drivers
would smoke or snooze.[2]

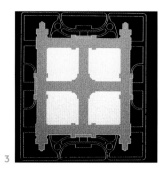

3

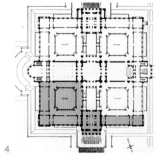

4

5

2

3

4

The depressing interior was consonant with the sad approach. The lobby had barely been altered since 1935, except that the mural in the ground-floor ambulatory, originally depicting Blackfoot Indian cosmology,[4] had been replaced by a photomural of an orbiting module. At the center of the ground floor was an orrery—a Copernican "planetarium" consisting of spherical brass "planets" suspended from tracks, which moved through their orbits while rotating on their axes.[3] Its audience sat on folding metal chairs. Upstairs was the famed Star Chamber. Thousands of New Yorkers and visitors remember the mystery and exoticism of the hemispherical volume and its insect-like star projector.[1] But apart from the dome itself, there was little that could serve a twenty-first-century museum's need for an up-to-date planetarium. Even the famed projector was well behind the times. Zeiss developed the star projector, which gave rise to the modern planetarium, in 1919.[5] The first one in the United States was installed in the Adler Planetarium in Chicago in 1930,[6] and the Hayden's Zeiss Mark VI, its third projector, had been installed in 1969.

On the morning of our interview we entered via the grand stairway of John Russell Pope's monumental Central Park West entrance. A museum guard directed us through the vast entry hall, a kind of Roman basilica, to the Portrait Room, where we met a committee of trustees. I made a brief slide presentation focusing on the dilapidated state of the building. When I was finished, several trustees noted other needs, including increased parking (in 1993 Roche Dinkeloo formulated a master plan that included a garage; it was later shelved), inexpensive food services and a high-end restaurant, a museum store, access for the disabled, and of course, efficient entry and drop-off for school and tour buses.

5

6

Just before Jeff was to begin his address, trustee Richard Gilder[2] called out, "What would you do if money was no object?" With images of Howard Roark in my head, I pantomimed the plunging of a dynamite detonator. The response was muted amusement, but later I came to understand that my theatrics might have spurred the conception of a new planetarium.

SECTION

1

2

3

4

A day after our interview, Ellen Futter invited me to her office. Her longtime assistant Linda Cahill was in attendance. Ellen asked whether I believed it was really possible to create a "new" Hayden Planetarium and at the same time satisfy the impromptu wish list from the committee meeting. This must have been a rhetorical question, for Ellen knew more than most about architects' egos. In response, I pointed to an image from our original presentation to the museum.[1] Then I asked for a week or two for a little more research.

I delved into the project—or at least the core idea of the project—with Todd Schliemann,[2] a partner at the firm, who would become the codesigner and the director of the design team. He grew up under the drawing board of his architect father, and his graphic abilities and inventive visual imagination are matched by a profound understanding of the science of building. He is also a near-professional sailor[3] whose knowledge of boat structure and mechanical details contributed significantly to the new building. Coincidentally, there is a lunar impact crater on the far side of the moon called the Schliemann Crater. It is named after Heinrich Schliemann, discoverer of Troy; I have always liked to believe that he is a distant relative of Todd's.

I thought it was important to keep the dome. This was not a question of nostalgia but of preservation. The original dome was one of the first sprayed thin-shell concrete structures in the country.[4] An engineer and naturalist named Carl Akeley had perfected the spray system.[5] Later, he became the chief curator of the Hall of African Mammals at the museum and "reskinned" elephants and other large mammal skeletons in a similar manner.[6]

5

6

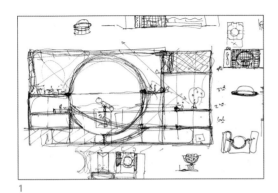

1

2

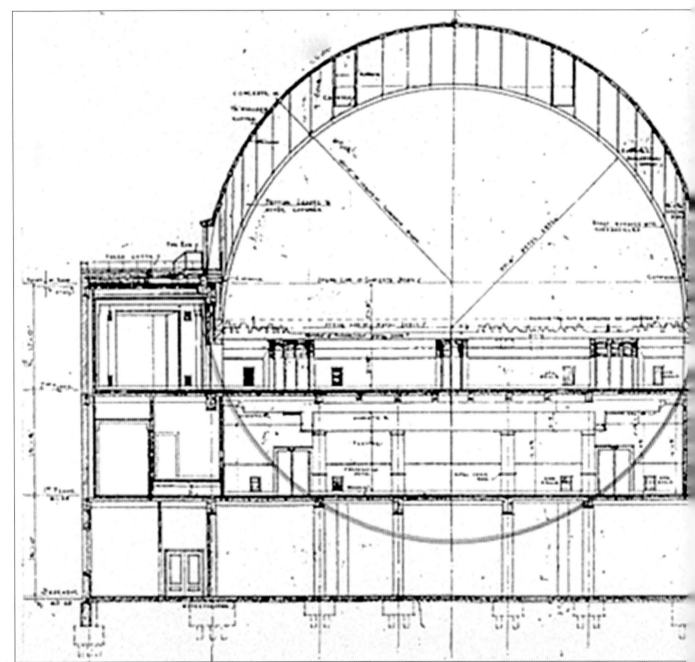

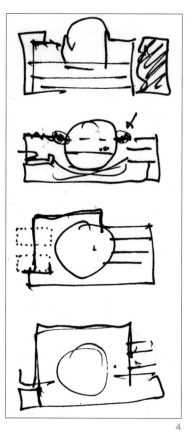

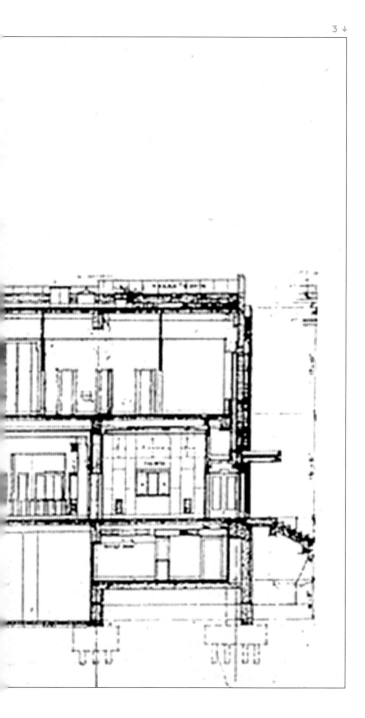

4

One of Trowbridge & Livingston's original working drawings, a cross-section through the building at midpoint, became our Rosetta Stone.[3] At one point I laid it out on the drawing board, picked up an old-fashioned compass, and located the center of the hemisphere. Then I very simply completed the sphere. The lowest point would hover approximately ten feet above the existing floor.[1] It appeared that we could save the dome, construct a new bottom half, enclose the completed sphere in a glass envelope, and array exhibits around it on several levels. Archimedes, alleged to be the inventor of the planetarium, would have said, "Eureka!"[2]

Todd and I returned to the museum to meet with Ellen. By this time we were armed with more sketches of an enclosed sphere.[4] She was intrigued by our ideas but also attuned to the internal and external politics of the situation. Would such a plan require the demolition of all or part of the existing building? And if so, would the museum need approval from the Landmarks Preservation Commission? My answers were "yes" and "probably."

ROSE CENTER FOR EARTH AND SPACE   325

1

2

With Ellen's backing, I decided to risk an off-the-record conversation with two former historic preservation students at Columbia, Alex Herrera[1] and Brian Hogg.[2] Both worked for Landmarks. I showed them a few rough sketches and plans for the planetarium.[3,4] The American Museum of Natural History complex was a New York City landmark and was listed on the National Register of Historic Places—but the Trowbridge & Livingston planetarium was not an individual landmark. Our intention was to use the centroid of the footprint of the existing building as the organizing point for a new structure; this would allow the museum to one day complete its northern face in accordance with J. Cleaveland Cady's original master plan.[5]

I concluded with the critical question: would the demolition and rebuilding of the Hayden Planetarium be likely to gain approval from the commission? Alex and Brian were cautiously optimistic but observed that our public presentations would need to be exhaustively documented and supported by experts, critics, and other respected New Yorkers. When I reported this informal meeting to Ellen, we both clearly understood that only one thing, other than lack of funds, could stop this project in its tracks: a negative assessment by the Landmarks Preservation Commission.

3

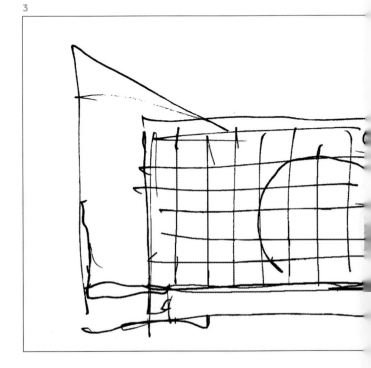

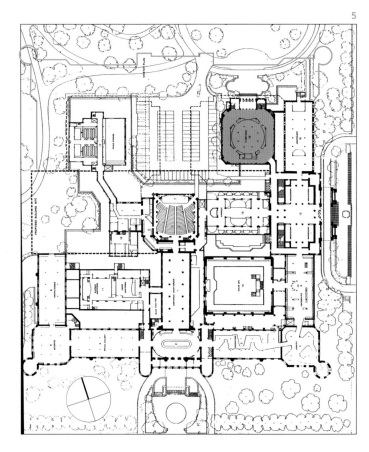

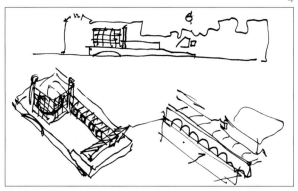

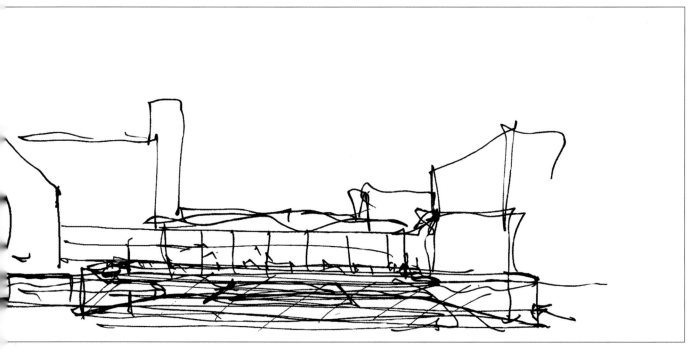

I have no memory of being appointed in any formal way. We were simply authorized to proceed. Todd and I determined that we would be able to save the dome but that the remainder of the existing building would indeed have to come down. Modifying the planetarium would not create an iconic presence on the museum's north face, nor would it satisfy the spatial needs of an ambitious exhibition program.

It was clear to Ellen Futter that the project would have to be funded by some kind of public-private partnership. Support of the city would be crucial financially as well as politically. Happily, the timing was perfect for such an ambitious venture. It was the second year of President Clinton's first term, the economy was robust, the Channel Tunnel had opened,[1] and space was in the news—a Russian cosmonaut had lived aboard *Mir* for 437 days.[2]

4

Ellen hoped that Fred Rose[4] would guide the planetarium committee. Fred had served on the museum's board of trustees for many years. A public-spirited real estate developer with an engineering degree from Yale, he had a puckish sense of humor, best exemplified by the origami animals he made out of dollar bills. Fred understood the complexities of architecture and construction in New York; as important, he would recognize an icon in the making. He enthusiastically accepted her offer to lead the committee with trustee Don Clifford. Fred and his wife, Sandy, made a large donation to jump-start the project; at first anonymous, the gift would eventually assure the couple's identification with what was to become the Frederick Phineas and Sandra Priest Rose Center for Earth and Space.

The size and depth of the adjacent garage we were proposing—no ordinary low-ceilinged automobile container—were behind some of the decisions we made as we developed the design.[3] In the early nineteenth century, the site had been a swamp—much like the site for the Bar Association in Albany—and its geology limited the extent of our excavation. The top floor of the garage would be at ground level; two additional floors would be submerged. In addition, the top floor would have to be eighteen feet in height to accommodate school buses. We wanted the roof of the structure to become a public terrace between the new building and the museum's old powerhouse to the west. The terrace would therefore set the height for the second floor of the planetarium. It was at this point that we finally realized we would not be able to preserve the existing concrete dome, despite our previous endeavors in that direction. Instead, we would create a new spherical steel structure sheathed in aluminum.

3 ↓

When we shared our progress with Ellen, we focused on the relationship of the new to the old: the profiles and materials that would define the exterior form of the new building exemplified this "merger." We also explained how maintaining the footprint of the old planetarium would one day allow for the completion of the original exterior envelope, if that day were to come. This consideration became a crucial part of the brief we eventually produced for the Landmarks Preservation Commission. One of the commission's guidelines is that alterations to a landmark must be reversible—and here they were.

Ellen's reaction was both joyful and fearful. She understood that the planetarium would announce to the world that the Museum of Natural History was ready to enter the twenty-first century. Yet she possessed a finely honed political sensibility and economic pragmatism, and she knew that there were still many hurdles to overcome.

As our work continued we had weekly progress meetings with a task force that included senior staff from the museum. It was imperative that both the task force and the trustee committee have confidence in the concept. A third constituency—the faculty of the institution's eleven academic departments—had to weigh in as well. As is true at any research university, there were tensions and a few Jungian shadows between the administration and the department heads. Ellen asked us to prepare an abbreviated master plan for the entire complex. The attendant analysis required that we interview each department head, discussing the relationship among the various subject areas covered by the museum, including the new department of astrophysics. These consultations also introduced the idea of a renewed planetarium.

Dean Michael Novacek,[1] an esteemed paleontologist who was also senior vice president and provost, represented the faculty on the planetarium task force. He had a scraggly beard, dressed like a country singer, and was more at home in the Gobi Desert than on the Upper West Side. He proved to be a brilliant mediator, diffusing suspicions and debunking the doubts of his fellow departmental heads. It wasn't until later in the process that we met the ebullient, verbose, and relentlessly

optimistic Neil deGrasse Tyson,[2] founder and chair of the Department of Astrophysics, director of the Rose Center, and star of astrophysical stage, screen, and radio. Neil was not initially enthusiastic about our scheme. He could not visualize how he and his staff would work in, as he put it, "a place with curved walls." But it was not long before his doubts turned into cheers, and he is still the Rose Center's booster-in-chief.

Ellen and her committees anticipated that the planetarium would join the roster of the museum's three-dimensional icons: the barosaurus display in the Theodore Roosevelt Rotunda,[4] the whale in the Hall of Ocean Life,[7] the giant sequoia in the Hall of North American Forests,[5] and the elephants in the Hall of African Mammals.[6] Ralph Appelbaum's[3] design for the Dinosaur Halls had opened to great acclaim during Ellen's first year as president, and it was no surprise that he replaced Jeff Kennedy as the exhibit designer.

Ralph and I had not worked together before, and at that time we had no idea we would soon be collaborating on Bill Clinton's presidential library. I admired the intellectual richness of his ideas and the elegant design of the hardware with which they were expressed. But both of us are competitive, and both of us wanted to expand the scope of our work within the project. One evening we met in my office to clarify our roles. I placed a tape recorder on the conference table to record our discussion—Ralph was clearly not expecting this—and a few minutes later we had an agreement. The materials and details of specific exhibits were Ralph's responsibility. All other visible surfaces, details, and materials were ours.

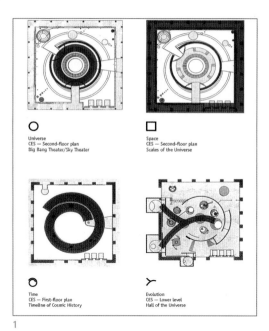

Universe
CES — Second-floor plan
Big Bang Theater/Sky Theater

Space
CES — Second-floor plan
Scales of the Universe

Time
CES — First-floor plan
Timeline of Cosmic History

Evolution
CES — Lower level
Hall of the Universe

1

2

Once we had managed to define our respective areas, our team, Ralph's team, and a small group of distinguished astrophysicists assembled by Neil began the work. We thought of the building—not just its circulation—as a "journey." Ralph's team created a framework for the interpretive material based on a "quartet" of themes—Universe, Space, Time, and Evolution[1]—that governed the organization of the facility as a whole.

The public approval process was never far from our minds, even at this stage of development, and as the team developed the technical aspects of our design, I began a parallel search for image precedents that would stir the imaginations of trustees, politicians, regulators, and journalists. Neil and the science committee were not always comfortable with my references to science fiction. To them, the word "astrology" does not exist. But most radical architectural ideas also have a romantic side. Among the depictions we found were illustrations and film stills from H. G. Wells's *Things to Come,*[3] Nathaniel Salisbury's *Moon Doom,*[5] and J. M. Walsh's *Vandals of the Void.*[4] We also used photos of giant soap bubbles, weather balloons, and Wallace Harrison's Perisphere from the 1939 World's Fair. Most eerie was an illustration of an imaginary asteroid, titanic in size, that appeared to have landed in Manhattan a few blocks south of the planetarium.[2]

3

4

5 "THE MOON DOOM" by Nathaniel Salzburg   February

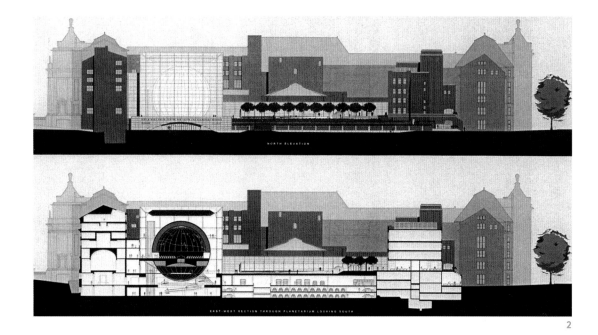

At Fred Rose's suggestion, Morse Diesel was contracted for construction management and budgeting and James Schmidt was retained as the owner's representative. Ellen convened a board retreat at Arrowwood, a conference center in Westchester, to review the financial issues and submit an update on the project. Morse Diesel and Jim Schmidt outlined cost projections and cost control methodologies. Dan Stoddard, a financial consultant, offered hypothetical fiscal scenarios relevant to the new building, all based on the assumption that project costs would not exceed $100 million (by opening day this had grown to $250 million). His speculative events included a one-time two-thousand-point drop in the Dow Jones; a major war involving the United States; even an 8.0 earthquake in the Northeast. In each of these situations, the museum's operations would be secure. We were excused so that the board could discuss our proposals. The next morning I received a call from Linda Cahill informing me that the group had approved the project. We were to move ahead.

A number of Ellen Futter's in-house advisors—Linda, Barbara Gunn, and Lisa Oppenheimer—had served under Ed Koch. So too had attorney and task force member Gordon Davis, an enthusiastic architect manqué (as a young man he worked for Los Angeles architect Paul R. Williams). All felt the time had come to present the project to the current city leadership,

headed by Rudolph Giuliani. First we met with Peter Powers, Giuliani's childhood friend and first deputy mayor. Next we saw Jennifer Raab, then chair of the Landmarks Preservation Commission and now president of Hunter College. We visited with Schuyler Chapin, commissioner of cultural affairs; he had played important roles in our Carnegie Hall and Santa Fe Opera projects. Our final audience was with Henry Stern, the commissioner of parks. He reminded us multiple times that not one tree in Theodore Roosevelt Park could be touched. Gordon Davis attended all meetings and quietly assured the museum that the city would support the project.

Working on the technical aspects and public portrayal of the building simultaneously shifted our work into high gear.[1,2] It was very much like planning an invasion, with equal emphasis on offense and defense. Meetings with the task force took on a sense of urgency—architecturally, politically, legally, and behind closed doors, fiscally. This was best exemplified by the endless pre-presentation rehearsals. Once Ellen opened a gathering by asking, "How are you all feeling?" This was not a pleasantry. She wanted to know if anyone had a health problem that might affect his or her participation as the project moved forward.

1

By this time, our most consequential agency presenta-tions were on the horizon: the Landmarks Preservation Commission, the Art Commission, and the local community board. The jurisdiction of Landmarks is restricted to the exterior envelope of the building plus eighteen inches inside. In this case it would also include the terrace. Bill Higgins and Elise Quasebarth, our preservation consultants, collected historic documents and contemporary precedents to support the project. Their eighty-five-page report was central in explaining why LPC should deem the design appropriate.

Among the elaborate materials we produced was a chronological depiction of post-1871 modifications to the museum complex. [5,6] Facsimiles of original draw-ings and timelines demonstrated how the institution had evolved over time. We also gathered a set of for-mal precedents: Buckminster Fuller's U.S. Pavilion at Expo 67, [2] Roche Dinkeloo's additions to the Metropoli-tan Museum of Art, [3] and I. M. Pei's pyramid at the Louvre. [4] We included some of this in our first press conference on January 26, 1995. Paul Goldberger wrote about the event in the *New York Times* in an article with the less than auspicious headline "Natural History Museum Plans Big Overhaul." At the same moment, lawsuit threats were realized. Our three lawyers, Ellen, Gordon Davis, and special counsel Fred-erick A. O. (Fritz) Schwarz, were prepared.

Legal challenges arose predominantly from unhappy Upper West Siders, including a few residents of the exclusive Beresford apartment tower opposite the museum on West Eighty-first Street. The principal concerns were increased traffic and construction noise, the "bogeymen" of many city dwellers. An envi-ronmental impact statement undertaken by the Planetarium Authority—a body established for this single purpose—addressed those issues specifically, and the New York State Appellate Division dismissed the petition and later denied an attempt to take the case to the Court of Appeals. But it was the Bull Moose Dog Run[1]—an emotionally charged patch of dirt in Roosevelt Park—that caused the most community hand-wringing. The museum agreed to spend half a million dollars to enlarge the animal recreation area, and the objections melted away.

Over the next eight months, we met many times with the Landmarks Preservation Commission (Jennifer Raab) as well as with Community Board 7, the Land-marks Conservancy (Peg Breen), the Municipal Arts Society (Kent Barwick), the Manhattan borough presi-dent (Ruth Messinger), the Art Commission, and the Commission of Cultural Affairs. The project was deemed to be of such importance that we even sched-uled a private session with the editorial board of the *New York Times*.

2

3

4

5 ↓

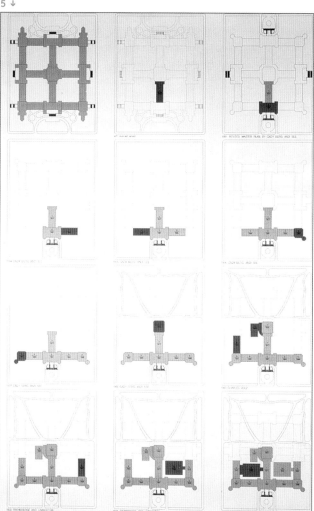

6 ↓

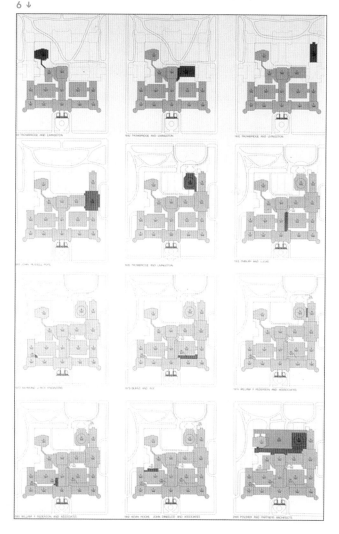

2

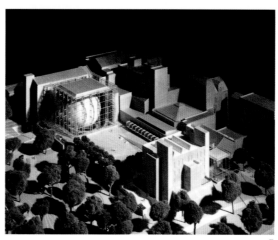

3

The drawings formulated for Landmarks showed a cubic volume approximately 120 feet on a side and 95 feet high.[1] The north and west sides were glass, and the south and east sides were nested into the existing museum complex, as those of the old building had been.[3] Within the cube was a hollow sphere 87 feet in diameter. Critical to the design concept was the disengagement of the sphere from the enclosing volume. The orb seemed weightless in the renderings, since only one of three sets of supports was visible.[2]

On November 11, 1995, all of our care and preparation, the endless rehearsals, the production of dozens of drawings and models, and most important, the support of government officials and private organizations paid off. The Landmarks Preservation Commission approved the project unanimously. Eighteen months after I had pushed the imaginary detonator, the design was finally fixed.

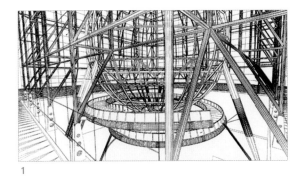

1

2

We were now ready to move from science fiction, historic imagery, and politics to twenty-first-century technology and construction. It took just over a year to assemble the working drawings. The demolition of the old Hayden Planetarium took place in January 1997, and in May 1997 ground was broken for the Rose Center. The two-and-a-half-year period of construction and exhibit installation is best described as the only inanimate heart transplant in history. The new building required myriad systems involving miles of cables, ducts, and connective hardware as well as service and public corridors to attach it to the main museum. Drawings from thirty-six consultants and dozens of suppliers augmented our working drawings.

One of the first consultants we retained was structural engineer Matthys Levy, a partner at Paul Weidlinger Associates. His contributions were central to the design of the complex steel understructure for the sphere.[3,4] He designed the three pairs of diagonal supports that connect to a steel truss "girdle" that carries the Space Theater in the upper portion of the sphere and an auditorium for a Big Bang presentation below. A thin skin of aluminum panels, perforated by 5,599,630 small openings, concealed the steel structure of the sphere.[2] These tiny apertures mitigated the acoustical reverberations produced by the glass envelope, the inner metal flat-panel walls, and the terrazzo floors.

The steel submissions, often Piranesi-like three-dimensional prints,[1] and the mechanical/electrical drawings resembled an anatomical model of the human circulation system. The scaffolding, which formed a simulacrum of the finished envelope, was a construction project unto itself.[5] As the steel for the sphere began to take its form, either (false) modesty or (true) secrecy prompted the museum to cover the west and north faces of the structure with a giant tarpaulin.

1

2

3

4

5

6

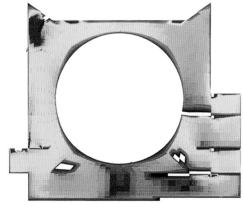

7

When the original museum complex was first built, the south and east fronts were elegant works of Romanesque Revival architecture; the north and west facades, however, were left for a later day. With the Rose Center, that day had come, for the north side, at least. In Ellen Futter's office hung a five-foot-long, sepia-toned, nineteenth-century photograph of the south facade of the building.[4] Its entranceway on West Seventy-seventh Street inspired in part the new north entry to the Rose Center: an arched, eighteen-foot-high portal that affords the museum's first accessible entrance.[5] While we initially selected Milford Pink granite for this new entry—it seemed prudent to use the stone of the museum's Central Park West range—the samples supplied were unacceptable. We substituted dark gray Jet Mist granite; its delicate white swirls suggested galaxies and the Milky Way.

When it was time to select the color and level of illumination for the sphere, nearby residents offered dozens of conflicting opinions and critiques. We conducted twilight and evening tests and finally agreed on a soft blue. Nowadays, in mild weather, young couples recline

on the lawn of Theodore Roosevelt Park, and Upper West Side retirees gaze on the building from the sidewalk. Drivers slow their vehicles, and buses occasionally pause for an extra moment.

A different color decision was needed for the thousands of square feet of interior walls. Ellen and her staff preferred a champagne tone, while we leaned toward a warm gray. We asked color consultant Donald Kaufman to mediate this impasse. Occasionally, the most trivial ploy can resolve a stalemate. At one of our meetings, Donald excused himself, went out into Roosevelt Park, and returned with a piece of tree bark. A matching paint sample was approved in short order.

The diaphanous walls of the glass cube that sits atop the stone and brick base are supported by a system of vertical tubular-steel wall trusses braced by horizontal high-strength stainless-steel tension cables.[1,6] The enclosure consists of monolithic five-by-fifteen-foot sheets of water-white glass.[2,3] Humidity inside the building is kept low to prevent condensation on cold days. Patterned glass on the lowest fifteen feet of the west wall and air-conditioning mitigate the heat and glare of late afternoon summer sun. Our mechanical engineers, Altieri Sebor Wieber, prepared brightly colored fluid dynamic studies to guide the design of the environmental control systems.[7] Matt Levy and the glazing consultant, Tri-Pyramid, focused on the structural system, especially issues of safety and security. If one pane of the glass were to shatter—whether from a natural wind accident or an act of vandalism—the rest of the wall would remain in place.

1

3

2

4

5

Inside the cube, Ralph Appelbaum's circulation diagrams were coming to life. The granite entry arch leads to the Tisch Grand Foyer, which has panoramic views of the exhibition area below and the exterior of the sphere above.[5] A monumental Busby Berkeley–style stair[1] and a tubular elevator guide museumgoers down to the many interpretive displays on modern astrophysics arrayed on the photomosaic floor of the Cullman Hall of the Universe. Also installed are modern iterations of the comparative gravity scales so beloved in the original planetarium.[4] On the south side of the hall are three glass elevators that rise the full height of the volume. The destination for most visitors is the third level, where a dark gathering space heightens anticipation for an "expedition into the universe." An enclosed glass bridge leads into the Hayden Planetarium Space Theater, where a retractable, $4 million Zeiss Mark IX projector depicts the skies above on a digital dome.

After the show, visitors take an escalator down to the second level. Circumnavigating the sphere is a walkway (an accidental evocation of the ambulatory of the old planetarium) with a railing-mounted exhibit, "Scales of the Universe."[2] An open bridge provides entry to the Big Bang Theater, which occupies the lower third of the sphere. The 360-foot-long Heilbrunn Cosmic Pathway, which explains the history of the universe, starts at the Big Bang exit and leads to the first level. Here museumgoers can visit the Gottesman Hall of Planet Earth, proceed to the rest of the museum, or exit the Rose Center—past the gift shop, of course.

One of the most popular artifacts in the hall is the 15.5-ton Willamette Meteorite, the largest found in the United States.[3] The meteor originally fell on Canada or Montana and was transported by a glacier to the lands of the Grand Ronde Indians in Oregon. Its political and legal history is notable. The meteorite was given to the museum in 1906, but the Grand Ronde Indians sued for its return when learning of its transfer to the planned building. The parties reached an agreement by which the meteorite would remain in the Rose Center and tribal members would be able to conduct a private ceremony around the sacred object once a year.

1

46 BUILD, MEMORY

2

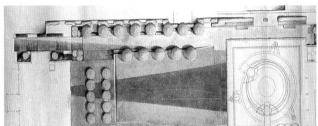

3

4

Ellen and Anne Sidamon-Eristoff, chair of the board of trustees, had decided to hold a limited competition for the new open space to the west of the building, to the north of a glass connector once intended to be the Milky Way Café, and atop the parking garage. Landscape architect Kathryn Gustafson's[2] submission was an elegant, metaphoric lunar eclipse and water feature, both intellectually rigorous and architecturally appropriate.[3] The one-acre Arthur Ross Terrace[1,4] is accessible via a broad stairway that rises from Theodore Roosevelt Park between the old powerhouse on Columbus Avenue and the new building.

1

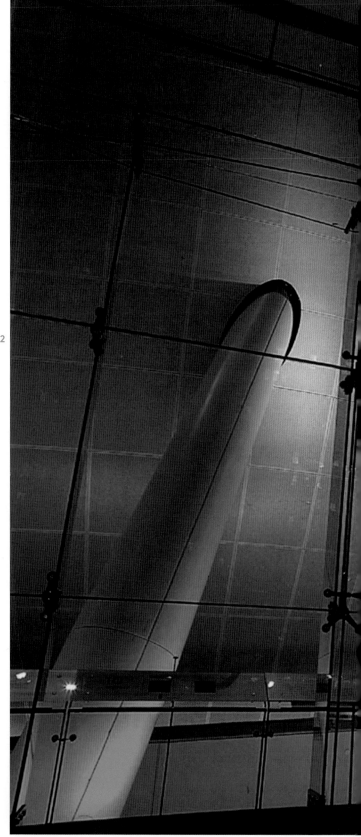

2

The Judy and Josh Weston Pavilion—smaller sibling to the Rose Center—is a forty-foot cube of glass that provides an entry off Columbus Avenue.[1] Within this glass space is a galactic armillary sphere eighteen feet in diameter. The pavilion is an important component in the museum's complex circulation system and offers accessible public entry on the west side of the museum. Santiago Calatrava's New York Times Capsule marks the approach to the glass jewel box. The welded-steel "fortune cookie," which contains cultural artifacts from all over the world, will be opened in the year 3000.

A week before the opening, Herbert Muschamp, then the architectural critic of the *New York Times,* visited the building at twilight. He brought along an Yma Sumac CD. The sound technicians played the disc over the thirty-two-speaker system. Herbert assumed the lotus position directly under the center of the sphere and closed his eyes. The only light was the blue glow of the sphere. A week later his review appeared in the *Times:* "The new Rose Center for Earth and Space at the American Museum of Natural History brings us face to face with something commensurate to our capacity for wonder...The planetarium is an aesthetic apparition as well as a major civic event...Like a quasar, a black hole or a subatomic particle, the planetarium defies easy comprehension...It's like finding another world."

1

2

3

On the evening of December 31, 1999, the temperature in New York City was thirty-nine degrees. A light wind blew and a soft drizzle fell. Taking place within the Rose Center was a most extraordinary New Year's Eve party. Over, under, and beside the bluish sphere, more than two thousand guests had gathered to cheer the new museum and a new year. [1,2]

More than any other single person, Fred Rose was responsible for this glorious evening. His enthusiasm, generosity, and knowledge were evident on the construction site, which he visited at least twice a week. He knew many of the workers by name, and he kept Ellen and the board informed on the project. Tragically, he passed away just a hundred days before the building was inaugurated.

Shortly after the building opened, Bruce Springsteen gave an outdoor concert on the Ross Terrace. [3] The steady rain did not dampen the spirits of the thousands of attendees. The Rose Center, a "cosmic cathedral" that will educate, entertain, and enthrall visitors for years to come, was a spectacle even more compelling than the Boss's music.

PHINEA   SANDRA PRIES

HAYDEN P

ROSE CENTER FOR EARTH

NETARIUM

Scandinavia House
New York, New York
1997–2000

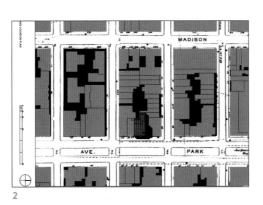

In 1995 the American-Scandina-vian Foundation decided that its headquarters, on East Sixty-fifth Street in Manhattan, had grown too small.

The group purchased two Park Avenue townhouses between Thirty-eighth and Thirty-ninth Streets;[1,2] the adjoining structures shared a party wall. The philanthropist Grace Rainey Rogers had lived in the northern, Beaux-Arts mansion. To her a "party" would have denoted a festive soiree. The East German mission to the United Nations occupied the southern building, a modern faux-Deco structure. There, "party" meant the Communist Party. The irony here—one of them—was that the private dwelling was, in essence, public, and the public government office building was strictly private. Scandinavia House unified the two concepts.

The commission to design a new building for the foundation was not my initial exposure to the Nordic countries and their extraordinary design traditions. Ellyn and I first visited Copenhagen in 1956, arriving on a subzero night in January. I had graduated from architecture school only six months earlier, and I was to begin a one-year fellowship courtesy of Senator J. William Fulbright and his grant program. Everything exceeded our expectations, from the temperature to the pastries.

My fellowship proposal had focused on studying low-cost housing and the development of prototypical systems that could be applied to the design of modular structures.[5] But it was immersion in the Scandinavian design culture that constituted the real core of my postgraduate studies. From Denmark we traveled to Norway, Sweden, and Finland, enjoying each country's distinctive folk art, contemporary crafts, and modern buildings. (We weren't able to visit Iceland, the fifth Scandinavian nation.) Denmark, represented by the architect Arne Jacobsen,[3,4] and Finland, by Alvar Aalto,[1,2] were the more architecturally sophisticated.

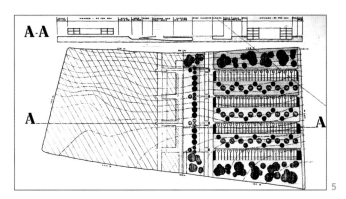

1

The Scandinavian sensitivity to the interdependence of natural and man-made environments is exemplary. Although each of the five countries has an individual identity—particularly Finland, with its singular language and ethnic base—they are defined as a group by expansive marine coastlines.[1] The Baltic, North, Norwegian, Barents, and Iceland Seas mark the cultures deeply. Comparative scale is also important, for it dramatically affects living and building in Scandinavia. Population densities in the Nordic lands are sparse, with Denmark the densest at 334 people per square mile and Iceland the least dense at 8.

While I was interested in contemporary buildings, I was equally fascinated by vernacular structures: factories, barns, castles, schools, churches,[2,7] hospitals, stone huts, wooden saunas, and cemeteries.[6] Outside the major cities, Scandinavian architecture and its natural context are indivisible. This might explain the balanced appreciation of both the historic and the modern. Architecture and craftsmanship are celebrated with the same enthusiasm as music, literature, and fine art. Everyday Scandinavian objects—ceramics, textiles, toys, furniture, clothing—form an enriching and colorful domestic landscape.[3,4,5] What a fertile environment in which to continue my studies in architecture!

3

4

5

6 ↑

7 ↓

1

2

3

In Copenhagen I was assigned to the Royal Academy of Fine Art[6] on Kongens Nytorv,[2] the elegant historic square close to the docks, bars, and cafés of Nyhavn, the gritty port area.[3] The director of the Royal Academy was Kay Fisker,[4] one of Denmark's most distinguished scholars and architects. Pencils and crayons sprouted like tulips from the pockets of his signature smock. My faculty advisor was Vilhelm Wohlert,[5] a young professor; a few years later, with Jørgen Bo, he won the competition to design the Louisiana Museum in Humlebaek, about thirty kilometers north of Copenhagen.

Denmark had not, in 1956, entirely recovered from World War II. But while its economy was depressed, its intellectual atmosphere and social life were robust. A popular watering hole was Galathea Kroen,[1] named after the boat that Steen Andersen Bille piloted around the world in 1845. The dark, Polynesian-themed, oddly sophisticated jazz bar was a magnet for African-American musicians, Danish jazz enthusiasts, artists, writers, students, drifters, and assorted European and American expatriates. The rather edgy and stimulating social context my wife and I encountered there was central to our intellectual experience. Architecture was as popular a conversation topic in Copenhagen as music in Vienna or ballet in Moscow. The high public regard for architects, and consequently their buildings, has stayed with me.

4

5

6

1

2

3 ↑

4 ↓

6

7

8

We hoped to develop a unique identity that would celebrate both the differences and the shared experiences of the participating countries. Scandinavian architecture has long been characterized by a mastery of material, texture, and detail, firmly rooted in the craft of traditional building. Nordic architects of the recent past—Aalto,[5] Saarinen, Lewerentz,[7] and Asplund—provided inspiration, as did contemporary practitioners such as Henning Larsen[8] and Sverre Fehn.[6]

Before going too far with the design, my wife and I revisited Norway, Sweden, and Denmark with Edward Gallagher,[1] president of the foundation. Our aim was to see recent contemporary architecture and to meet with historians, architects, critics, and potential donors. Almost as soon as we arrived, I asked to visit Wohlert and Bo's Louisiana Museum, which, in many ways, epitomized my Scandinavian experience. The rambling set of structures—a classical villa, glass connecting corridors, discrete pavilions, underground galleries, and sculpture gardens—remains, to this day, an exemplar of authentically organic architecture.[2,3,4] It is beautifully constructed, modest in form, generous to its visitors, and protective of its natural habitat. All of these architectural values have, for over fifty years, influenced the work of myself and my colleagues.

1

We looked at the zoning for the property to determine whether the available bulk should be maximized. This would allow rental apartments to be built above the cultural facilities.[2] But the board was not interested in playing landlord. Instead, we decided on a seven-story structure with one floor below grade and six floors above.[3] The Scandinavians very much wanted a "green" building, but our consultants insisted this would be too expensive. The dollar beat the krone/krona/króna.

The Park Avenue site is east of the New York Public Library,[5] south of Grand Central Station,[6] and most important, four blocks west of the United Nations.[7] The foundation originally intended to restore the northern townhouse—the one that belonged to Grace Rainey Rogers—and to create a new building connected to the mansion on the site of the southern structure. An architect member of the foundation board had prepared a rendering of such a hybrid scheme, showing an all-glass envelope merged with a restored classical neighbor.[1] However, our analysis exposed the challenges inherent in repurposing the residentially scaled rooms of the Rogers house. And the American-Scandinavian Foundation wanted to unify the cultural contributions of the five countries, not to present a bifurcated image.

Our solution was a single new building on the double site. We proposed an open stack of loftlike volumes unified behind one facade. These lofts would be linked vertically by circulation and service cores. This flexible system would accommodate a variety of social events and gallery shows and, simultaneously, would emphasize spatial coherence and institutional identity.

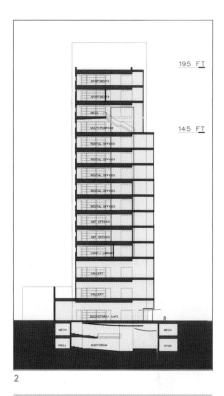

2

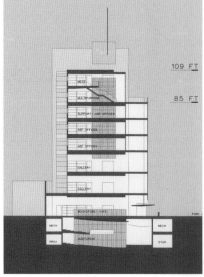

3

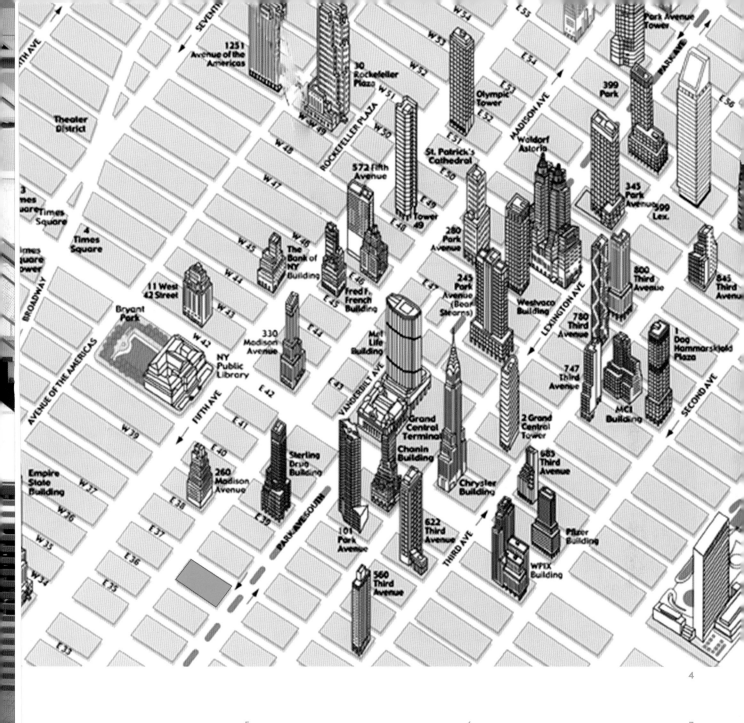

Theater District

1251 Avenue of the Americas

SEVENTH AVE

W 54

W 53

W 52

W 51

W 50

W 49

ROCKEFELLER PLAZA

30 Rockefeller Plaza

Olympic Tower

MADISON AVE

Park Avenue Tower

E 55

E 54

E 53

399 Park

Waldorf Astoria

E 52

St. Patrick's Cathedral

W 48

572 Fifth Avenue

W 47

E 50

Tower 49

E 49

E 48

PARK AVE

E 56

345 Park Avenue

390 Lex.

FIFTH AVE

Times Square

Times Square

4 Times Square

Times Square Tower

BROADWAY

W 46

W 45

The Bank of NY Building

W 44

E 47

Fred F. French Building

280 Park Avenue

E 46

245 Park Avenue (Bear Stearns)

Westvaco Building

LEXINGTON AVE

845 Third Avenue

800 Third Avenue

780 Third Avenue

11 West 42 Street

Bryant Park

AVENUE OF THE AMERICAS

W 43

W 42

E 44

330 Madison Avenue

NY Public Library

E 43

Met Life Building

E 42

VANDERBILT AVE

Grand Central Terminal

Chanin Building

2 Grand Central Tower

747 Third Avenue

One Dag Hammarskjöld Plaza

SECOND AVE

MCI Building

W 39

E 41

Chrysler Building

685 Third Avenue

E 40

Sterling Drug Building

260 Madison Avenue

W 38

E 39

Empire State Building

W 37

E 38

W 36

E 37

PARK AVE SOUTH

101 Park Avenue

THIRD AVE

622 Third Avenue

Pfizer Building

W 35

E 36

WPIX Building

W 34

E 35

560 Third Avenue

E 34

E 33

4

5

6

7

1

2

3

4

5

6

7

At the rear of the ground floor a public stair, illuminated by a skylight on the second-floor terrace, descends to the below-grade floor, which accommodates Volvo Hall,[1] a 165-seat auditorium for screenings, music performances, and symposiums. A simple and elegantly proportioned space, the hall is defined by its birch walls and ceiling. The textural wall panels are perforated in an arrangement determined by the acoustic consultant.

Working with us was an interior design committee consisting of board members Lena Kaplan, Inger Elliott, and Monika Heimbold. All loose furniture and textiles are Scandinavian. Aalto-designed circular ceiling fixtures accompany the Henningsen Artichokes. Birch, generally with a natural finish, is used throughout the interior. On the ground-floor wall adjacent to the café,[2] horizontal wood strips are painted white, hinting at the textures of vernacular Scandinavian structures. The strips give scale to the space and also provide a flexible system for displaying crafts and posters.

The selection of the seat color for Volvo Hall was as sensitive as the one that took place a decade earlier for Carnegie Hall. Charmian Place, the director of interior design in our office, had selected a bright blue fabric, intending to cool the warm wood box of the auditorium. Inger Elliott preferred red. I thought the answer might lie in a tribute to the entertainer Victor Borge,[6] who had given a gift toward the hall. Ed Gallagher discovered that Borge's favorite seat for watching a piano recital was the left aisle seat in the fifth row. I suggested that we insert one red seat, for Borge, amid rows of blue seats.[7] Resolution!

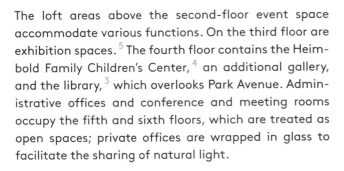

The loft areas above the second-floor event space accommodate various functions. On the third floor are exhibition spaces.[5] The fourth floor contains the Heimbold Family Children's Center,[4] an additional gallery, and the library,[3] which overlooks Park Avenue. Administrative offices and conference and meeting rooms occupy the fifth and sixth floors, which are treated as open spaces; private offices are wrapped in glass to facilitate the sharing of natural light.

1

2

The day of the dedication began with a reception for Volvo Hall. Ed Gallagher walked me over to Victor Borge. When Ed introduced me, Borge responded in his soft Danish accent with what I hoped was mock seriousness: "Oh, I didn't know we had an architect!" We had a laugh and a nice chat about his red seat and the design in general.

The formal ceremony, attended by kings, queens,[1] princes, and princesses, took place on the sidewalk of Park Avenue. The ground floor was draped in blue.[2] After a few short speeches, the curtain was drawn back to reveal the five flags of Scandinavia.[3] Honking horns, champagne pops, and applause completed the street-side celebration.

EGUR

ENMA   S

ISLAND

FIN

RJA

SVÍÞJÓÐ

ED STATES OF AMERI

CELA

NLAND

TANSKA   ISL

LAND

ORWA

N

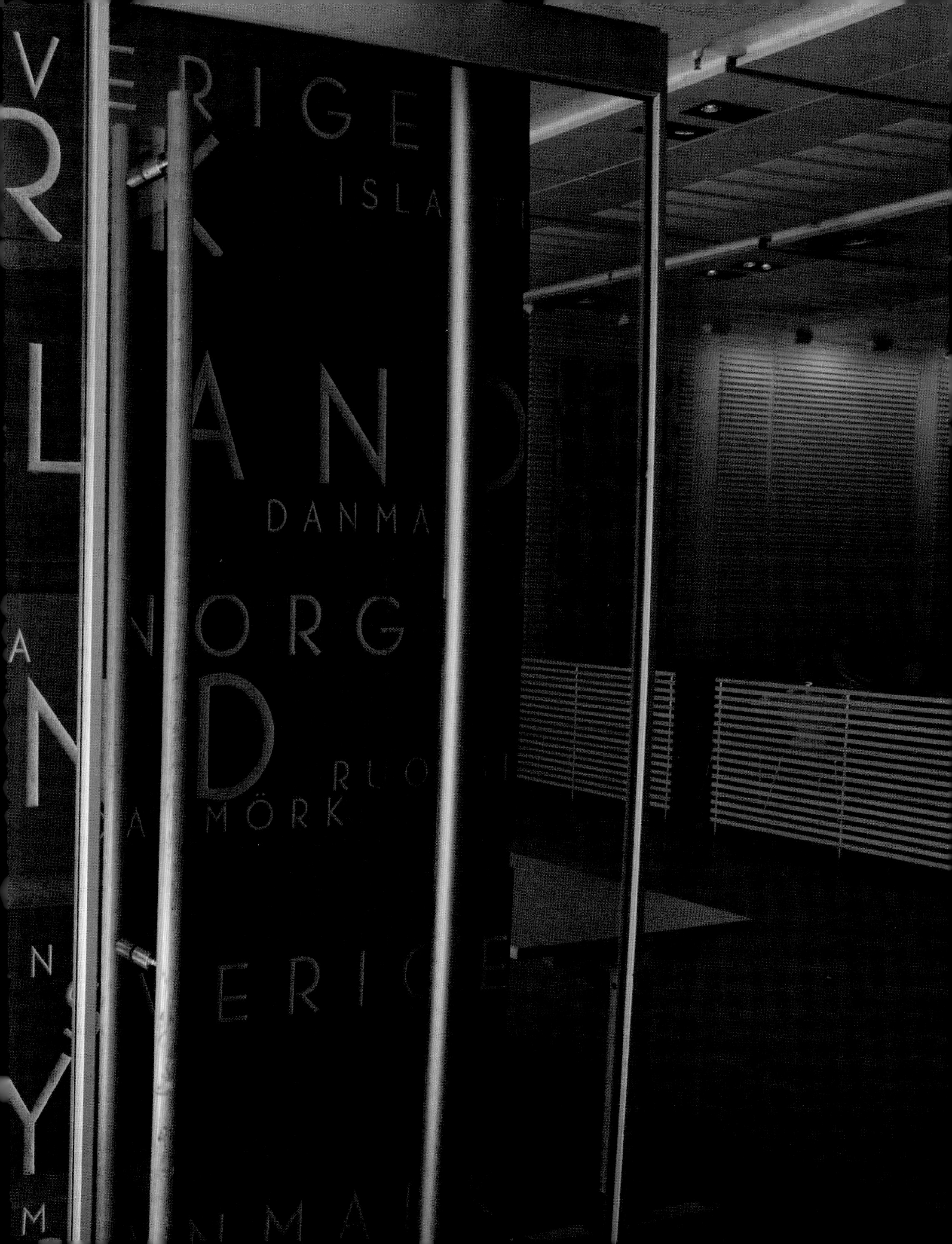
VERIGE
ISLA
DANMA
NORG
RUO
MÖRK
ERIC

William J. Clinton Presidential Center
Little Rock, Arkansas
1999–2004

Most presidential libraries express the particular character of their namesakes the way that dogs, after a time, seem to resemble their masters. [2]

FDR's at Hyde Park, New York, is aristocratic and genteel (and the first presidential library, opening in 1941); JFK's in Charlestown, Massachusetts, sophisticated and cool; Carter's in Atlanta, folksy and gentle; Johnson's in Austin, Texas, imperious; Reagan's in Simi Valley, California, cowboyish and hokey; George H. W. Bush's in College Station, Texas, pretentious and corporate; George W. Bush's in Dallas, Texas, moderne manqué. Those for Hoover, Truman, Eisenhower, Nixon, and Ford can be summed up in one word, bland!

Presidential centers do not fit into the genre construed by the term "library." The portion that most approximates a library is the research archive, which is used only by scholars and is visited perhaps one or two hundred times per year. More accurately described as presidential history museums, or even political memory banks, presidential libraries are popular for their publicly accessible museum components, landscapes, and educational facilities. Their construction is privately funded and intended to promote the understanding of a specific presidency and to celebrate the American experience.

President Bill Clinton set in motion the design and planning for his own presidential center toward the end of his second term. It was Kaki Hockersmith, [4] a vivacious, tiny ball of energy, who started the process that brought us to his attention. Kaki is an interior designer who lives and works in Little Rock, Arkansas. She had decorated public and family rooms at the White House and would later design the executive conference center on the top floor of the new presidential library. A longtime friend of the Clintons, she often dined with them in the family quarters of the White House. At one of these dinners, late in 1998, there was discussion about the ongoing but still inconclusive selection of an architect.

The president had first called I. M. Pei, designer of the Kennedy Library. [1] He had also given the Clintons a private tour of the Louvre. However, Pei was not interested in taking on a second presidential library and suggested his longtime partner James Ingo Freed. [5] Sadly, Freed was in a late stage of Parkinson's disease and communication with him was difficult—and communication was of central importance to Clinton.

Kaki was enlisted in the search and called a friend in New York who was prominent in cultural public relations. By happy coincidence the husband of one of her staff members was my partner Richard Olcott. [6] Kaki knew that the president was interested in a multigenerational design team and learned of our extensive experience with cultural institutions. It turned out that the president or first lady had visited several of our projects, including the Rose Center and the National Inventors Hall of Fame in Akron, Ohio. [3] Chelsea had been impressed by our Cantor Center for Visual Arts at Stanford. [2] It seemed to be a "perfect storm." The next day we received a call asking us to send a portfolio of our work to the White House.

Three months later Nicole Seligman, the president's outside counsel, called to make arrangements for us to meet with the president. Richard and I were joined by Kevin McClurkan, a young architect in our firm. He was born in Little Rock, attended architecture school in Fayetteville, and still had family in Little Rock. He knew most of the principal building professionals in town, and most of them knew Bill Clinton. Chemistry was also important to the president, and I sensed the homeboy connection would be a good fit.

1

2

3

The New York Times

NEW YORK, WEDNESDAY, FEBRUARY 24, 1999

, in Reversal,
gn Peace Pact
eks to Consult People

1

On February 23, 1999, a little before 11:00 a.m., we rang the bell at the West Wing gate. A marine appeared; we stated our names and he replied, "We were expecting you." It was the first in a series of unreal experiences that we were to have over the next six years.

An aide escorted us to a reception room; about twenty minutes later we were directed to Betty Currie's post outside the Oval Office. Suddenly Senate Majority Leader Tom Daschle, House Speaker Dennis Hastert, and House Majority Leader Dick Armey emerged from a conference with the president. Immediately, Bruce Lindsey, an advisor, escorted us into the inner sanctum.[1] Lindsey, Clinton's childhood friend, assistant, and deputy White House counsel, would be ever present. He is as short as the president is tall, not at all loquacious, and "tough but oh, so gentle." If the president was "Mr. Spend," Bruce was "Mr. Save." He is now CEO of the William J. Clinton Foundation.

I turned to President Clinton and said that he would probably recognize Kevin's accent. He laughed, took Kevin's hand in the two of his, and asked if he was related to another family of McClurkans that he knew.[2] Kaki and Nicole Seligman joined us, and the president settled into his wing chair, which was flanked by two sofas. Bruce and Richard sat to his right; Kevin and I to his left. He spoke about his primary concerns. First and foremost was the site.[4] His preference was for one located on the south side of the Arkansas River, east of downtown, as opposed to one that local architects and planners preferred, on the north side of the river, across from the central business district. A location on the river, to support a long-range plan for a river-edge park system, was critical. Next came program. There were three principal components: the library/museum (the public portion of the center), the archive building (which would house 80 million documents and eighty thousand objects), and the Clinton School of Public Service (which would become part of the University of Arkansas).

It seemed that we had barely spoken when a young woman entered and informed the president that our forty-minute appointment had five minutes left. Clinton waved her off, as a signal officer might wave off

4

an incoming aircraft on a carrier deck. Our meeting continued for another thirty minutes.

Richard asked Clinton what his favorite presidential library was; without hesitation he responded, "Pei's Kennedy Library." He went on to note that the Kennedy, Reagan, Carter, and Bush Libraries were all located in places that discouraged visitors. He stressed his concern for geographic accessibility. Schedule was also an issue for Clinton. With an expression between a smile and a smirk, he mentioned George W. Bush, who expected to have a second term in office and, after losing the election, had little time to create the kind of library he wanted. The president knew that we had worked with Ralph Appelbaum on the Rose Center and spoke of how impressed he had been with the interpretive material at the United States Holocaust Memorial Museum in Washington, D.C. He wanted Appelbaum on the team. No one addressed the budget, but Bruce Lindsey's expression made it clear that this was likely to be an issue as well. As we left the meeting, he said, "I'd like you fellas to go down to Little Rock. You'll meet Skip Rutherford and he'll show you the site I prefer. See what you think, get a feel for the town, and come back with some thoughts scribbled on one of those little napkins you architects use."

The day after the meeting, a photograph of Daschle, Hastert, and Armey appeared on the front page of the *New York Times*.[3] In our office a slightly different version of the front page made the rounds.

On March 23, 1999, exactly one month after our meeting, my phone rang. I summarized the astonishing conversation for the team:

I received a call from Nicole Seligman at about 2:30 pm today. She said that the President had pretty much made up his mind to go forward with us. However, he asked that she convey his desire that we be "singing off the same sheet." After visiting the site the President would like us to "Sketch up something—not fancy." She said that he really liked our work but that it was extremely important to him to know he'd be able to talk to us. She said the decision on teaming with a local architect would be up to the President and could come later. She (Nicole) was extremely warm and easy to speak with. Sooo off we go.

The next week Richard, Kevin, and I flew to Little Rock for two days. Kevin was to act as our guide to local architecture, local lore, and local fare. Little Rock has a very specific feel that is hard to describe. While it is in the Deep South—the local accents confirm that—it doesn't feel provincial. Politics and cultural life are close to one another. The downtown has a sense of hometown pride and a distinct energy.

The next morning we met Skip Rutherford.[1] The word "ebullient" doesn't do him justice. The old F.O.B. (friend of Bill's) has a personality not unlike Clinton's, whom he has known for his entire life. Skip was the former administrative assistant to Senator David Pryor, and after the presidential center was completed, he became the first dean of the Clinton School of Public Service. He was our shepherd and Seeing Eye dog for the journey we were about to embark upon. Skip introduced us to other members of the Clinton "family," most important, the president's director of scheduling, now executive director of the William J. Clinton Foundation, Stephanie Streett.[2]

3
A. CHOCTAW STATION
B. ROCK ISLAND BRIDGE
C. MARKHAM STREET
(PRESIDENT CLINTON AVENUE)

1

The twenty-seven-acre site was in a derelict industrial area on the Arkansas River at a point where it is 1,200 feet wide and where the 1899 Rock Island Bridge crosses onto the property. Union Pacific trains once stopped at the historic Choctaw Station[2] on the plot. Bridge and station gave the place a character both gritty and grand and became inspiration for the design. It was immediately evident to us that they had to be preserved and restored.

We visited Central High School, where in 1957 Governor Orval Faubus denied entry to nine African American students.[1] President Eisenhower ended the standoff by sending in the 101st Airborne Division, though the struggle against segregation would continue. From there we went to the Old State House,[4] where in 1991 Clinton announced his candidacy, and to the State Capitol,[3] where he served as governor. Last we swung by some tiny historic "dog trot" houses—their front porches ultimately became part of the new building's narrative.

1

2

3

4

5

On Tuesday, April 20, we flew to Washington for our next meeting with the president. Our destination was the Map Room, on the ground floor. It derives its name from its use by FDR as a war room during World War II.[1] The day of our visit saw a "war" of a different kind. President Clinton walked through the door about forty-five minutes behind schedule. He was flushed and agitated, and his first words were, "They're killing our children as we speak." It was the day of the Columbine massacre outside of Denver.[2] He said he was certain to be interrupted by aides and likely to leave to speak to the nation.

In spite of this crushing news, we started our presentation. We had prepared a twenty-foot-long, accordion-like portfolio with a "Presidential blue" silk cover. The contents of the document were organized into seven topics: locale, urban analysis, site analysis, programming/building typology, technology, inspiration, design approach. The president studied the full length of the document. He pointed out buildings he was familiar with and asked for explanations of some of the more abstract sketches.

When the inspiration section appeared,[6] the president commented, "Hey, there are more pictures of Hillary than there are of me." I explained that three women in the office, Susan Strauss,[4] Felicia Berger,[5] and Molly McGowan,[3] had compiled the document. But before he could respond, an aide passed him a piece of paper and he quickly excused himself. Our presentation was over.

After that we heard nothing from the White House or from Little Rock for three months. Finally, sometime late in July, positive vibes started to drift out of Little Rock from Kevin's professional colleagues. We never received an official letter from the administration notifying us that we had been selected. It just happened. Publicly our selection was announced by David Dunlap in the New York Times. On August 9, 1999, he wrote that after more than a year of "coast-to-coast conjecture," "The answer, it turns out, was in the stars. Or at least in the new Hayden Planetarium at the American Museum of Natural History in Manhattan. The team responsible for that project...has been chosen to design the library."

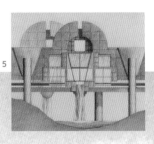

1 ↓ 2   3   4   5

6   7

The first formal meeting after our selection was scheduled for October 20. Its purpose was to engage the president, first lady, and senior staff in a discussion of various design issues. But first the president, a frustrated guide, led us on a tour. We followed him into the Lincoln Bedroom, where Churchill, as well as many other distinguished people—and donors—had slept. Next, we were led into the Treaty Room, which Clinton used as his office. There, we encountered endless mementos, photos of heads of state, gifts, and the hundreds of leather-bound books that must go with each presidency. He showed us JFK's golf putter as well as photographs of the Clintons at Rabin's funeral[7] and a young Bill Clinton with his mother.[6]

Once the meeting started—we were in the family quarters—we asked the president to describe his thoughts about the future library. "I want it to make folks feel good," he said. "And I want them to be *lifted up*." He described a vision of the place as both "grand and inviting—a general feeling of being *elevated*." His use of "lifting up" and "elevated" was serendipitous. He especially mentioned the Rock Island Bridge (whose middle section also "lifted up").[1] The president reminded us, not for the last time, that "bridge to the future" was his 1996 campaign theme. I could not help thinking about (but not mentioning, at least at that point) buildings as bridges—our own Quinco,[4] designs by Steven Holl[2] and Michael Graves,[5] the Pont Notre-Dame in Paris,[3] and many more. At that time there was no way we could have guessed we would end up with a scheme reflecting these notions.

1

2

The president claimed that most other presidential libraries did not successfully achieve these goals—and that the exhibits in particular often seemed like afterthoughts: "Both physical affect and intellectual effect must be equally meaningful. I would rather err on the side of too much than too little." He suggested a general theme for the institution—"hope and change in a virulent time."

Suddenly there was a hush. Through the door came Hillary Clinton [2] with her dignified bearing and quiet air of command. When I introduced myself, I mentioned that we had met. It is common in my experience that "important" people often move onto the next handshake, leaving your last words hanging. Not Hillary. She instantly stopped and asked me to explain. I reminded her of the dedication of the King Juan Carlos I Center at New York University with the king, queen, and then university president John Brademas. [1] "Of course, at NYU—it's a lovely space," she said. Hillary said little to begin with, but at a pause in the conversation she asked, "Are we tape-recording my husband so that we can refer to his thoughts at a later date?" A young staffer jumped up like a jackrabbit, and a tape recorder appeared almost instantly.

Terry McAuliffe, a longtime Democratic operative who was about to become chair of the Democratic National Committee, asked if we had an idea of the timeline for the project. I said, "Four years." The president looked up in surprise. I described the Rose Center and the Pequot Museum as comparable examples that took more than four years to complete.

We all took seats surrounding a large coffee table. We had prepared three schemes. [4] Richard placed on the table a site model, a roll of yellow tracing paper, and an architect's scale. We placed individual models into

3

the base one at a time, noting the historic precedent for each as well as its pros and cons. While the president was interested in the precedents, he was more fascinated by the wood and Plexiglas models and quickly learned how to fit them into the site model. [3]

All three schemes were oriented roughly east-west and faced north, toward the Arkansas River. The president observed that the northern orientation meant that the building could not have too much glass. Richard pointed out that more glass can lower the cost of energy. Clinton replied, "Energy conservation would be splendid and we should explore it. Ya know, everybody thinks Gore is the environmental 'pinko,' but in fact, it's me."

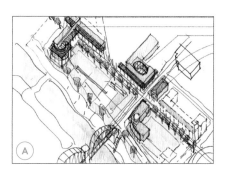

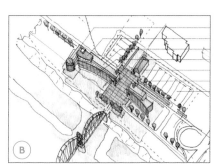

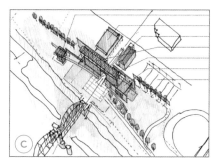

4   A. CAMPUS
      B. PIAZZA
      C. VILLA

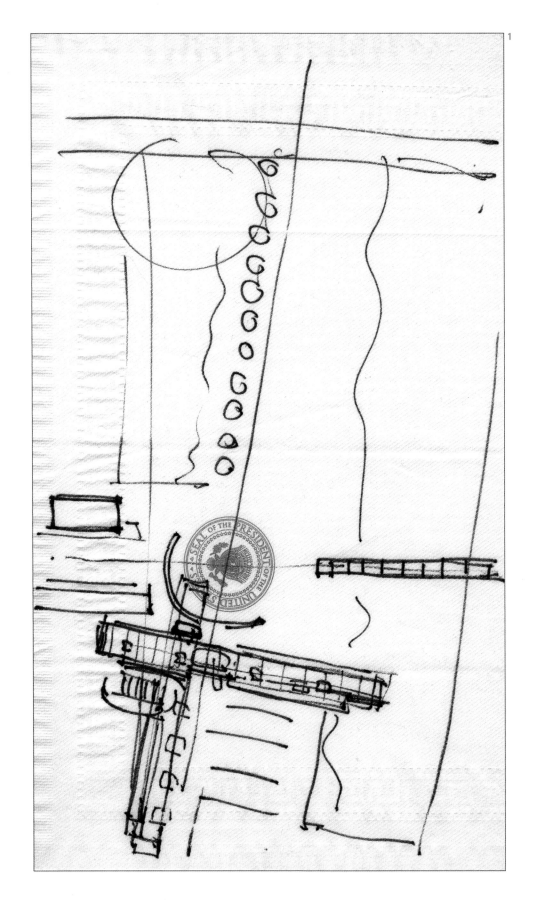

2

3

Although we had prepared our initial schemes with care, certain issues emerged that raised some doubts. In addition to the president's question about windows on the north facade, it was clear that an east-west alignment would not offer a view of Little Rock's evolving downtown skyline. Also, none of the schemes made a strong case for keeping the Rock Island Bridge.[2] And none was particularly conducive for development of the river's edge as a public park.

We started looking at a north-south orientation. In this case the principal facade and entry would face west, perpendicular to Markham Street (which would be renamed President Clinton Avenue) and parallel to Choctaw Station.[3] The building would also parallel the approach to the Rock Island Bridge, and it would have a sunset view. One more advantage was that the archives could be located farther away from the river.

A napkin sketch captures the decisions we made that day.[1] We used the presidential seal to represent a circular plaza that would organize the major building components of the complex and its open spaces. The

location was generated by the intersection of two main axes: the extension of President Clinton Avenue, creating an east-west pedestrian promenade from downtown straight to the front door of the center, and the north-south extension of the axis of Rock Island Railroad Bridge. The napkin has since been considered the conceptual Holy Grail.

When we returned from D.C., Joseph Fleischer, the senior managing partner, Richard, Kevin, other members of the now expanded team,[4] and I reviewed how to move forward with the design and the process of managing the project's development. We now had a better idea of the president's thoughts; Ralph Appelbaum had furnished some embryonic concepts for the interpretive material. The decision to rotate the building was taking hold, and by Thanksgiving we would be ready to show the new idea to the president.

We wanted to avoid a building that would be a "wall" separating the approach from downtown from the eastern half of the site, particularly at the river's edge. Elevating the structure because of the flood plain would offer better views and also allow the exhibition halls and conference center to float above the ground. A gracious reception level on grade would provide transparency between the east and the west portions of the site.

4

1

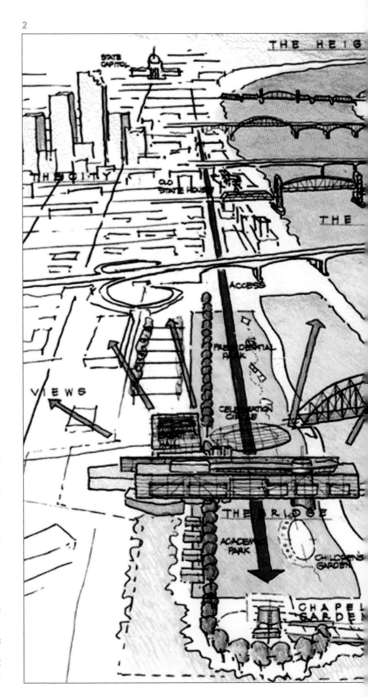

2

In our minds at least, this was a new "bridge to the future." The presidential library would become the "lucky seventh" of Little Rock's six existing bridges.[2] We hoped this image would have emotional and intellectual resonance for the president. Additionally, the new scheme would reinforce the urban park concepts of the city planners and create a dramatic presence when viewed from upstream or down.

The west facade of the structure would be a challenge. Late afternoon sun produces the maximum heat gain and glare. The theme of transparency drew us irresistibly to the idea of a four-hundred-foot-long wall of glass.[3] For the opaque portions of the building, the spirit of a metallic bridge pointed to the use of panelized metal—particularly for the east wall because of the requirements to control daylight (for the exhibits) and to conserve energy.

The president's office informed us that he would be able to meet the day before Thanksgiving just before the annual turkey "pardon."[1] I was out of the country, so Richard and Ralph attended the meeting. It was uneventful, as it was reported to me, but at the end the president turned to my colleagues and said, "So what else do you have for me?" This was the moment to pull the rabbit—an aerial view of the site, showing the relationship of the new building to downtown and the old bridge—out of the hat. The president was delighted.

January 27, 2000, was the president's final State of the Union address, and what an honor it was to be invited. It was a gala evening at the White House. The president, with his white hair and flushed face, was a beacon in the crowd. He found a way to say a little something to everyone. When he spotted Ellyn and me, he referred to Paul Goldberger's *New Yorker* review of the Rose Center, which had appeared ten days earlier: "If I had your press, Pole-check, I'd get me a third term!"

3

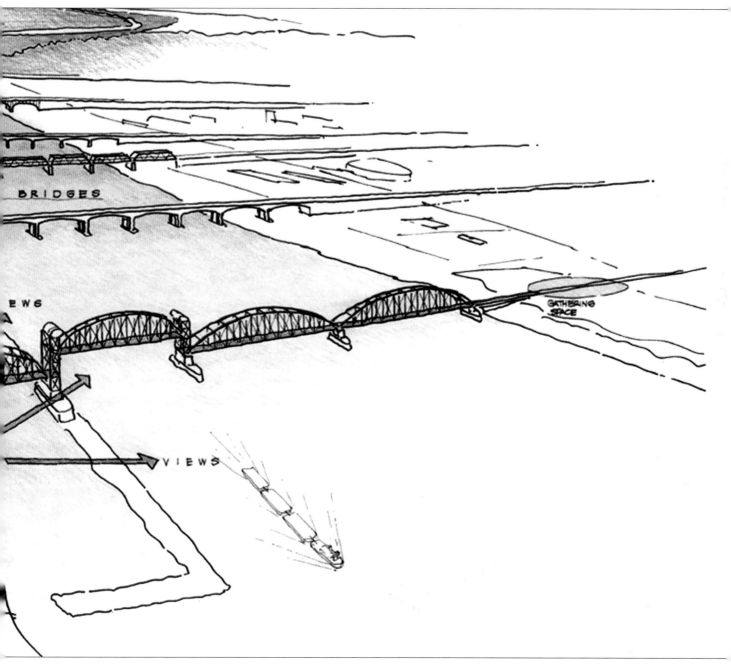

BRIDGES

EWS

VIEWS

GATHERING SPACE

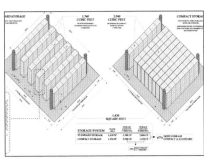

1

2

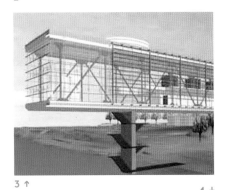

3 ↑

4 ↓

5 GROUND FLOOR PLAN
A. ARCHIVE STORAGE
B. SCHOLAR ENTRY
C. CORRIDOR
D. TEMPORARY GALLERY
E. RECEPTION DESK
F. ENTRY SECURITY ZONE

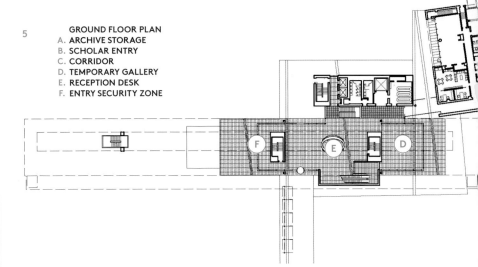

6 BASEMENT PLAN
A. ARCHIVE STORAGE
B. OBJECT STORAGE
C. CIRCULATION/SERVICE CORE
D. CAFÉ
E. CAFÉ TERRACE
F. CANTILEVER OVERLOOK

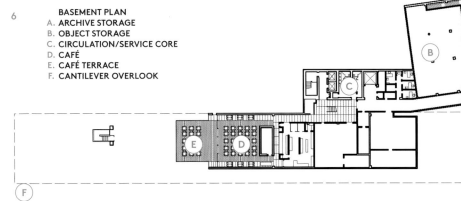

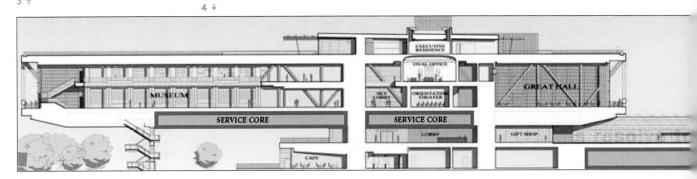

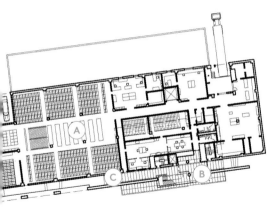

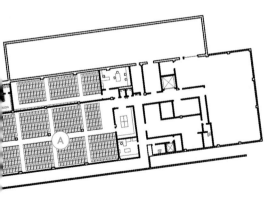

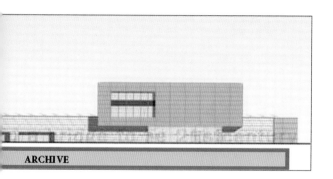

ARCHIVE

For all our progress on the design, we still had many hurdles to overcome. The National Archives and Records Administration, the agency with overall responsibility for presidential libraries, coordinates major construction and renovation projects at the thirteen centers. To say that agency officials were startled the first time they saw the new bridge concept is too tame a description of the reaction.

NARA officials had four concerns. First was quantity—the size of the archive.[1] The agency believed that the storage area for the millions of documents and thousands of objects (which included the president's Mustang) should be larger than that of the Reagan Library—also built for a two-term presidency. Second was control of daylight—NARA wanted exhibition materials to be protected from direct sunlight, whereas Clinton (and his architects) wanted transparency.[2] Third was security for materials placed in public exhibition spaces. Fourth was topography—no part of the project could be built within the hundred-year flood plain. We were grateful for this last requirement, for it allowed for the location of storage below grade,[4] thereby reducing the above-ground bulk of the future archive building.

Security concerns would also affect the site plan, particularly the seventy-five-foot security perimeter around the building. This buffer zone resulted in a virtual "zipper" of bollards around the above-ground structure. NARA also wanted to reduce the small portion of the building that was cantilevered over the river.[3] In this way we would not have to involve the Army Corps of Engineers, and it allayed concerns of the Secret Service that a boat loaded with explosives could be detonated under the cantilever.

1

At the next White House meeting, we brought a more precisely detailed site plan. We were once again in the family quarters, and there was no conference table for the drawing, so we laid it on a coffee table and sat around it.[1] The president stared at the plan for a few minutes and asked why the old bridge was on one north-south axis and the building on a different north-south axis[3]—something he had not previously noticed. We explained that the Little Rock street grid differed by a few degrees from the old railroad grid. We used the city grid for the museum and the railroad grid for the archives to differentiate the major program areas—the museum, elevated and transparent; the archive, partly buried and translucent. The angles of the grids would also align various pathways in the park, under development by landscape architects George Hargreaves and Cinde Drilling.[2]

2

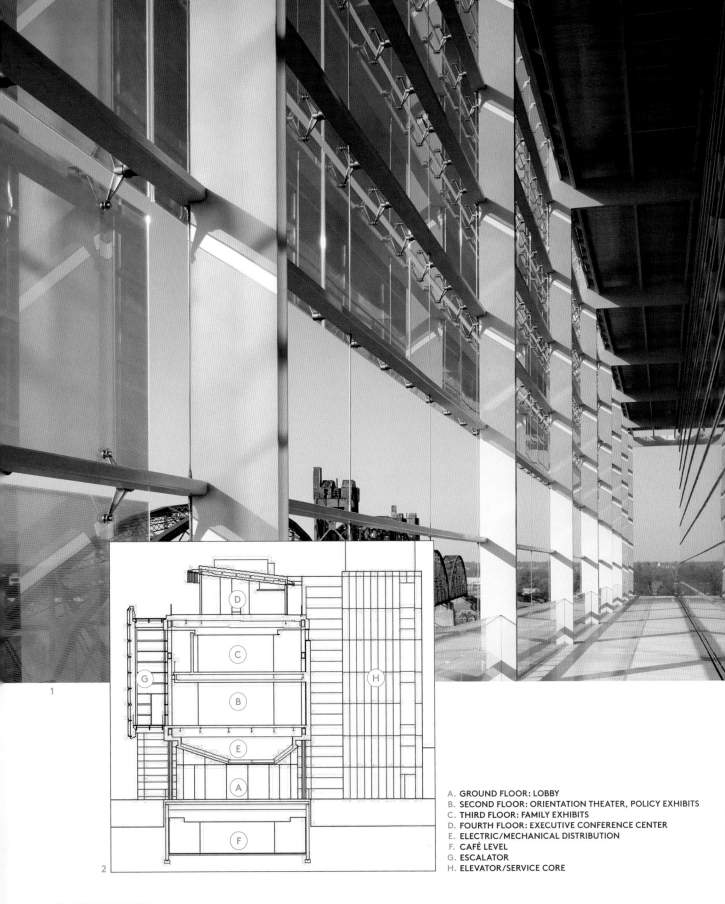

A. GROUND FLOOR: LOBBY
B. SECOND FLOOR: ORIENTATION THEATER, POLICY EXHIBITS
C. THIRD FLOOR: FAMILY EXHIBITS
D. FOURTH FLOOR: EXECUTIVE CONFERENCE CENTER
E. ELECTRIC/MECHANICAL DISTRIBUTION
F. CAFÉ LEVEL
G. ESCALATOR
H. ELEVATOR/SERVICE CORE

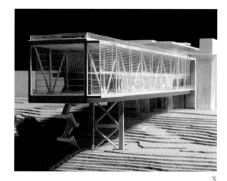

3

4

The choice of enclosure systems was dictated by the long west facade. Lightness was of paramount importance. "Lightness" refers to luminosity, reflectivity, and filtered daylight and also to weight. The tiny Plexiglas model we had presented in one of our early meetings at the White House was taken by the president more literally than we had anticipated. Months later, when we presented a more detailed model with a metal-and-glass skin, the president asked, what happened to "that nice glowing feeling on the one you showed me before? What I see here now looks like jalousie windows." Then "I just hate this." Stomachs dropped. We tried to explain that the earlier model was only to demonstrate the relationship of building to site.

It was good luck that later models of the double-glass west wall and an explanation of its solar gain advantages turned hate to love.[3] The west face of the building consisted of two glass skins separated by a twelve-foot "porch"[1]—our nod to the historic dog trot houses. This space acts as a sunscreen for the museum, protecting papers and objects and substantially reducing the air-conditioning required to cool the interior. We selected a special laminated glass with an inner layer of white and black dots. From the interior, the wall is transparent, maximizing views of the park and the city beyond; from the exterior, it reflects light and glare.

The structural system of the building and its spatial organization are interdependent. Schematically, the library is a 420-by-90-foot box raised 20 feet above the ground. Supporting the box are two service cores and a double column at the cantilevered north end. Suspended from the box is an undercarriage that distributes communications, mechanical, and electrical systems—the building's nervous system. Service and passenger elevators, fire egress stairs, and lavatories are located in a "backpack" appended to the east side of the box. An escalator with views of the downtown skyline and river provides access to the second and third levels.[4]

1

2

On December 9, 2000, approximately seventeen months after our appointment, the design of the presidential center was publicly unveiled in the Roosevelt Room of the White House.[3] I remember the experience as a circus because of the press and the excitable, over-controlling young staff. In some ways it was closer to the introduction of a new car than to a historic event.

Foundation chair Skip Rutherford made opening remarks and introduced me. I had been taken aside by the communications people and told when to appear, where to stand, where to sit, and most important, how long to speak—three minutes. Three minutes for a 170,000-square-foot, $2 million presidential center on twenty-seven acres? Impossible! In spite of the rolling eyeballs of the aides, I took only seventeen minutes longer than I had been allotted. My explanation of the siting of the refuse dumpsters—next to the plant for the *Arkansas Democrat-Gazette,* whose editor was a lifelong opponent of the president—occasioned the biggest laugh. The day after the unveiling saw the debut of commentary on the design. Much of it was positive, some of it was humorous, and of course we couldn't entirely avoid the negative.[1,2]

After January 2001, the end of the president's eighth year in office, we were no longer to experience the thrill of working in the White House. We met with the president either in Little Rock or at his new office in Harlem. On June 22, we met in an empty Chevrolet dealership in Little Rock[5] where the archives had been transferred by Air Force C-47s on the last day of Clinton's presidency.

3

The discussion was focused around a detailed eighth-inch scale model. Early in our presentation President Clinton pointed to an exit stair projecting from the building near the support for the cantilever and said, "I don't like that. It looks like a fire escape." To which I politely responded, "Sir, it *is* a fire escape." Within weeks the team found a way of integrating the stair with the dual columnar support for the cantilever.[4]

4

5

1

2

3

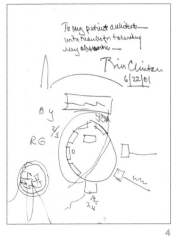

4

The president had often spoken of his admiration for the eighteenth-century library of Trinity College Dublin.[3] He especially liked the Long Room, where double-story alcoves flank a voluminous reading area. This became the historic precedent for the exhibition hall. Ralph Appelbaum suggested that we bifurcate the upper floor parallel to the long axis. His intention was to have "issue alcoves" on the lower level and open exhibition spaces above. The exhibition team ultimately created "towers" containing eight years of White House Day Books (hour-by-hour records), which both supported the upper-level exhibits and defined the alcoves.[2]

The northernmost portion of the glass and steel box was initially intended to be a display of selected gifts. Instead, these were moved to the upper levels of the exhibition area, and this spacious volume became a grand stairway linking the "lighter" exhibits above (family, White House life, and so on) to the "darker" exhibits below (politics, administration, policy, and the like). Perched over the river's edge, this space formed a connector between nature and nurture.[1]

The central portion of the structure contains what we considered the "soul" of the building, the replica of the Oval Office, on the third level. Directly below, on the second level, is the orientation theater. And below that, on grade, is the lobby reception desk. At the very top of the building are the Clintons' living quarters and an executive conference room. The southernmost portion of the elevated structure, farthest from the river, is a two-story conference center and meeting hall.

At our Little Rock meeting, the president said he loved the sunlight coming through the windows of the Oval Office in the White House; he hoped we would be able to achieve an identical effect in its replica. Richard said jokingly, "We could, sir, if you can find a way to turn the sun around." We demonstrated that the light from the glass wall would provide an illusion of sunlight. The president then took out a pen and asked for a piece of our graph paper. He made a small sketch of the Oval Office showing the Rose Garden ("RG"), the Washington Monument, and some additional cryptic notations. When asked, he signed it with enthusiasm: "To my patient architects—with thanks for tolerating my obsessions."[4]

1

The last item on our agenda was the Rock Island Bridge.[1] The president wanted to turn it into a "green" bridge—a sustainable organic garden in the sky.[2] Eventually we would add a ramp to the permanently raised center span. It was ten years before the Rock Island Bridge was completed by the firm of Polk Stanley Wilcox, our local associates. The pond area below is now the William E. Clark Presidential Park Wetlands, named in honor of the man who was responsible for construction of the library.[3]

There were still hundreds of decisions to be made. The architecture and engineering drawings were moving forward, but not as quickly as we wished. Lawsuit threats, NARA requirements, Appelbaum's interpretive research, cost estimates, and city, state, and federal regulatory approvals were slowing down the process. One issue was the outer glass wall.[4] The "spider" glazing supports were similar to what we had used at the Rose Center. But here the wall was a true membrane, open to the elements on both sides. Elaborate wind tunnel tests were required to satisfy the Little Rock Building Department.

Details and material selection were now our central focus. We made sustainability a first priority, researching radiant heating, "breathable" bamboo flooring,[5] the double-glass facade, and a green roof[6] (occasionally used by the president to hit·golf balls into the river). In 2004 the building was certified LEED Silver for new construction, and in 2007 LEED Platinum for existing buildings.

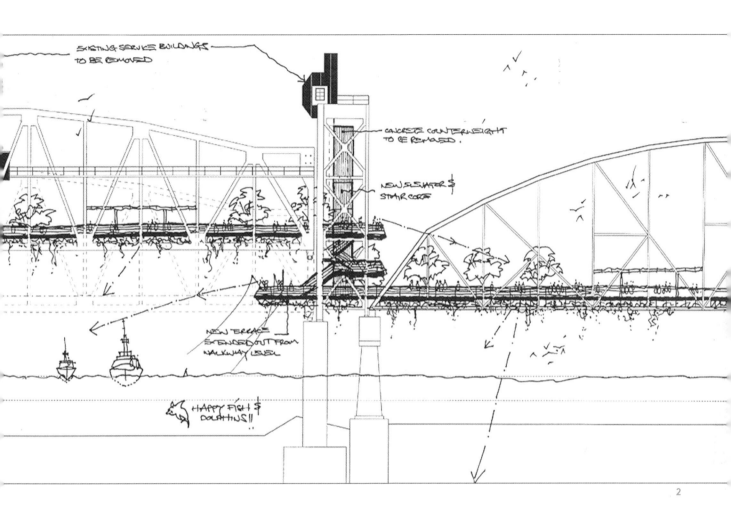

EXISTING SERVICE BUILDINGS TO BE REMOVED

CONCRETE COUNTERWEIGHT TO BE REMOVED.

NEW ELEVATOR $ STAIR CORE

NEW TERRACE EXTENDED OUT FROM WALKWAY LEVEL

HAPPY FISH $ DOLPHINS!!

2

3

4

5 ↑

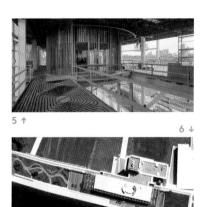

6 ↓

1

2

3

4

5

The groundbreaking took place on December 5, 2001.[5] The formal dedication would not occur until November 18, 2004. Normally, it would not take two years and ten months to build a building and landscape thirty acres, but investigations into the pardons President Clinton granted on his last day in office, donor doubts, and grand jury appearances brought major fundraising to a halt.

In July 2002 the concrete subcontractor poured the foundation and vertical cores.[1] The elevated truss structure and the logic of the structure's undercarriage were immediately evident.[4] In June 2003 steel erection was complete. The silhouette against the sky was dramatic and validated the visual intersection of the two "bridges."[2] The next year and a half was devoted to closing the building envelope,[3] completing interiors and systems, and installing the exhibitions. Owner's representative Gary Eikenhorst controlled every aspect of budget and construction.

1

2

3

The downside of living and working at a great distance from a project is that you don't get to see it every day during construction. That had certainly been the case with the Teijin Institute in Japan. On the other hand, it means that there is a moment of joy and astonishment you experience when the building that was initially imagined is finally observed and experienced.

Two days before the opening, my wife and I flew to Little Rock via Dallas. The clear autumn afternoon in New York gave us hope for fine weather on the day of the dedication in the state capital. But that hope was to be dashed. It was cloudy as we approached Texas and turbulent as we reached Little Rock. But I had my moment nonetheless. As the plane dropped below the low clouds, I looked out the window and saw a luminous horizontal form that appeared as if it were also about to land.[3] On the way to the hotel, our taxi passed the glowing silhouette of the library. It was a fleeting glance that will remain with me forever.

The next day (the day before the ceremony) we woke up early to misty sunshine. We walked from the Capital Hotel down the newly renamed President Clinton Avenue and entered the site under the I-30 overpass. A new road leads to Celebration Circle, the plaza once denoted on the "napkin" by the presidential seal. It is the metaphoric "red carpet" to the front door of the William J. Clinton Presidential Center. We were met by docents radiating the legendary Little Rock charm and workers doing a final cleaning. Just beyond the reception desk was the president's bombproof limo.[1] We took ourselves on a quick tour of the building, from issue alcoves,[6] Cabinet Room,[5] and Oval Office[2] to café.[4]

4

5

6

1

2

3

4

Only as architects could we be ever so slightly disappointed by the preparations that were underway. A white tent and stage partially concealed the west facade, thousands of chairs covered the green landscape, and media vans were lined up on the approach road.[4]

That evening the weather was perfect, and we returned to the building for a lavish preopening party. It was a magical evening for all of us who had worked on the project.[1] Fireworks over the river celebrated the building's completion, the end of a six-year odyssey.[2]

Most everyone remembers waking up on Christmas mornings. The inauguration of the Clinton Presidential Center was a grown-up's version of that, for me at least. There was a light drizzle, and low-hanging clouds scudded in from the west.[3] Ellyn and I were driven to an entry point off the service road on the southern edge of the site. We showed our credentials and entry tickets—not for the first time—and passed through metal detectors.

The drizzle had turned to serious rain. The Secret Service had confiscated all umbrellas, but the event planners had another ten thousand (approved, apparently) as well as ponchos at the ready. In any case, the downpour could not diminish the spirits of the thirty-five thousand people gathered.

It was truly a spectacle of biblical proportions. Bono's music ushered in President Clinton, President Bush, and former Presidents Carter and Bush Sr. After a number of short speeches, President Clinton rose. A marine held an umbrella for him.[1] He was ecstatic, and his words, as always, were inspiring.

After Clinton spoke we were walked to the building by the Secret Service. Ralph Appelbaum, Richard, and I had been asked to stand in different locations on the route that the presidential party would take through the museum. We were supposed to introduce ourselves and answer any questions from the presidents and their families. From where I stood I could watch the four presidents leave the platform and enter the building. After about twenty minutes I heard a few steps and down came not the presidential entourage, but Karl Rove and Stephen Hadley, Bush's national security advisor.

Rove appeared to be an affable fellow.[2] He asked about the glass and whether or not it was bulletproof (it is not), and then inquired, "How much did this place cost?" Nothing else seemed to interest him. As they left I called after Rove (I knew this would be my only chance), "Mr. Rove, you're not such a scary guy!" Without a second of hesitation, he muttered, "Thank you. Now I can go back to Washington to red-line the constitution, put churches in our schools, and cut down the redwoods!"

Moments later four "fathers" of our country appeared.[4] There were more introductions and small talk, then questions. Ralph Appelbaum told me later that Bush Jr., gazing out the window at the river, had said he'd sure like to be back in Texas for the bass fishing. Ralph pointed out that there were plenty of bass right here but that because of the Coast Guard gun boats, it was impossible to fish.[3] Bush, even before Ralph finished his sentence, interjected, "Lucky they're here—a submarine could pop up right out of the creek and blow us all to hell!"

2

3 ↑

 ↓ 4

After the tour we attended a private luncheon in a large tent. Shimon Peres, former prime minister of Israel, still dripping wet, was the main speaker at the lunch. After that were congratulatory encomiums. Celebrity-spotting neck-swivelings were common, and women guests used napkins to dry their hair while nibbling hors d'oeuvres. After the luncheon we walked back to the hotel. On the way we made our first stop at the Clinton Museum Store—a renovated brick building just west of the underpass—where we bought a few "presidential" trinkets to mark the occasion.

At the very beginning of this project, I had asked myself, "How will we define an architecture that represents democracy?" The answer was found as we responded, both conceptually and architecturally, to five principal policy initiatives articulated by the president:

Human and Civil Rights: openness and accessibility: material transparency
Sustainability: energy conservation: LEED recognition
Education: public assembly: Clinton School of Public Service, outdoor amphitheater, Celebration Circle, and Clark Wetlands Nature Center
Health Care: recreation and contemplation: River Walk and Children's Garden
Historic Preservation: importance of the past: adaptive reuse of Choctaw Station and Rock Island Bridge

In so many ways, President Clinton made this building possible. His inspiring metaphors, his focused intelligence, and the generosity of his personal involvement animated our efforts; but it was his belief in the future that truly galvanized the specific design concepts. His policy initiatives inspired the confidence, generosity, and boldness of the unique form of the building elements that comprise the William J. Clinton Presidential Center.

2

This library tells the story of America at the end of the 20th century, of a dramatically different time in the way we worked and lived. We moved out of the Cold War into an age of interdependence, with new possibilities and new dangers. We moved out of an industrial economy into an information-age economy. We moved out of a period when we were obsessed with overcoming the legacy of slavery and discrimination against African-Americans to a point where we were challenged to deal with an explosion of diversity of people from all races and ethnic groups and religions from around the world. And we had to change the role of government to deal with that.

President William J. Clinton
November 18, 2004

National Museum
of American Jewish History
Philadelphia, Pennsylvania
1999–2010

1
2
3

Throughout history the Jewish people roamed the world, rarely by choice, and a sense of impermanence became a way of life for many.

The Old Testament refers to Solomon's temple, but otherwise lasting architecture is rarely introduced. A single tree or an oasis of palms was enough for a rudimentary shelter for people who wished to gather for religious services. Two temporary structures, the *chuppa*[5] and the *sukkah*,[6] can be considered ceremonial "archetypal huts." The former is a cloth-covered canopy supported by four poles that in its openness symbolizes Abraham's home; the latter is a hut covered by branches that represents both the shelters of the Israelites as they wandered in the desert for forty years and the huts erected in the fields and used during the frantic final days of the fall harvest.

The narrative of permanent Jewish architecture in the United States begins in 1654, when a group of Dutch Sephardic refugees left Brazil for the American colonies. A century later the first known American synagogues were completed—Touro in Newport (1763)[1] and Mikveh Israel in Philadelphia (1782).[2] The congregation of Mikveh Israel initially held services in a private residence on Cherry Street in downtown Philadelphia. The first purpose-built home for the synagogue, designed by William Strickland, was constructed nearby in 1782.[3] The stylistic choice—Egyptian Revival—was odd considering the biblical relationship between Hebrews and Egyptians. Between 1825 and 1976 the board of managers of the congregation commissioned four new buildings, the last the current edifice close to Independence Mall.

RELIGIOUS LIBERTY.

4

5

6

1

2

3

H2L2, the legacy firm of Paul Philippe Cret, who had designed the Barnes Foundation and Rodin Museum in Philadelphia, designed Mikveh Israel's new synagogue. A workable but undistinguished building, it opened on the Bicentennial, July 4, 1976, and inaugurated the National Museum of American Jewish History. In the late 1990s, a group of influential Philadelphians, led by George Ross,[1] a Goldman Sachs executive, decided that the museum should have an identity of its own, distinct from that of the synagogue, and began to develop the idea of a separate building on the same site. Immediately on receiving a request for qualifications, I visited the existing building just off Independence Mall, a three-block-long open space that also accommodates the National Constitution Center, the Independence Visitor Center, and the Liberty Bell Center. [4,5]

An anonymous entrance off a tree-lined allée that connects Fifth Street (Independence Mall East) and Fourth Street led to a deserted lobby that served both the synagogue and the museum. The exhibition space, a single poorly lit volume, contained a number of vitrines devoted to different subjects: sports, the American labor movement, temple sisterhoods, science, comedy, music, and so forth. Fewer than one hundred objects were on display, and on the day I stopped by, there was only one other visitor. Nevertheless I came away impressed by the scope of the subject matter. A compelling project generally includes three ingredients: a prominent site, interesting subject matter, and a progressive institutional mission. This future museum possessed all three.

My colleague Joseph Fleischer accompanied me to the interview, which was held in a windowless conference room. George Ross and Ronald Rubin, a prominent real estate developer, cochaired the building committee. Three other developers; George's wife, Lyn Ross;[2] and acting director Gwen Goodman[3] completed the group. At the end of the interview, the group asked why we wanted to undertake this project. I answered emotion-

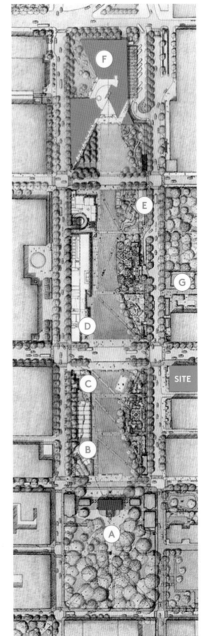

4   A. INDEPENDENCE HALL
     B. LIBERTY BELL CENTER
     C. PRESIDENT'S HOUSE SITE
     D. INDEPENDENCE VISITOR CENTER
     E. FREE QUAKER MEETING HOUSE
     F. NATIONAL CONSTITUTION CENTER
     G. MIKVEH ISRAEL

ally, not architecturally. I noted that my upbringing had been secular and that I viewed this commission as an opportunity to rediscover, to some extent, my cultural and religious roots. This assertion appeared to carry more weight with the selection committee than any of our credentials.

1

2

3

4

Our early schemes drew on ideas of opacity and transparency, concepts that would prove fruitful throughout. One design featured two prominent volumes—a stone tower surmounted by a live flame and a facade of glass elevated above the ground—on the site of Mikveh Israel, as envisaged. [1,4] In the end, negotiations with the synagogue proved to be near impossible, and the museum board began looking for another site. At the time, local television station KYW was planning to move. The board secured an option on the station's building, about two hundred feet south of the synagogue at the southeast corner of Fifth and Market Streets. [2] The property is next to the historic Bourse, [3] built in 1895 as a commodity exchange, and across the street from Independence Hall and the Liberty Bell.

Corner sites are often problematic, and this one was particularly so, for both philosophical and practical reasons. On the original site, a new building would have coexisted with other national symbols, including the historic Christ Church Cemetery. But any building on the new site would be a stand-alone structure. Some on the building committee were concerned that the prominent location might invite commentary on the flaunting of Jewish achievements.

We also had to consider where to put the "front door"—on Market Street (perpendicular to the Mall) or on Fifth Street (parallel to the Mall). On the Fifth Street side is one of the city's most active metro stations. A major tourist pedestrian route, the roadway does not allow vehicle drop-offs. Our decision to place the public entry on Market Street, close to the corner, respected the dignity of the Mall.

1

2

Luminosity remained critical to our approach, and the Jewish eternal light[1] and the Statue of Liberty's torch[2] inspired our designs. For the waves of Jewish immigrants coming to the United States in pursuit of freedom, acceptance and rejection were two sides of the same coin, one light and one dark, one transparent and one opaque.[3,4]

Light is fundamental in any expression of Judaism. The eternal light that hangs over the ark in Jewish houses of worship symbolizes God's eternal presence. Never extinguished, the light conveys the parallels between God and fire that are emphasized throughout Exodus. Freedom, representing the bond between newcomers and their adopted land, was the key to reconciling these points. The reconciliation implies unity and harmony, an optimistic interpretation of the immigrant experience in America.

4

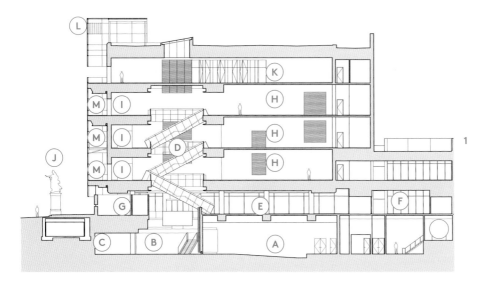

1   A. DELL FAMILY THEATER
     B. CONCOURSE/GALLERY SPACE
     C. EDUCATION CENTER
     D. ATRIUM
     E. ONLY IN AMERICA
     F. BOOKSTORE AND CAFÉ
     G. DONOR WALL
     H. PERMANENT GALLERY
     I. PRE-GALLERY
     J. RELIGIOUS LIBERTY
     K. TEMPORARY GALLERY
     L. BEACON
     M. FREEDOM EXPERIENCE

MARKET STREET

FIFTH STREET

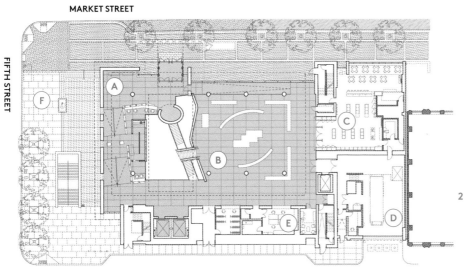

2   ENTRY LEVEL PLAN
     A. TICKETING
     B. ONLY IN AMERICA
     C. MUSEUM STORE AND CAFÉ
     D. LOADING DOCK
     E. CURATORIAL CENTER
     F. RELIGIOUS LIBERTY

MARKET STREET

FIFTH STREET

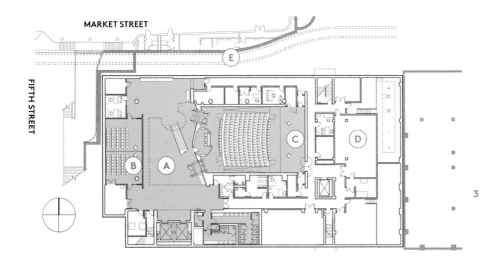

3   CONCOURSE PLAN
     A. LOWER LOBBY
     B. EDUCATION CENTER
     C. DELL FAMILY THEATER
     D. PHYSICAL PLANT
     E. SUBWAY

4

Sketch models embodied this conception in a building form of two interlocked volumes, one transparent and open and the other opaque and enigmatic. [4,5] The first, a narrow rectilinear block facing the Mall, is intended to welcome people of all ethnicities and religions. Light emanating from this prism reminds visitors of the complex culture of America. The second, wider and lower than the transparent volume, is clad in terra-cotta. It is appropriate both contextually—the adjacent Bourse is one of Philadelphia's earliest terra-cotta buildings—and symbolically, as a metaphor that represents the permanence of Jewish culture and theology. Housed within the terra-cotta block would be the entry atrium, exhibit spaces, and main circulation core and offices.

The unique structure consists of an elevated four-story box supported by eight columns; [6] these columns transfer loads down to the complex transportation tunnels under the site. Dan Sesil of Leslie E. Robertson Associates, the principal structural engineer, says that the configuration was "born out of a deep respect for the artifacts and shared stories housed within and from the need to support a series of sophisticated architectural gestures." The wall truss system he developed incorporates triangulated steel assemblies sized to fit on a truck. [7,8] Supported on a small number of concrete-encased steel columns, the steel components create a continuous braced frame that loops around the box. These trussed wall panels work together with the floor framing to allow the building to cantilever to the west while opening up from within, thereby creating the internal atrium and balconies with expansive views of Independence Mall.

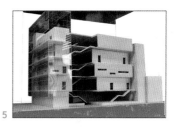

5

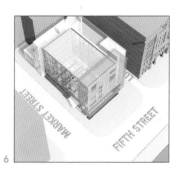

6

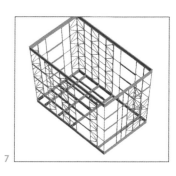

7

8

4   5   6

Pennsylvania governor Edward Rendell, Senator Arlen Spector, and the building committee broke ground on September 30, 2007.[2] The design/construction process in New York City, my hometown as an architect, can be like a civil war. Architects, engineers, and ultimately, the client are at the mercy of many different trades and their arbitrary pricing, conflicts between unions and subcontractors, feeble excuses for delays, and general miscommunication (not always accidental). But building in Philadelphia was instead a happy "Philadelphia story."[1,3]

Ron Rubin, with many years of development in the city behind him, brought in the builder, Intech, and the owner's representative, Becker & Frondorf. Three young men—Charles Moleski[4] from the owner's rep, Zach Baron[5] from the construction manager, and Josh Frankel[6] from our office—ran the project economically and on schedule. Not a single design detail was sacrificed. Problems during construction, stemming from physical conditions, material unavailability, drawing interpretation, city inspectors, and so forth, are normal. In this case the efficiency of their resolution was abnormal. After a year of fund-raising, permitting, and regulatory approvals, the building and its exhibitions were completed in twenty-four months.

1

2

Two icons identify the museum. Facing the Mall from the west side of the building is *Religious Liberty,* a twenty-four-foot-high Victorian sculpture rendered in white marble.[4] A gift to the city of Philadelphia from its Jewish community in honor of the 1876 Centennial, the work was originally installed at the synagogue. I wanted to move the sculpture to the new building: the juxtaposition of classical symbol and minimal glass facade would emphasize the union of past and future.[1] The budget could not support the sculpture's relocation, but fortunately Dan and Joanna Rose, friends and philanthropists in New York, sponsored its restoration and transfer.

The second piece, *Beacon,* is a contemporary artwork installed in the highest corner of the glass volume.[2] Artist Ben Rubin reinterpreted the eternal light and the torch of the Statue of Liberty in a sculptural LED construction. Seven computer-animated layers are based on the unique graphic structure of the Talmud, in which each page is a rendition of a conversation, with primary text, commentary, dissent, and counterargument arrayed together.

The entrance, from Market Street, leads to an atrium crisscrossed by stairs.[3] The stairs, which connect the exhibition floors and also the concourse level, have been likened to the gangplanks that led immigrants off ships to new homes in New York, Galveston, or San Francisco in the early part of the twentieth century. The glass treads dramatize the movement of museumgoers. On the concourse level are the Dell Family Theater and the education center. A ramp from the entry passes a bust of Sidney Kimmell, Philadelphia native and founding donor of the museum.

3

4

1

2 ↑

3 ↓

5

6

The installation "Only in America" occupies most of the first level. [6] This "hall of fame" illustrates the life stories of eighteen notable Jewish Americans in an audiovisual installation visible in part from the exterior. The second, third, and fourth floors of the terra-cotta volume are devoted to interpretive exhibits designed by Gallagher & Associates. Organized chronologically, the permanent installation includes "Foundations of Freedom: 1654–1880," "Dreams of Freedom: 1880–1945," and "Choices and Challenges of Freedom: 1945–Today." [4]

The transparent volume is devoted, for the most part, to the Freedom Experience, three twelve-foot-wide galleries that overlook the Mall. [5] A weave of vertical and horizontal lines makes up the pattern of the baked-on ceramic frit on the glass curtain wall facing the Mall. [1] The open rooms provide quiet sanctuaries for reflection after the intensity and richness of the core exhibits. Visitors can gaze on the historic structures of Independence Mall, enriching their museum stay with a new perception of past and present. Audiovisual exhibits will one day relate the experiences of other immigrant groups to those of the Jews, expanding the welcome offered by the institution.

The top floor of the terra-cotta block has access to an outdoor balcony overlooking the Mall and the city to the west. [2] Also on this level are a temporary exhibition gallery and skylit event space with a floor partly of translucent glass. [3] The temporary gallery, lower concourse spaces, and auditorium constitute the public program areas.

1

The three-day opening weekend commenced on Friday, November 12, 2010, with private tours of the building and a symposium featuring two panel discussions.[3] One of the panels, "Crafting American Public Space," focused on the architecture and was moderated by Paul Goldberger. The group included designers who had worked on civic and monumental projects in Philadelphia: the late Bernard Cywinski of Bohlin Cywinski Jackson (Liberty Bell Center); Laurie Olin (redesign of Independence Mall); Billie Tsien of Tod Williams Billie Tsien Architects (Barnes Foundation); and me. Henry Cobb of Pei Cobb Freed & Partners (National Constitution Center) was absent due to illness. Five hundred people attended the program, asked dozens of questions, and offered even more opinions. It *is* the National Museum of American Jewish History, after all!

Festivities continued on Saturday with an evening gala: a reception in the museum, dinner in a transparent roofed tent on the Mall, and performances by Bette Midler and Jerry Seinfeld. The weekend culminated in an opening ceremony on a brilliant Sunday afternoon.[4] Assembled on the Mall was a crowd of nearly two thousand—elected officials, community leaders, and dignitaries from across the country, including Vice President Joe Biden.

After the ceremony I led three generations of my family on a tour. Relations had traveled from New York; Louisville, Kentucky; and Buenos Aires, Argentina. My cousin Ann Klein,[1] ninety years old and a survivor of Auschwitz, insisted on climbing the many open stairways. As I had hoped it would, the celebration merged, for me, the personal and the professional.

Lycée Français de New York
New York, New York
2000–2003

1

2

Napoleon may have lost the battle of Waterloo, but he assured the future of the French educational system.[2]

The American and French Revolutions of the late eighteenth century generated substantial political unrest and economic stress. The French upheaval is most commonly remembered for acts of terrorism, often by guillotine; it is paradoxical, and not widely known, that the leaders of the revolution were concerned with education. In 1793 the Committee of Public Instruction reordered the country's educational system. The committee looked at "the duties and prerogatives of the state, the rights of parents, the potential benefits of higher education...the necessity for training teachers, and the suitable status of the teaching profession." One of the earliest French high schools, or lycées, in Paris is the Lycée Condorcet, originally the Lycée Napoleon.[1]

Once Napoleon was elevated to emperor in 1804, he almost immediately made education a priority, particularly for the military, the civil service, and the middle class. He believed that an educated and successful populace would be a less rebellious populace. The Napoleonic system of education in France has survived, more or less intact, for more than two hundred years. More hierarchically structured and intellectually rigorous than its American counterpart, it is also more stratified and elitist in nature. Most American educational institutions consider the final year of lycée to be the equivalent of the first year of college.

Over the years the French system expanded beyond French-speaking countries. In New York the distinctive aspects of French public education may be found on the Upper East Side, at the Lycée Français de New York. The independent school offers a *maternelle,* or preschool, as well as primary and secondary education. After the fourth grade, both English and French are mandatory subjects; in other respects, the Lycée follows a French curriculum and prepares students for the demanding *baccalauréat* exam.

3

A. ORIGINAL BUILDINGS
B. NEW LYCÉE FRANÇAIS

2   3

4

The idea of a bilingual private school in the city was initiated in 1935 by Charles Ferry de Fontnouvelle, the French consul general in New York.[3] At the time the Great Depression had taken a turn for the worse and Franco-American relations were barely tepid. The consul general enlisted moral and financial support from the board chair of the Alliance Française, the attorney general of New York, the president of Columbia University, the U.S. ambassador to France, and the director of cultural affairs of the French Ministry of Foreign Affairs.

The prospects of the school were intimately tied to the political situation in Europe leading up to World War II. Enrollment in 1935—at the time, the Lycée was housed in the French Institute on East Sixtieth Street—was twenty-four children in three classes. The school expanded in student body and in real estate, first with the five-story Carhart Mansion at 3 East Ninety-fifth Street.[4] Designed by Horace Trumbauer, this elegant Beaux-Arts building would initially accommodate eighty students. Over the next decades the Lycée purchased five other properties: 5 East Ninety-fifth Street (adjacent to the Carhart Mansion); the Sloane Mansion, a double house on East Seventy-second Street designed by Carrère and Hastings;[2] a structure on East Ninety-third Street; and a final building on East Seventy-third Street.

While these expansions allowed the school to increase the number of students, stabilizing its tuition-driven finances, the resulting decentralization affected faculty and student morale. There were no communal facilities, such as an auditorium, gymnasium, cafeteria, or private outdoor play spaces. The fragmentation led to cliques forming among students and parents. Finally, the cost of maintenance and operations led the board of trustees of the Lycée to a momentous and wrenching option: to sell all six properties and build a completely new school.[1]

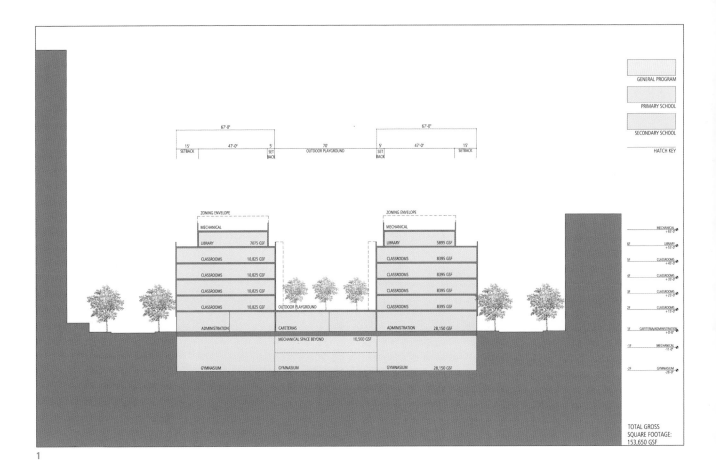

GENERAL PROGRAM

PRIMARY SCHOOL

SECONDARY SCHOOL

HATCH KEY

67'-0"

67'-0"

15'
SETBACK

47'-0"

5'
SET
BACK

70
OUTDOOR PLAYGROUND

5'
SET
BACK

47'-0"

15'
SETBACK

ZONING ENVELOPE

MECHANICAL

LIBRARY 7075 GSF

CLASSROOMS 10,825 GSF

CLASSROOMS 10,825 GSF

CLASSROOMS 10,825 GSF

CLASSROOMS 10,825 GSF

ADMINISTRATION

OUTDOOR PLAYGROUND

CAFETERIAS

MECHANICAL SPACE BEYOND 10,500 GSF

GYMNASIUM

GYMNASIUM

ZONING ENVELOPE

MECHANICAL

LIBRARY 5895 GSF

CLASSROOMS 8395 GSF

CLASSROOMS 8395 GSF

CLASSROOMS 8395 GSF

CLASSROOMS 8395 GSF

ADMINISTRATION 28,150 GSF

GYMNASIUM 28,150 GSF

MECHANICAL +65'-0"

6F LIBRARY +55'-0"

5F CLASSROOMS +45'-0"

4F CLASSROOMS +35'-0"

3F CLASSROOMS +25'-0"

2F CLASSROOMS +15'-0"

1F CAFETERIA/ADMINISTRATION +0'-0"

-1F MECHANICAL -11'-0"

-2F GYMNASIUM -26'-0"

TOTAL GROSS
SQUARE FOOTAGE:
153,650 GSF

1

The appropriately named chair of the board at that time was Elsa Berry Bankier, an investment banker at BNP Paribas and alumna of the Lycée.[2] The board put together a building committee of François Chateau, François Macheras, and Robert Pine, all in banking; Mark Cunha, an attorney; and Australian-born architect Don Zivcovic.[3] The members had one thing in common—they had children at the school. This state of affairs would prove extremely important in tense discussions with the parent body and the faculty.

The radical and risky venture required exceptional real estate and planning advisors. Richard Speciale, who had been with J. P. Morgan for many years, extended both financial and real estate expertise. He introduced the committee to the Albanese Development Group. Vincent Albanese and his son Russell had recently abandoned plans to build a thirty-one-story residential building on a through-block site between Seventy-fifth and Seventy-sixth Streets and between First Avenue and the East River, and they agreed to develop the site with the Lycée instead.[4]

2   3

Next, architects Thomas Phifer and Jean Parker Phifer were retained to produce a feasibility study. They analyzed the possible build-out square footage of the site.[1] The study demonstrated that building to the maximum allowable limits would double the size of the school's six existing buildings. The new program of 158,000 square feet included ground-floor communal areas and many academic and recreational spaces that the Lycée had never enjoyed.

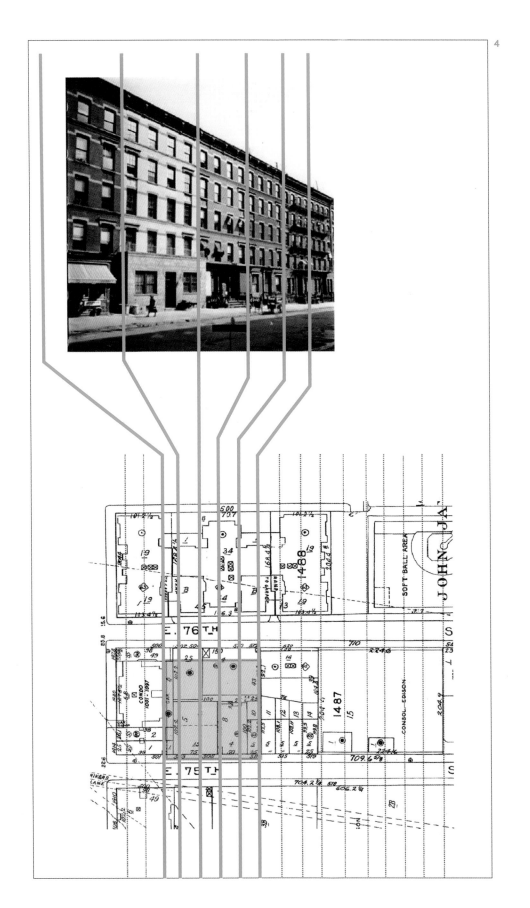

1

2

3

7

4

6

8

The selection of an architect for the Lycée was complex. There was pressure from some parents, a few members of the board, and even the French government (which subsidizes the tuition of students from Francophone countries) to select a French architect. Consequently Jean Nouvel and Bernard Tschumi,[7] my successor as dean of the Columbia School of Architecture, were put forward. Our inclusion on the list was roundabout, to say the least. While attending the University of Western Australia, Don Zivcovic had met Lawrence Speck, a Texas architect visiting Australia as a Fulbright scholar. The committee had asked Larry to compete for the project; distance and other obligations were a hurdle, and so he suggested that the Polshek office be considered.

Susan Rodriguez, who had recently become a partner in the firm, accompanied me to the interview.[8] Particularly interested in the design of educational facilities, she is both a gifted designer and a skilled program developer. She would be the codesigner and day-to-day team leader. At the interview I spoke briefly of my forty-

year love affair with Paris and French culture in general. My first visit to the country was in 1957, and in 1987 Ellyn and I purchased a pied-à-terre on the Left Bank.[1,2]

Other than my design of a new campus for Rosemary Hall at the Choate School, our experience with educational projects was slim. Yet a potpourri of private and public ventures included almost every program element of a secondary school: an addition to the Glenfield Middle School in Montclair, New Jersey;[3] a physical education center at CUNY's Kingsborough Community College;[6] a new theater and photography department at Phillips Academy in Andover, Massachusetts;[4] and studio art facilities and an art library in the Brown Fine Arts Center at Smith College.[5] At the end of the interview, a member of the committee asked, "What would be distinctively French about your design?" I was tempted to answer, "It will be covered in fleurs-de-lis," but I was wise enough to respond, "It will be indisputably rational—a testament to French culture." The group wanted to move quickly. Don called the next day and said, "Let's get to work."

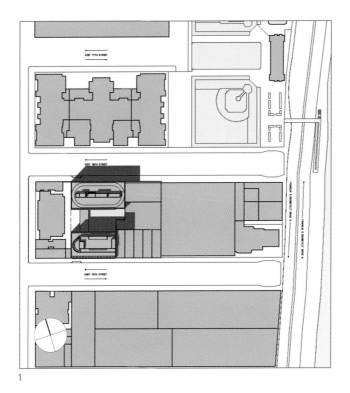

1

The site had once been part of a district of low-scale carriage houses and residential buildings. Light industrial facilities and large-scale postwar apartments had long since disrupted that consistent rhythm. We wanted the new school to connect back to the memory of the scale, texture, and dimensions of the original neighborhood. It happens that twenty-five feet is both the width of the typical neighborhood building and also the ideal long dimension for a lycée classroom. We used this dimension as our overall structural and planning module.

The New York City zoning envelope for the two-hundred-foot-long, through-block plot allowed, above grade, two five-story structures with rear yards. We started with two buildings, one to the north and one to the south, with a 7,300-square-foot void in the center.[1,2] By excavating the bedrock to a depth of thirty feet, we could provide underground volumes for the auditorium, gymnasiums, lounge, and mechanical plant.[3,4,5]

1

2

3

4

5

6

7

The building committee asked me to present the evolving design to the faculty and student body. I was apprehensive about this—friends had warned me that such a group could be extremely difficult. But Elsa Berry's self-confidence and discipline must have been contagious, because those same qualities characterized the cooperative spirit of the faculty and parents. Since I had promised rationalism at the interview, I decided to title my presentation "Descartes in (less than) Ninety Minutes."[6] Among the images were an aerial view of Paris; Le Thoronet, the monastery in the South of France;[2] Charles Perrault's east facade of the Louvre;[3] the Bibliothèque Ste. Geneviève;[1] Jean Nouvel's Fondation Cartier;[4] the Charles de Gaulle Airport;[5] a man standing on two blocks of ice being pulled around the Place de la Concorde by a Citroën (nonrational!);[7] and the logo of the Lycée with a caricature of Descartes within its oval frame. Offering even a wisp of French architectural history was a risky venture; I received one challenging question from a French professor, but it did not mar our successful presentation.

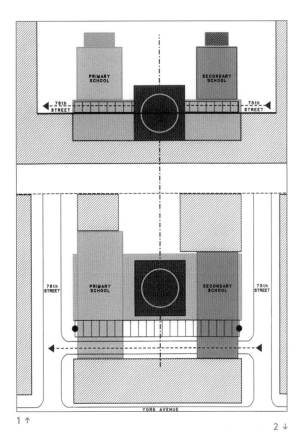

The base of the building occupies the full area of the site. On this ground level are street entries, a two-story central lobby, libraries for the primary and secondary schools, a café, and vehicular drop-off with an entry on Seventy-sixth Street and an exit on Seventy-fifth Street. A grand stair leads from the lobby up to an exterior landscaped terrace[3] and down to the 350-seat auditorium and two gymnasiums. These communal facilities are the *coeur* of the school, its symbolic and functional heart.[1]

Above the base the building divides into two volumes, one facing south to Seventh-fifth Street and the other facing north to Seventy-sixth Street. The secondary school occupies the south structure; the *maternelle* and primary school, the north structure. Each has four floors of classrooms. The sixth floor of the secondary school contains the art department and a terrace, and the sixth level of the primary school is an outdoor play area.

1 ↑   2 ↓

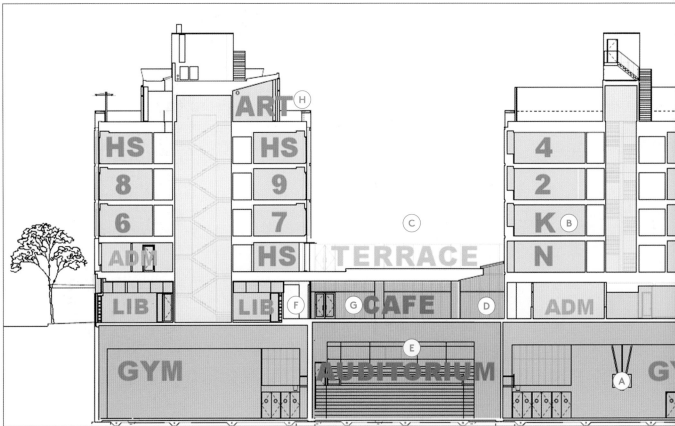

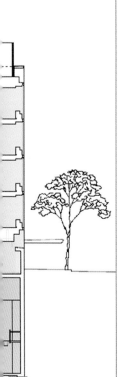

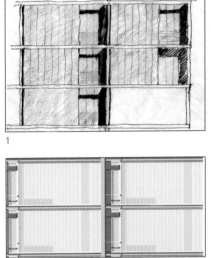

1

2 ↑   3 ↓

4

5

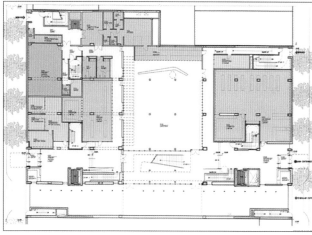

6

In addition to the two street-facing facades, the school has two internal facades looking over the terrace. The choice of materials—vertical planks of translucent channel glass on the north fronts,[1,2] precast concrete on the south—was determined by solar orientation and heat loads more than any other factors. The beige precast concrete is intended to recall the limestone facades of the school's original buildings. The floor-to-ceiling channel glass, commonly used in France for industrial buildings, has several desirable characteristics: the translucency blocks distractions from the outside streets; defused daylight creates an ideal environment for learning.[3,4] In each of the north faces is one "French window" for vision and ventilation. Jet Mist granite at the building base discourages graffiti and insures visual and auditory privacy for the libraries. Clerestory windows at the top of the stone admit ample daylight.

1

2

While we were worrying about glass and limestone, the trustees were worrying about money and schedule. The school had to be ready for 1,100 children by September 2003. The institution's six properties had to sell not only at the right price but at the right time, and the sales agreements had to allow the students to stay put while the new building was under construction. The events of 9/11 and the Internet bubble had depressed the real estate market enough that the Lycée would require additional financing even after the houses were sold.

In August 2002 the emir of Qatar purchased the last of the six buildings, the great double mansion on Seventy-second Street, for $26 million. A few months later the Lycée floated three bonds that were underwritten by J. P. Morgan and totaled $94 million. The bonds, the proceeds from the six houses, and private donations allowed the project to proceed.

At our suggestion the Albanese Group had retained Frank Sciame as construction manager. Sciame's excavators broke ground in January 2002, preparing the way for the large communal volumes that were so critical to the school.[1] We had only eighteen months—a brief moment in construction time—and fortunately most work proceeded according to that schedule. Only the discovery of oil-contaminated bedrock in the excavation and late delivery of the channel glass threatened (but did not derail) our target date.

1

3

For the base of the building, I had suggested to the client that we create a "texture of literacy" by engraving the names of significant French artists, poets, diplomats, and other intellectuals in the granite.[2] Nearly 3,000 individuals were nominated by a faculty committee; 450 were chosen, primarily French and American with a few international, to enrich the street walls. Napoleon made the list but Nazi sympathizers Charles Lindbergh and Coco Chanel did not.

In September 2003 French president Jacques Chirac, accompanied by Simone Veil, minister of health, and Dominique de Villepin, former prime minister and graduate of the Lycée, arrived with great fanfare.[1] After Chirac's warm dedicatory address, legendary restaurateur Daniel Boulud, whose daughter attended the school, served hors d'oeuvres fit for Napoleon, or at least for a French president.

Our greatest accolade came during the first month of school. Yves Thézé, then the head of school, walked me through the halls. Classes were in session, and one teacher, who recognized me as I peeped into a classroom, motioned for us to enter. The students stood up— the young men wore navy ties and white shirts (shirttails hanging out of their navy trousers); the young women were more neatly dressed—and broke into applause when the teacher introduced me. Napoleon stressed certain military qualities in his schools: uniforms, music, discipline. Add the attribute of charm and little has changed.[3]

Newseum/Freedom Forum
Foundation World Headquarters
Washington, D.C.
2000–2008

1

Pennsylvania Avenue,
"America's Main Street,"
is one of Washington, D.C.'s
grand diagonal boulevards.[1]

The French-born architect Pierre L'Enfant, who served George Washington in the Revolutionary War, drew up the plan for the city that bears the first president's name. Pennsylvania Avenue was one of the earliest streets in the city; in fact, for years it was only a dirt road.

Every president since Thomas Jefferson—Ronald Reagan excepted—has marched down the boulevard, from the U.S. Capitol to the White House, on his inaugural parade. The avenue has also provided the funeral route for the eight presidents who have died in office.[3] American citizens and others—suffragettes, Ku Klux Klansmen, the Bonus Army, rabbis protesting government inaction on the Holocaust, Civil Rights supporters, pro-Native American rights Long Walkers, the farm strikers of Tractorcade, lesbian and gay rights activists, the Million Men, and the Million Moms—have used this photogenic path to support or protest just about everything.[4,5] Thousands and tens of thousands will continue to march, mourn, and celebrate on this short but nationally prominent stretch of roadway. It is thus wholly appropriate that the Newseum, an institution devoted to historic and contemporary news gathering, sits along this storied avenue.

2

3

4

5

1

2

3

anonymous museum. The interpretive material, however, was astounding. The Newseum brings together all journalistic genres: advocacy, broadcast, investigation, tabloid, even sensationalism. It was easy to understand how the museum had enticed visitors to cross the Potomac.

At the top of the building was the headquarters of the Freedom Forum, the parent foundation. Founder Al Neuharth,[4] who died in 2013, was the self-made press mogul who created *USA Today*. Old-guard journalists have long resented the colorful paper's popular success. But the officers and trustees of the foundation inherited that newspaper's feisty spirit and independence, sponsoring the museum's expansion.

We interviewed with Newseum CEO and trustee Charles Overby and president Peter Prichard,[2] and afterward Ralph told us that they were considering only our firm and Richard Meier's. Richard had recently completed the headquarters for Canal+ in Paris; the Rose Center in New York was our most recent commission. As for direct newspaper experience, mine was limited to a delivery route for the *Akron Beacon Journal*— I learned to fold the daily issues so that they would land accurately when I tossed them from my bicycle. Overby (from Mississippi) and Prichard (from New England) were both modest and soft-spoken journalists who grew up in the chaotic newsrooms of daily papers, and it occurred to me that the two men would feel more comfortable in our sloppy and relaxed workplace than in Meier's ordered, all-white studio. We set up a visit to New York, and several days later, Charles called to invite us to design the largest public building of our forty-one-year practice.

The Newseum was founded in Arlington, Virginia, in 1997 and in 2000 purchased a site for a new building in the capital proper. Ralph Appelbaum had designed the original exhibits for the organization and had already been enlisted for those in the new museum. We had just completed work with him on the Hall of Biodiversity at the American Museum of Natural History,[1] and he proposed us as architects for the project. We submitted our qualifications and made plans to see the Virginia facility. It was located in a banal office building;[3] a portion of a white sphere—the auditorium—projected from the roof in an attempt to identify the otherwise

1

Overby, Prichard, and the building committee had secured the Pennsylvania Avenue site in a transaction with the District of Columbia. At the time of President John F. Kennedy's inauguration, the north side of the avenue was badly run-down. Kennedy instructed his assistant secretary of labor, Daniel Patrick Moynihan, to set up a committee to encourage private interests to develop new buildings on the avenue. Moynihan had a grander vision, one that only the powers and coffers of federal government could fulfill. His "Guiding Principles for Federal Architecture" of 1962 proposed redeveloping Pennsylvania Avenue, and Nathaniel Owings of Skidmore, Owings & Merrill was retained to create a master plan.

After the Dallas tragedy the next year, Jacqueline Kennedy asked President Lyndon Johnson to move ahead with the plan. The politically torturous process was finally resolved in 1972, when the bill authorizing the Pennsylvania Avenue Development Corporation was signed by President Richard Nixon.[2] By that time, Moynihan was ambassador to India. The rehabilitation of the avenue proceeded slowly but steadily, and by 2000 the District of Columbia's Department of Employment Services, a near-derelict building at the corner of Pennsylvania Avenue and Sixth Street NW, was one of the few vestiges of the formerly shabby roadway.

President George W. Bush intended to use the property, next to the Arthur Erickson–designed Canadian Embassy,[1] for a new embassy for Mexico. But the Freedom Forum bought the land for $100 million, thwarting his plan. The prominent site[3] is directly across from John Russell Pope's National Gallery of Art (West Building) at a junction between L'Enfant's diagonal and orthogonal grids. The 643,000-square-foot structure that would arise on the commanding location would respect both the federal and the local precincts.

2

3

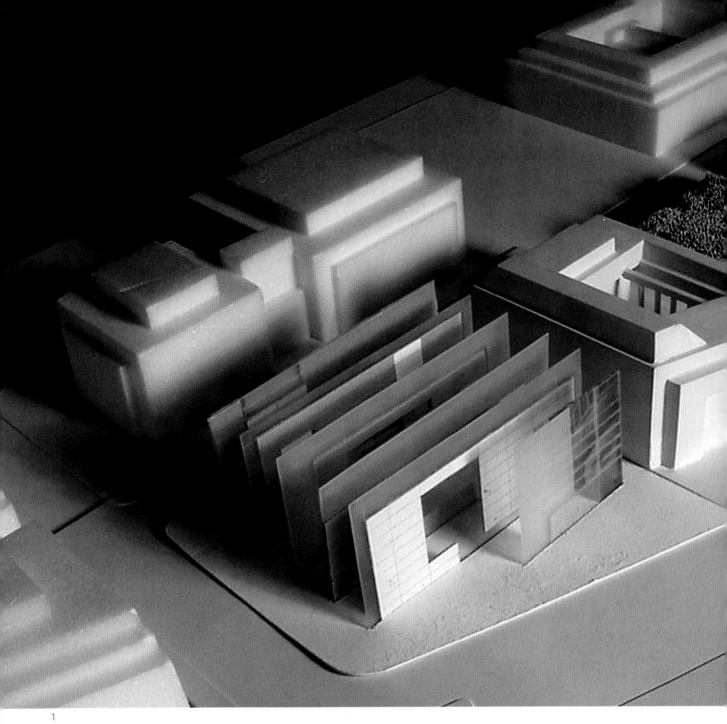

1

2

3

On the project team in our office was Robert Young, my codesigner and team leader; Joseph Fleischer, assisted by Tyler Donaldson, would direct all technical and managerial aspects of the building, in particular the dozens of consultants and the construction management. On occasion our in-house project meetings were taken over by jokes about the Newseum's name. My colleagues invented imaginary institutions such as the Blueseum (jazz), Mooseum (cows), Shoeseum (pumps), and Boozeum (libations).

Charles and Peter were hands-on clients from day one, unhurried, open to new ideas, unconcerned with "bean counting," and always enthusiastic. We were especially excited about the unhurried part. We were able to work with Appelbaum's office on research and analysis for almost a year and a half before the formal start of work.

As part of that research, the clients and I went to Paris. We visited contemporary buildings that used materials, assemblies, and details of the quality (and cost) we anticipated for Washington, including Jean Nouvel's Institut du Monde Arabe,[3] Piano and Rogers's Centre Pompidou,[4] and Paul Andreu's Charles de Gaulle Airport.[2] Another part of the predesign period was an in-house ideas competition. The proposals were not to address the program but to respond to one particular question: "How would you best express the mission of an institution committed to emphasizing the importance of a free press and free speech?"

Ralph Appelbaum had once casually asked whether the new building could be arranged like the pages of a newspaper. That literal notion must also have occurred to junior designer James Ke. His scheme was composed of thin plastic layers—almost like pages of newsprint. Robert and I quickly recognized that this abstract notion could evolve into a "big idea" that would both organize the complex building program and rationalize the challenging site.[1]

1

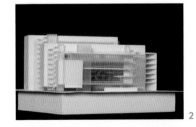

2

3

After the ideas competition we began working with four resonant metaphors: proscenium, transparency-democracy, the newspaper, and window on the world.[5] Our clients also participated in the predesign research with two specific goals. Both Charles and Peter aspired to present breaking news to large numbers of people both outside and inside the building. And Charles wanted the First Amendment of the Constitution to appear somewhere in or on the building.

Notebooks from the museum archives included images of people observing or participating in the delivery of news:[1] individuals and small groups looking at information posted on walls, issuing from ticker tape machines, displayed in newspaper company windows, or pinned on bulletin boards. Radios and loudspeakers, televisions, and smartphones are newer but extremely influential devices that transmit the news. The scheme began to evolve as Robert Young created tiny three-dimensional models of various ideas.[2,3] A "window on the world" within a glass "proscenium" facing Pennsylvania Avenue became the venue for breaking news. Adjacent to the proscenium was a stone surface destined to bear the First Amendment.

5

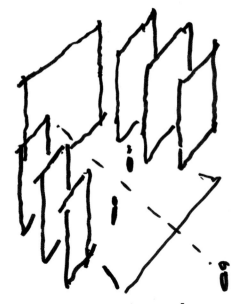

THE PROSCENIUM
(ALL THE WORLDS A STAGE)

TRANSPARENCY = DEMOCRACY

'THE NEWSPAPER'

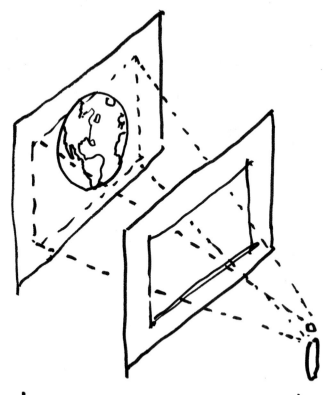

'WINDOW ON THE WORLD'

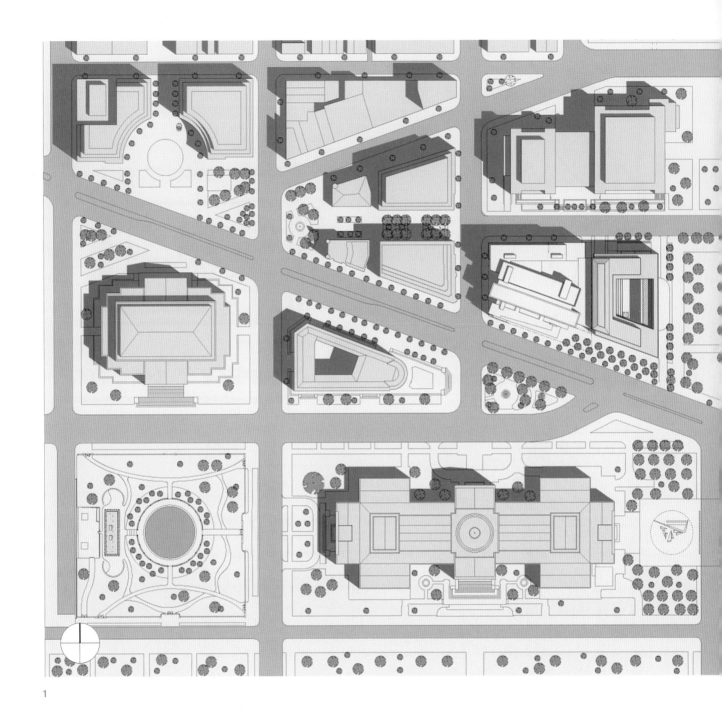

1

2

3

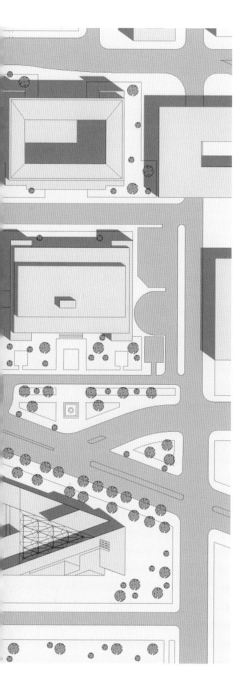

4

5

Finally we presented a detailed rendition of the design to Charles and Peter. [4,5] To say that the response was positive hardly explains the rest of that day. Charles left the conference room and returned with the news that Senator Moynihan (by this time retired) would like to see us. We were whisked to his office, where the tall, thin, and ever so slightly bent senator said, in his inimitable accent, that the museum would be an extraordinary addition to the avenue and to all of Washington. He nodded toward a full-scale papier-mâché sculpture of Thomas Jefferson—his son's creation—and said, "President Jefferson would be pleased." Moynihan sent us to Tony Williams, the mayor of the District of Columbia. Williams was delighted with our brief presentation and said that the city would do whatever it could to help move the project forward. The acclaim we received that day was a precursor to later, more consequential approvals: the U.S. Commission of Fine Arts, the National Capital Planning Commission, and the National Park Service.

After our star-studded tour we took a cab to Reagan Airport, stopping at the site on the way. The old building was not yet demolished. The day was sunny, and both halves of the National Gallery—Pope's neoclassical West Building[2] and I. M. Pei's contemporary East Building[3]—were glowing. These two structures would frame the view from the Mall to the Newseum.

As we developed the design, we expanded the thin layers of the concept model into the idea of three bars, Bars A, B, and C. These volumes, parallel to the diagonal course of Pennsylvania Avenue, would contain program elements. Bar D, a fourth bar, parallel to Sixth Street and the city's underlying orthogonal grid, would contain market-rate housing, which was required by the sale agreement. Between the bars would be skylit circulation spaces. After the Department of Employment Services building was torn down, we arranged to have the plan inscribed on the site to explain it to the building committee.[5]

The components of the program—entry sequence, atrium, exhibits, minitheaters, Annenberg Forum, broadcast studios, offices, residences, retail, restaurants, and parking—are organized within the bars according to the availability of daylight. The "extroverted" program (café and terrace, First Amendment wall, galleries with Capitol and Mall views) is in Bar A, the low front bar; the "introverted" program (day-lit galleries, conference center, and atrium) occupies Bar B; and the "black box" program (news history galleries, minitheaters, and broadcast studios) is in Bar C and below grade. Between the bars are skylit circulation spaces.

The three bars of the museum increase in height as they step back from the avenue. The lowest, the public face of the building, harmonizes with the Canadian Embassy in terms of size. It also acts as a transition between the embassy to the east and the older buildings to the west. A cantilevered portion creates a covered pedestrian zone along the sidewalk where front pages of selected national newspapers are displayed.

After the year and a half of predesign and two years of preparing design and construction drawings, we were finally ready to begin construction with Turner Construction Company as the general contractor. The cost cutting that any project is subject to at this stage was painful but ultimately did not compromise the design, though Peter Prichard, usually the most cheerful of our client collaborators, grew longer and longer in the face as construction tensions arose. Happily, our project architect, John Lowery, was unflappable as he quietly used his experience, charm, and height to mediate daily conflicts.

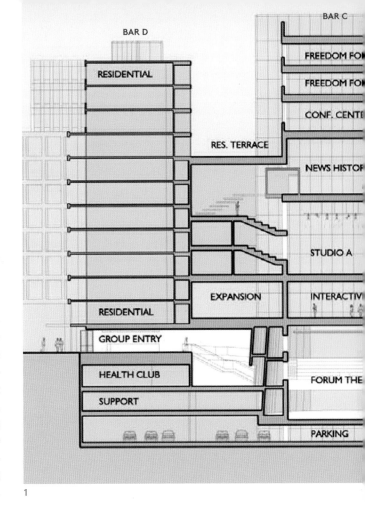

1

The structural design of the building, like the architecture, reflects the sources and technologies of the news.[4] Daniel Sesil of Leslie E. Robertson Associates, the principal structural engineer, describes the building in this way:

Each [of the structural systems] was chosen with a common aspiration: to define the spaces of the complex in a way consistent with the design themes of transparency and openness...The design intentionally asks the structure to do more than simply support the building's architecture...The structure is brought forward and asked to participate in the creation of space that serves as both a functional and a metaphorical public forum.

The Newseum's glass walls expose much of the steel structure. The support connections are limited in both number and complexity to keep the walls as transparent as possible.[2,3]

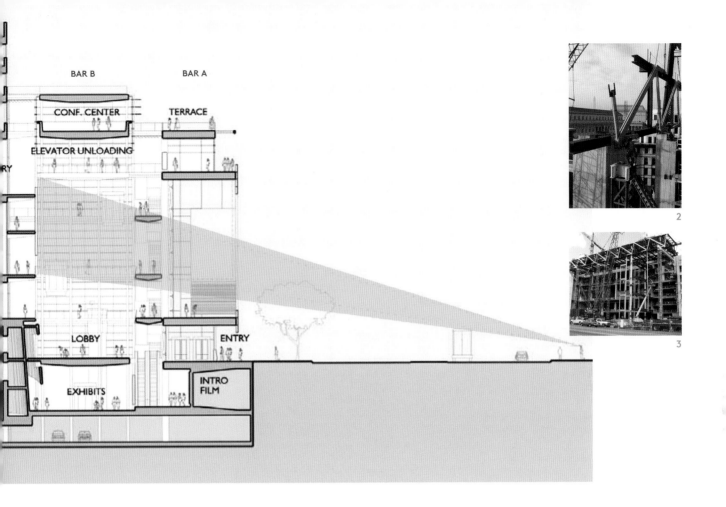

BAR B   BAR A

CONF. CENTER   TERRACE

ELEVATOR UNLOADING

LOBBY   ENTRY

EXHIBITS   INTRO FILM

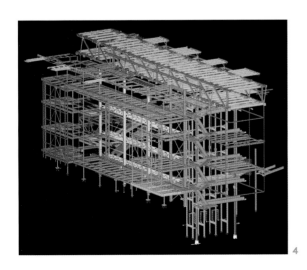

2

3

4

5

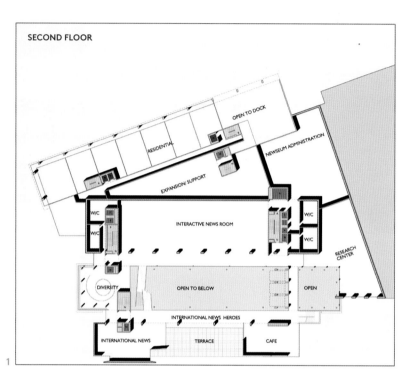

SECOND FLOOR

RESIDENTIAL

OPEN TO DOCK

NEWSEUM ADMINISTRATION

EXPANSION/ SUPPORT

W/C

W/C

INTERACTIVE NEWS ROOM

W/C

W/C

RESEARCH CENTER

DIVERSITY

OPEN TO BELOW

OPEN

INTERNATIONAL NEWS HEROES

INTERNATIONAL NEWS

TERRACE

CAFE

1

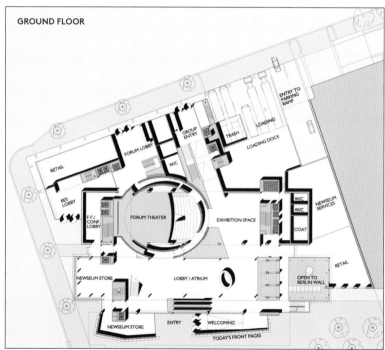

GROUND FLOOR

RETAIL

FORUM LOBBY

GROUP ENTRY

TRASH

LOADING

ENTRY TO PARKING RAMP

LOADING DOCK

W/C

RES. LOBBY

F.F./ CONF. LOBBY

FORUM THEATER

EXHIBITION SPACE

W/C

W/C

NEWSEUM SERVICES

COAT

RETAIL

NEWSEUM STORE

LOBBY / ATRIUM

OPEN TO BERLIN WALL

NEWSEUM STORE

ENTRY

WELCOMING

TODAY'S FRONT PAGES

2

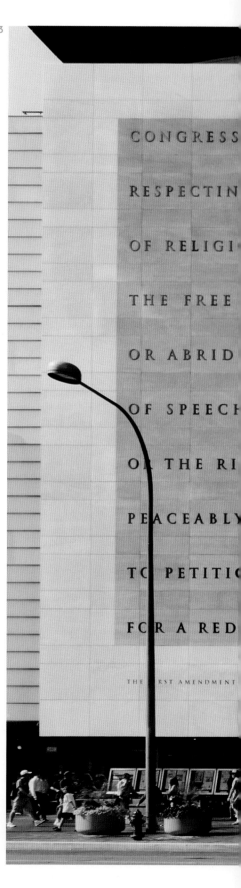

3

CONGRESS

RESPECTIN

OF RELIGI

THE FREE

OR ABRID

OF SPEECH

OL THE RI

PEACEABLY

TO PETITIO

FOR A RED

THE FIRST AMENDMENT

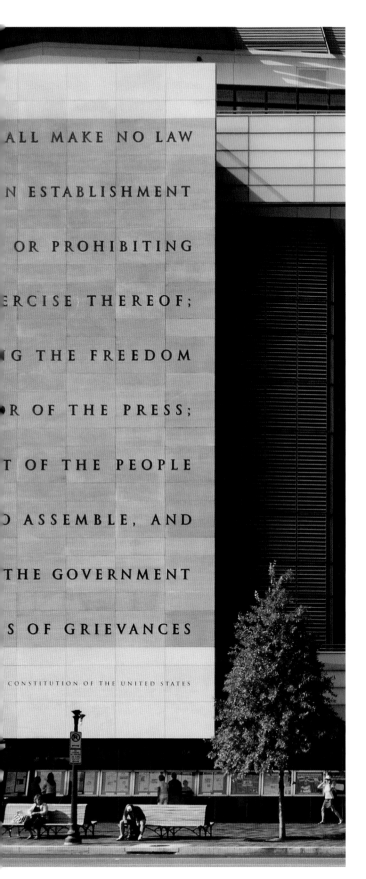

ALL MAKE NO LAW

N ESTABLISHMENT

OR PROHIBITING

RCISE THEREOF;

G THE FREEDOM

R OF THE PRESS;

T OF THE PEOPLE

D ASSEMBLE, AND

THE GOVERNMENT

S OF GRIEVANCES

CONSTITUTION OF THE UNITED STATES

4

5

The exterior envelope of the museum had to express, both in form and in narrative, a commitment to freedom of the press. The most obvious declaration is the huge iteration of the First Amendment. [3] The words are carved into a fifty-two-by-seventy-four-foot wall of Tennessee marble suspended from the Pennsylvania Avenue facade. A second assertion, different in scale and content, is the sidewalk display of front pages. [4,5] More than eight hundred newspapers send their electronic versions to the museum each day. The pedestrian area affords room for fifty-six of them, enlarged and mounted under glass. On occasion, one story dominates most of the papers, but more often the front-page articles reflect the interests and events of a local community.

1

Washington's predominant architectural vocabulary is a neutral but nonetheless ideological classicism. This imagery was entirely inappropriate for a building charged with conveying historic and contemporary communications. We chose to clad the bars in contrasting materials, each of which admitted and emitted different amounts of light. The envelope of the low bar consists almost entirely of translucent and clear glass. Projecting off the glass skin of the middle volume are nine-inch-deep translucent glass fins that control sunlight and provide a distinctive texture. The tallest, innermost bar emerges only at the top of the building in a smooth skin of semireflective, heavily tinted glass. The residential block has exposed floor slabs separated on the south and west facades by glass infill and on the north front by a staccato pattern of glass and aluminum panels.

The "window on the world" on the principal facade serves to impart the Newseum's mission. The 4,500-square-foot, water-white glass area is framed within the white-translucent-glass proscenium and in turn frames a 30-by-50-foot LED screen within the building. Images of breaking news displayed on the screen are visible from Pennsylvania Avenue day and night. The First Amendment, the newspaper display, and the Internet projections represent the technology and history of news delivery from stone to paper to ether.[1]

1

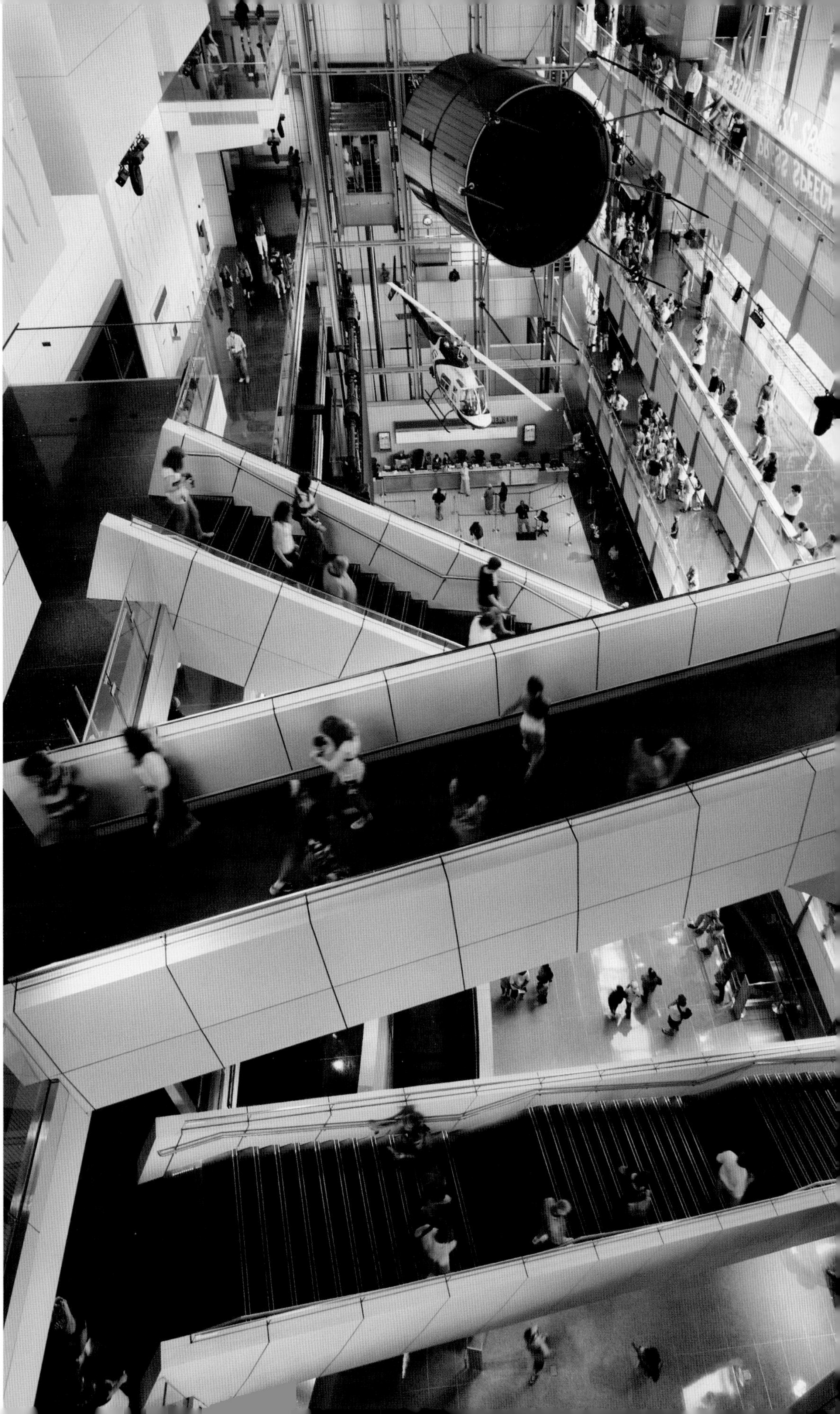

The interdependent relationship between multi-faceted architectural/structural expression and the varied technological/communications strategies is evident upon approach to the building from the National Mall. Almost all visitors enter from Pennsylvania Avenue through the expansive atrium on the ground floor;[2] school and tour groups arrive via Sixth Street. Multiple but easily grasped routes depart from the atrium, making it effortless for visitors to decide where to go and how to get there. Museumgoers may descend to minitheaters on the lower level for an introductory film or ascend by means of a room-size glass elevator—the tallest hydraulic elevator in the world—to the top floor to begin the exhibit sequence. As visitors spiral down through the galleries and around the atrium, they look out to sweeping views of the Capitol, Pennsylvania Avenue, and the Mall and in to a suspended news helicopter.[1,3]

1

2

The museum's exhibits total 250,000 square feet. The success of any topical museum relies on a symbiotic relationship between installations and architecture, and we worked with Ralph Appelbaum to integrate design and content, from the sequencing of spaces to the detailed development of exhibit casework. Architectural and interpretive visions reinforce one another throughout the building. Among the principal display spaces is the three-story 9/11 Gallery. [3] The central focus of the room is a large section of the antenna from Building 1 of the World Trade Center. This artifact was saved by an alert museum curator who traced it to a Boston junkyard just days after the terrorist attack. A gallery wall puts on view headlines from that grotesque day.

A second triple-height space, the Berlin Wall Gallery, is on the lowest level of the institution. Installed are eight twelve-foot-tall sections of the original concrete wall, each weighing about three tons—the largest display outside Germany. [1] Also exhibited is an East German guard tower that was near Checkpoint Charlie, Berlin's infamous east-west crossing. [2]

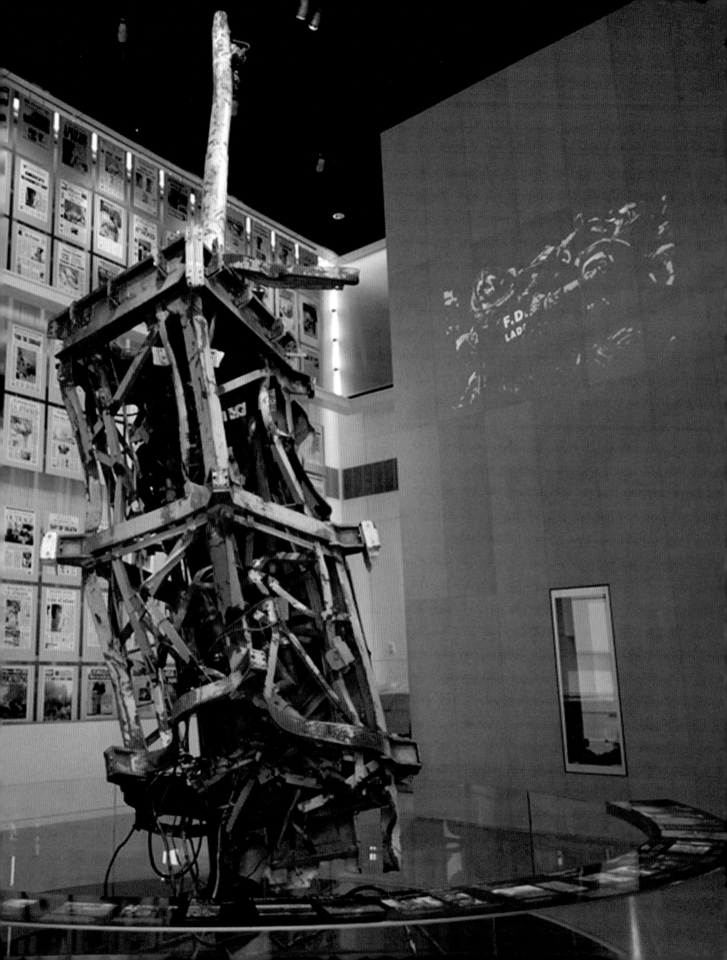

2

3

4

5

On the third level, sheltered under a two-story curved glass form, is the Journalists Memorial; this area is dedicated to reporters, photographers, editors, and broadcasters who have lost their lives in the line of duty.[1] Also on this floor is the Internet, television, and radio gallery.[3] The Pulitzer Prize Photographs Gallery is on the ground floor and features a comprehensive collection of images as well as filmed interviews with many of the photographers.[2] The 450-seat Annenberg Forum on the lower level hosts public programs, music and drama, and film screenings.[4] We consider the final "exhibit" to be the U.S. Capitol, visible from a terrace at the upper level.[5]

Charles Overby is an old-fashioned southern gentleman in many ways, and as the opening drew close, he asked me to come to Washington. When I arrived at the Newseum he escorted me out to Pennsylvania Avenue, to a section of the granite base that had been draped in white. In the company of Peter Prichard and a few others, he removed the cloth. There, engraved in the stone, was the name of our firm. It's unusual, these days, to place the name of an architect on a building. To me, this act, and this ceremony, typified the attitude of our clients—generous in spirit and respectful of professionalism, journalistic, of course, and also architectural.

The Newseum opened on April 11, 2008. The festivities included a public dedication on Pennsylvania Avenue. Newseum chair Alberto Ibarguen, Neuharth, Overby, Prichard, and many more were in attendance. [3] A block party, private dedication in the Annenberg Forum, and other events followed. [2] Among the participants at the private ceremony were Speaker of the House Nancy Pelosi; Arthur Sulzberger Jr., publisher of the *New York Times* and chairman of the New York Times Company; Chief Justice of the United States John Roberts; and Representative John Lewis, Democrat of Georgia. Lewis stated, "Without the American press, the civil rights movement would have been like a bird without wings." [4] Less than a year later, the Newseum was to witness its first Pennsylvania Avenue inaugural parade. [1] Wrapping the building was 5,000 square feet of signage celebrating new president Barack Obama.

CONGRESS SHALL MAKE NO LAW

RESPECTING AN ESTABLISHMENT

OF RELIGION, OR PROHIBITING

THE FREE EXERCISE THEREOF:

OR ABRIDGING THE FREEDOM

OF SPEECH, OR OF THE PRESS:

OR THE RIGHT OF THE PEOPLE

PEACEABLY TO ASSEMBLE; AND

TO PETITION THE GOVERNMENT

FOR A REDRESS OF GRIEVANCES

James Stewart Polshek

James Stewart Polshek is an internationally recognized architect, public advocate, and educator. Polshek received a Master of Architecture degree from Yale University's Graduate School of Architecture in 1955 and spent the 1956–57 academic year at the Royal Academy of Fine Arts in Copenhagen as a Fulbright Fellow. In 1962 he founded James Stewart Polshek, Architects, which subsequently became Polshek Partnership. From 1972 to 1987 Polshek was dean of the faculty of the Graduate School of Architecture, Planning and Preservation at Columbia University. During his tenure, he created the Temple Hoyne Buell Center for the Study of American Architecture. In 1980 he cofounded Architects and Planners (now Architects/Designers/Planners) for Social Responsibility. He is the author of *Context and Responsibility* (1988).

Polshek has received honorary degrees from Pratt Institute, Parsons The New School for Design, and the New Jersey Institute of Technology. In 2002 he was awarded the Municipal Art Society's Jacqueline Kennedy Onassis Medal and was inducted into the American Academy of Arts and Sciences. Polshek was elected to the American Academy of Arts and Letters in 2005. In 2006 he was named the William Bernoudy Fellow at the American Academy in Rome, and in 2009 he received the Brooklyn Museum's Augustus Graham Medal for excellence in architecture. Since 2006, Polshek has been a member of the New York City Public Design Commission.

Acknowledgments

This book would not exist without three creative, committed, and collaborative muses. Andrea Whitfill integrated image and text with imagination, impeccable design judgment, persistence, and unerring focus. Andrea Monfried refined and enriched the narrative with a comprehensive knowledge of language and an insistence on accuracy. Paula Scher supported the idea of the book in its early stages and then applied boundless invention to the overall design concept.

Peter Polshek, Jennifer Polshek, and Nina Hofer encouraged me when the book was little more than a notion. They went on to clarify language, suggest images, and provide enthusiasm and motivation.

Finally, and most important, Ellyn Polshek acted as counselor, editor, critic, cheerleader, and memory bank. Her past lives as editor and lawyer, not to mention the fifty years during which she shared the joys and frustrations of this architect's life, were brought to bear on every word and every picture in this volume.

At The Monacelli Press, I particularly want to thank Elizabeth White, managing editor, as well as Gianfranco Monacelli, Alan Rapp, and Michael Vagnetti, and at Pentagram, Jeff Close.

The architects and support staff who have been responsible for the hundreds of completed works that I have been privileged to attach my name to number an amazing 1028. Twelve in particular have made specific contributions to the realization of this book: Penny Chung, Greg Clawson, Josh Frankel, Michael Hassett, Molly McGowan, Adam Mead, Charmian Place, Damu Radheshwar, Jim Sinks, Joanne Sliker, Susan Strauss, and Aislinn Wiedle.

I am grateful to the current partners of the legacy firm that continues to maintain a half-century of design excellence represented by the stories in this book—Timothy Hartung, Duncan Hazard, Guy Maxwell, Kevin McClurkan, Richard Olcott, Susan Rodriguez, Tomas Rossant, Todd Schliemann, Don Weinreich, Thomas Wong—and especially Joseph Fleischer, who has selflessly supported me since 1966.

So many others have participated in the making of this book and the buildings in this book: Ralph Appelbaum, Elsa Berry Bankier, Norton Belknap, Richard Berry, Jim Bickel, Lorna Bieber, Rhonda Bolner, Patricia K. Bucklin, Linda Cahill, Joan Darragh, Anna Dorfman, David Dunlap, Inger Elliott, Denis Finnin, Gino Francisconi, Ellen Futter, Edward Gallagher, James Garrison, Gwen Goodman, J. Reid Herlihy, Eric Himmel, Kaki Hockersmith, Jay Holleran, Sophie Horay, Maira Kalman, Yoshiyuki Koshiyama, Cindy Layman, Patrick Markle, Huguette Martel, Barbara Mathé, Victoria McGann, Charles Moleski, Lydia Muniz, Victoria Newhouse, Guy Nordenson, Otis Pearsall, Peter Prichard, Jimmy Pynn, Herbert H. Ragan IV, Lyn Ross, Ben Rubin, Skip Rutherford, Kathleen Sabogal, Matthew Shanley, Rollene Saal, Whitney North Seymour Jr., Dan Stoddard, Stephanie Streett, Jonathan Thayer, Nancy Thorne, David Thurm, Joseph Toussaint, Oliver Trager, Neil deGrasse Tyson, Hélène Veret, Ann Webster, William Whittaker, Robert Young, Nancy Zeckendorf, and Don Zivkovic. I thank them all.

Build,
Memory
Volume
Two

500 Park Tower,
New York, New York

Sulzberger Hall,
Barnard College,
New York, New York

Lam Research Theater,
Yerba Buena Center
for the Arts, San
Francisco, California

Museum of the
City of New York,
New York, New York

National Inventors
Hall of Fame,
Akron, Ohio

Flushing Regional
Branch, Queens
Borough Public Library,
Queens, New York

Jerome L. Greene Hall,
Columbia University
Law School,
New York, New York

Mashantucket Pequot
Museum and Research
Center, Mashantucket,
Connecticut

Iris and B. Gerald Cantor
Center for Visual Arts,
Stanford University,
Stanford, California

Museum of the
American Indian,
Suitland, Maryland

Joseph Papp
Public Theater,
New York, New York

Brown Fine Arts Center,
Smith College,
Northampton,
Massachusetts

Kahn Building Renovation
and Expansion, Yale
University Art Gallery,
New Haven, Connecticut

Holland Performing
Arts Center,
Omaha, Nebraska

Roosevelt House,
Hunter College, City
University of New York,
New York, New York

Master Plan for
St. John the Divine,
New York, New York

Credits

Teijin Institute for Biomedical Research
Teijin Applied Textile Science Center
Andors & Company 21.3
Architalk/Wordpress 55.4
© chai kian shin/Shutterstock Stock Photo 14–15
© 2010 Evan Chakroff 18.1
© Xavier de Jaureguiberry 33.4
© Darren Epstein 16.4
Flickr/courtesy of Okinawa Soba 25.3
Fuente/The Japan Times 37.3
© Ishimoto Yasuhiro 19.3
Cary James, Frank Lloyd Wright's Imperial Hotel 27.3, 54.1, 54.2
juergenspecht.com 37.4
© Barnabas Juhasz-Dora 19.2
© Akio Kawasumi/PPA 17.4
Kawasumi Architectural Photographic Office 15 (inset) 30.3, 31.4, 32.4, 33.1,34.3, 35.4, 35.5, 36.6, 42.1, 44.1, 45.2, 45.3, 46.3, 47.4, 47.5, 47.6, 56–57
© Kyoto Bon Fire 17.6
Courtesy of Le Corbusier Archive © FLC/ARS 29.6
Julie Lemberger/Oregon Dance Live 16.1
Library of Congress: Paul Rudolph Collection 33.5
M_Strasser/Flickr 17.7
Osamo Murai 48.1, 48.2, 48.3, 49.4, 50.1, 50.2, 50.3, 50.4, 50.5, 52.2, 52.3, 53.4
Courtesy of the Nakashima Archives 21.4
Perfect Blue 16.3
© James Stewart Polshek 20.1, 21.5, 22.1, 22.2, 24.1, 24.2, 26.1, 26.2, 28.2, 28.4, 28.5, 32.1, 37.2, 37.6, 40.1, 40.1, 40.3, 43.3, 43.4, 43.5, 49.5, 52.1
Peter Polshek and Nina Hofer 45.4
© PPA 30.1, 30.2, 30.3, 31.4, 33.2, 33.3, 34.1, 34.2, 35.3, 36.1, 37.5, 51.6, 51.7
Potential in Space:Teijin Central Research Laboratory © Kajimavision Productions Co., LTD 38.1, 38.2, 46.1, 46.2
© President and Fellows of Harvard University, Peabody Museum of Archaeology and Ethnology, 98470030 23.3
runningmaps/creative commons 27.4
Courtesy of Society of Fukuoka Prefecture 54.3
S/S 2007 Photo by Anthea Simms 16.2
© Ezra Stoller/Esto 15 (inset), 22.4, 23.5
© Théatre National du Bunraku avec Minosuke Yoshida III, Trésor National Vivant 15.5
Pepe Bernad Torá 28.1
© Zen Hokusai litsu hitsu 26.4

New York State Bar Center
Albany Times Union 69.4, 71.5
Courtesy of Pamela Babey 76.1
Paola Costi Baldi/Wiki Commons 61.5
© Bettman/Corbis 79.3
© Robert Breckford/PPA 62.1
© Burns Photographic, Inc./PPA 59 (inset)
© George Cserna 62.3, 67.2, 71.4, 76.2, 76.3, 77.5, 77.6, 78.1, 80.2, 82
© 2009 Hildreth Meière Dunn 77.4
Courtesy of Eisenman Architects 72.3
© Konrad Fiedler 64.1
© Michael Fredericks/courtesy of the NYSBA 79.2, 80.1
Gorucci/Portuguese Wikipedia Project 61.4
Chester Higgins Jr./New York Times 63.4
Jer21999/Wikipedia Commons 60.1
© Nathaniel Lieberman/PPA 62.2
Collections of the Louvre/Creative Commons 58–59
© Mapplethorpe Foundation 72.1
© Clare McGregor 66.1
© Richard Meier & Partners Architects 72.2

Olivetti and post modernism/Wordpress 69.3
© 2012 Jessica Painter Photography 60.2
James Stewart Polshek 64.2, 65.3
© PPA 70.1, 71.2, 73.4, 73.5, 74.1, 74.1, 74.3
Progressive Architecture (Jan. 1969) 75.4
Librado Romero/New York Times 71.3
Seier + Seier/Wikimedia 68.1
© Alan Stuart/PPA 81.3
© vimla.patil 61.3
© Matt Wade Photography/Wikimedia 62.G, 67.3
Marilynn K. Yee/New York Times 63.5
Albany Times Union 69.4, 71.5
Courtesy of Pamela Babey 76.1
Paola Costi Baldi/Wiki Commons 61.5
© Bettman/Corbis 79.3

Quinco Regional Mental Health Center
© Gil Amiaga/PPA 96.1
Arnaudet, "Living Bridges," *The Inhabited Bridge: Past, Present and Future*, p. 71 fig. 91 93.5
© Ricky Berkey 88.3
© 2013 Centerstone Columbus, Indiana 87.3
courtesy of Columbus, Indiana, Archives 89.7
© 2013 Columbus Regional Health 90.2
© George Cserna/PPA 99.3, 99.4, 99.5, 100.1
cyrilyne/centerblog.net 93.3
© Barry Denwitt 96.3
Designophy 88.2
© Don DiBernardo 88.4
Eliel Saarinen file/Wikimedia Commons 88.1
© Freud Museum London 84–85
© Balthazar Korab/PPA 85 (inset), 86.1, 98.2, 102
Courtesy of Milestone Contractors 88.5
© James Stewart Polshek 90.1
© PPA 91.3, 95.2, 95.3, 95.3, 95.4, 97.4, 98.1
Purple Pen 19/Wikimedia Commons 96.2
Rainerkruckenberg/Wikimedia Commons 94.1
Abbie Rowe: White House Photographs/John F. Kennedy Presidential Library and Museum, Boston 87.2
Shutterstock 93.2
Taxiarchos228/Wikipedia 92.1
© Wagner International Photos/American Audio Visual 101.2

Carnegie Hall
© Josef Astor 110.5
© Clive Barda 132.3
Carnegie Hall Archives 106.3, 108.2, 109.4, 110.3, 110.4, 110.6, 113.5, 117.4, 118.4, 123.4, 128.1, 132.1, 135.3, 135.5
Cité de la Musique 133.5
William D. Cohan, *The Last Tycoon* 132.2
© Dave Darnell 127.3
© TheFitzyreport/Wordpress 140–41
© Jeff Goldberg/Esto 136.1, 137.2, 137.3
© Henry Grossman 118.3, 119.5, 126.1
© Roy Gumpel/1986 110.1, 110.2
© Erich Hartmann/Magnum 118.1
© Chester Higgins Jr./New York Times 122.1
© Ken Howard 108.1
© imdb.com 123.3
© Helmut Jacoby 109.6
Courtesy of Kirkegaard Associates 123.2
Bob Kosovsky, Library for the Performing Arts, Music Division/New York Public Library 108.3
© Michel LeGrand/Carnegie Hall Archives 124.2, 125.4
Library of Congress/George Grantham Bain Collection 106.2
Library of Congress/Marceau 106.1
© Bjorg Magnea/PPA 105 (inset)

© The M. C. Escher Company, The Netherlands 114.3
Michele McDonald/Globe Staff 137.3
© Nan Melville 138.1
Abe Melzner/Carnegie Hall Archives 123.5
© Music of Vienna 133.6
© New Yorker/Cover/January 18, 1988 by Roxie Munro 127.2
Vinh X. Nguyen 104–105
© 2013 Pelli Clarke Pelli Architects 129.3
© PPA 113.3, 113.4, 114.1, 114.2, 118.2, 128.2, 129.4, 129.6, 130.1, 131.2, 131.3, 133.4, 134.1, 135.2, 137.4, 137.5, 137.6, 136.2
© Al Ravenna 109.5
© Cervin Robinson/PPA 107.4, 120.1, 120.2, 120.3, 120.4
© Laura Rosen/PPA 113.2
© Steve J. Sherman 116.2, 116.3, 125.3
© Jan Staller 115.4
Courtesy of Teachers College/Columbia University 135.4
© Paul Warchol/PPA 116.1
Wikipedia 121.5

United States Embassy, Oman
Courtesy of AIA/architect/this week/allen.cfm 151.8
© Al Hamra/Falaj/The Sultanate of Oman/Hill and Hill 158.1, 158.4
© Emily Andrews 151.10
Courtesy of ansar.ru/world/2011 144.1
© Bernardo Ricci Armani 144.2
© Art Institute of Chicago Archives 165.5
© Daily Star of Lebanon 145.4
© Dwell 165.2
© Egyptian Revival Architecture 163.2
© ehdwalls.com 142–43
© everest700/Wikimedia Commons 145.3
© Federal Aviation Administration 148.5
© Fox Film Corporation, 1921 153.4
© Ben Geach 168.1
© Getty Images 152.1
Courtesy of Eric and Emma Gimon/photograph by Kathrina Simonen 149.6
© Jeff Goldberg/Esto 143 (inset), 166.1, 166.2, 169.2, 169.3, 169.4, 169.5, 170.2, 171.1, 171.2, 172.1, 172.3, 174–75
© James Gordon/Wikimedia Commons 162.1
© Gyanibash/Creative Commons 154.2
Courtesy of Reid Herlihy 151.11
© InterContinental Muscat 154.1
© Mimi Jacobs/Smithsonian Institution, Archives of American Art 148.2
Louis I. Kahn Collection, University of Pennsylvania and Pennsylvania Historical and Museum Commission 163.3, 163.4
Le Corbusier Archive 150.1, 150.2
© lifeat55mph.blogspot.com 146.3
© Mai–Sachme/Wikimedia Commons 156.4
© Marx Toys 167.5
© James Mitchell/Wikimedia Commons 147.6
© Mush Emmons/Virgina Tech Archives 148.4
© Bob Narod, Photographer 150.3
© Chris Nevins/Flickr 150.4
© photolyric/Shutterstock 156.3
Courtesy Platt Byard Dovell White Architects 151.9
© James Stewart Polshek 155.4, 156.1, 160.2
© PPA 155.3, 158.2, 159.5, 159.6, 161.1, 164.1, 166.3, 166.4, 170.1
© PRI Public Radio International 165.4
© Tristan Schmurr/Flickr 156.2
© Tangier Restaurant & Cabaret 160.1

© United States Department of Defense
(DF-ST-82-06554) 152.2
© United States Department of State 150.5, 150.6
© University of Victoria 165.3
© Victorwkf/Virtual Tourist 158.3
© Henry Waxman 146.2
© Charles F. Wetherall 146.4
© Wurster/WBE Collection, Environmental Design
Archives, University of California, Berkeley 148.3
Courtesy of Yale University Art Gallery/Archives
147.5

Brooklyn Museum
© The Baltimore Sun 195.6
© Richard Barnes 177 (inset), 200.1, 204.1, 205.3,
207.2, 210–11
© Diane Bondareff/AP Images 202.2
© Brooklyn Museum Archive 180.1, 180.2, 181.4,
181.5, 181.6, 181.7, 181.8, 181.9, 182.1, 182.2, 182.3,
182.4, 184.1, 185.2, 185.3, 185.4, 186.1, 186.2, 186.3,
187.5, 192.1, 192.2, 193.3, 194.1, 194.2, 194.4, 204.2
© Iris & B. Gerald Cantor Foundation 189.3, 194.3
Courtesy of Chicago Historical Society 178.4
Columbia University Archives 195.7
© Fred R. Conrad/The New York Times 206.1
© Jeff Goldberg/Esto 196.1
© Google Earth 189.3
LGBT Religious Archives Network 178.2
National Archives: Mathew Brady 178.1
© Jeanne Noonan/New York Daily News 197.3
© James Stewart Polshek 180.3, 199.2
© PPA 190.1, 191.3, 191.4, 194.5, 196.2, 198.1, 201.2,
201.3, 201.4, 203.4
© PPA/Arata Isozaki & Associates 191.2
© PPA (section) © Patricia Bazelon/Brooklyn
Museum (images) 195.8
© Ben Rahn 202.3
© Ben Rahn/A-Frame 179.6, 182.5
© SkyView Survey 178.3, 183.6
© Carl Stahl/H.G.Esch 202.1
tourofegypt.net 176.177
© Kate Turner 188.2
© Steve Turner 201.5
Makoto Shin Watanabe 188.1
© Aislinn Weidele/PPA 209.2
© Carin Whitney/PPA 208.1, 209.3, 209.4
Wikipedia 178.5
http://zukan.exblog.jp/4775617 186.4

Seamen's Church Institute
Courtesy of Dick Berry 218.2
© Jeff Goldberg/Esto 213 (inset), 215.4, 220.1, 221.5,
222.1, 223.4, 223.5, 223.6, 223.7, 224.1, 224.2, 225.3,
226.3, 227.4, 227.5, 228.1, 230.2, 231.1
© Ken Grant 216.4
© Shalom Jacobovitz/Wikimedia Commons 212–213
© Phillip Lange 214.1
© Andy Madelt 230.1
William H. Miller Jr., Luxury Liners 1927–1954: A
Photographic Record 218.3
Courtesy of Richard Olcott 218.4, 220.2
© James Stewart Polshek 221.4
© PPA 218.5, 219.6, 219.7, 220.3, 222.3, 226.2
© Courtesy of the Franklin D. Roosevelt Library,
Hyde Park, New York 214.2
© Laurent D. Ruamps 222.2
Courtesy of Frank Sciame 218.1© Seamens Church
Institute 214.3, 216.2, 216.3, 217.5, 225.4, 226.1,
229.2, 229.3

Santa Fe Opera House
Courtesy of Auerbach Pollock Friedlander 250.1

© Dan Barsotti/Santa Fe Opera 238.1
© Jay Blakesberg 250.3
© Blossom Music Center 242.3
Courtesy of Sarah Caples 243.6
Michael Conroy/Associated Press 295.6
© Hans Fahrmeyer/Santa Fe Opera 237.2
© Raphael Azevedo Franca 240.1
© Jeff Goldberg/Esto 236.1, 253.2, 253.3
© Henry Grossman 239.3
© Al Hamra/Falaj/The Sultanate of Oman/Hill
and Hill 243.9
© Ken Howard 244.3
© Alex Irvin 242.2
© Robert Llewellyn 242.4
© McNay Art Museum 248.1
Courtesy of Blake Middleton 243.7
National Science Digital Library 237.3
© James Stewart Polshek 243.8, 243.10
© PPA 243.5, 247.3, 248.2, 248.3, 248.4, 248.5,
250.4, 250.5, 250.6, 251.7, 251.8, 252.1, 254.1
© Princeton University 250.2
© Damu Radheshwar 254.3
© ready4c/wunderground 234–35.
© Robert Reck 235 (inset), 256.1, 256.2, 256.3,
256.4, 257.5, 258.1, 258.2, 259.1, 260.1
© Treye Rice 242.1
© Santa Fe Opera Archives 240.3, 241.4, 246.1
SiefkinDR/Wikimedia Commons 243.11
© Waldemar Swierzy 239.1
© Vivaverdi/Wikimedia Commons 246.2
© Kathy Weiser/Legends of America 254.2
© Judy Purcell Wilson 240.2
© Robert Workman 245.4
Courtesy of Nancy Zeckendorf 244.1, 244.2

Newtown Creek Wastewater Treatment Plant
© Adams/Daily News 271.6
© Sara Ambalu/PPA 280.2
© Kate Ascher, The Works: Anatomy of a City, p.
179 285.3
© Victoria Belanger 286.1
© Al Camardella Jr./Flickr 265.8
© Greg Clawson/PPA 273.2
© 2009 Stefano Colzani 267.3
© Walter DuFresne 283.3
Four Freedoms Park Conservancy, Inc. Base
Photograph: www.amiaga.com. Digital
Rendering: Christopher Shelley 268.1
© Jeff Goldberg/Esto 263, 264.4, 278.2, 280.1,
280.4, 284.1, 288.289
© Google Maps 269.2
© Maira Kalman, And the Pursuit of Happiness
286.2, 286.3
© Matthew C. Marshall 265.7
© McGill School of Architecture 265.5
© Michael Sporn Animation 282.2
© http://michaelwalch.wordpress.com/ 287.4
© Newtown Creek Alliance 279.4
© New York Historical Society 265.9
© James Stewart Polshek 281.5
© The Poop Project: The People's Own Organic
Power Project 278.1
© Jock Pottle/Esto 274.1, 274.2
© PPA 270.1, 270.2, 270.2, 270.3, 275.3, 275.4, 276.1,
276.2, 277.3, 279.3, 279.6
Courtesy of the Public Design Commission of the
City of New York 269.3, 271.4, 271.5, 284.2
© Andy Roberts/Wikipedia Commons 266.1
© Leo Roubos/Flickr 267.4
Stockphoto 272.1
© Roger Stoller/Buckminster Fuller
Foundation 265.6

© George Trakas 283.4
© Joop van Houdt/Wikimedia Commons 266.2
© Mitch Waxman/Flickr 279.5
© Aislinn Weidele/PPA 280.3, 282.1, 283.5
© Andrea Whitfill 275.5
© Yayimages 262–63

New York Times Printing Plant
© Bettman/Corbis 296.1
© George Cserna/PPA 298.1
Alfred Eisenstaedt, V-J Day 1945/Life Magazine/
Wikimedia 292.3
© Fresh Air Fund 295.3
© Carlos Avila Gonzales/The Chronicle 297.7
© Jeff Goldberg/Esto 291 (inset), 293.5, 294.1,
298.3, 302.1, 302.2, 304.2, 305.4, 306.1, 306.2,
306.3, 308.1, 308.2, 310–11
© Google Earth 300.2
© Dick Halstead/Time & Life/Getty Images 298.2
Bozhong Li and Jan Luiten van Zanden/CEPR
Discussion Paper 8023 293.6
Library of Congress 292.1
© Trevor Little 307.4
© MADMAN 290–91
Robert D. McFadden 296.4
Modern Times © Roy Export S.A.S. Scan courtesy
Cineteca di Bologna 296.6
© New-Historical Society 296.5
© New York Post 296.3
© New York Times 309.3, 309.4
© Rebecca Garcia Nieto 295.4
© James Stewart Polshek 305.4
© PPA 299.5, 301.1, 302.3, 303.4, 303.5
Syracuse University Archive Library 294.2, 295.7
Courtesy of David Thurm 296.2
Wealth-X Research 295.5
Wikipedia 292.2, 292.4
Woodblock/netease 293

Rose Center for Earth and Space
© American Museum of Natural History 316.1,
317.3, 318.1, 320.1, 321.2, 321.3, 321.4, 321.5, 321.6,
322.4, 323.5, 329.4, 330.1, 330.2, 330.3, 331.4,
331.5, 331.6, 340.2, 341.3, 341.4, 341.5, 341.6,
342.4, 350.1, 352.1
Courtesy of the Annenberg Rare Book &
Manuscript Library, University of Penn-
sylvania 324.2
© Richard Barnes 342.1, 342.2, 344.2, 345.6
Courtesy of Bibliotheque Nationale, Paris 315.3,
315.4, 315.5
Chicago Architectural Metals and Chicago
Ornamental Iron Company 340.1
© D-Box 328.3, 338.1
© Eurotunnel 328.1
© farm1/Flickr 337.3
© Denis Finnin/AMNH 313.2, 344.5, 348.1, 348.2
© Jeff Goldberg/Esto 314.2, 318.2
© janettravels.uk 337.4
© Vincent Lafort 346.1
© New York Landmarks Conservancy 326.1
Gustafson Guthrie Nichol 347.2, 347.3
© James Stewart Polshek 344.4
© PPA 317.4, 319.1, 319.2, 319.3, 322.1, 322.3, 323.6,
324.1, 324.3, 325.4, 326.3, 327.4, 327.5, 331.7, 332.1,
334.1, 335.2, 337.5, 337.6, 339.2, 339.3, 342.3, 342.5,
344.3, 347.4, 351.3
© Russian Federal Space Agency 328.2
© RWDI 343.7
© Nathaniel Salisbury 333.5
© SardineTea/Flickr 336.1
© Skyscrapercity.com 337.2